THE SINGLE ADULT MINISTRY SOLUTION

Leader Manual

THE SINGLE ADULT MINISTRY SOLUTION

Leader Manual

COMPILED BY TIM CLEARY

LifeWay Press
Nashville, Tennessee

Warning! This resource is user-friendly.

Single-Adult Ministry Toolboxes, placed strategically throughout this resource, provide practical resources
for training single-adult leaders and for developing single-adult ministry plans and strategies.
You have permission to duplicate the toolboxes in this book for use in your local church.
Other duplication is prohibited.

Printed in the United States of America

LifeWay Press
127 Ninth Avenue, North
Nashville, Tennessee 37234

contributors

George Barna is an internationally acclaimed demographer, author, and speaker, as well as the president of Barna Research Institute in Glendale, California.

Hazel Bell is an accomplished writer and single-adult director, as well as the editor of *Singles and Leaders Newsletter*, based in Norman, Oklahoma.

Jon Bodin is a staff minister at WillowCreek Community Church in Southern Barrington, Illinois.

Ken Brumley is a well-known single-adult minister, speaker, storyteller, and dramatist in Tyler, Texas.

Tim Cleary is a single-adult minister, writer, trainer, and national single-adult ministry specialist with Christian Single Resources, based in Nashville, Tennessee.

Steve Cretin is an experienced single-adult minister and Christian educator and the director of Sunday School consultative ministries for Southern Baptists, based in Nashville, Tennessee.

Chris Elkins is a noted author, speaker, and minister with single adults and media in Dallas, Texas.

Doug Fagerstrom is a nationally known author, speaker, and single-adult minister, as well as the national director of the Network of Single-Adult Leaders, based in Grand Rapids, Michigan.

Larry Garner is an author and Christian educator in Jackson, Mississippi.

Karen Gibson is the consultant for Texas Baptist single-adult work and a single-adult minister in Plano, Texas.

Ron Hill is a minister with single adults in San Antonio, Texas.

Rich Hurst is a nationally known author and motivational speaker with Single-Adult Ministry Resources in Colorado Springs, Colorado.

Carolyn Koons is a nationally known author and speaker, as well as the director of the Institute of Outreach Ministries, Azusa Pacific University, in Azusa, California.

Bruce Moore, a single adult, serves as a single-adult minister to more than one thousand single adults in Jacksonville, Florida.

Bill Morgan is an experienced single-adult minister in Springdale, Arkansas.

Bill Pentak is a marketing specialist and a single-adult minister in Houston, Texas.

Ron Proctor is an evangelism specialist and a single-adult minister in Euless, Texas.

Candy Smith is an experienced single-adult minister and conference leader in Richardson, Texas.

Harold Ivan Smith is an internationally renowned author, speaker, and research specialist, as well as the president of Harold Ivan Smith and Associates in Kansas City, Missouri.

Steve Smith is the single-adult minister with one of America's largest single-adult ministries in Dallas, Texas.

Ralph Starling is an experienced single-adult minister and media specialist in Richmond, Virginia.

Bill Taylor is an author, a leading Christian educator, and the director of Sunday School ministries for Southern Baptists, based in Nashville, Tennessee.

Jerry Wilkinson is an experienced writer, counselor, conference leader, and single-adult minister in Tucson, Arizona.

Ben Young is the host of the popular Houston radio program "The Single Connection" and directs America's largest Sunday School ministry for single adults.

Norm Yukers is a seasoned national single-adult ministry leader and the president of the Network of Single-Adult Leaders, based in Tucker, Georgia.

contents

internet Zai

AoL Net find

introduction

Tim Cleary

How to Use *The Single-Adult Ministry Solution Resource Pack*

The Single-Adult Ministry Solution Resource Pack provides you three strategic resources that, when used together, will create dynamic synergy in developing single-adult ministry in your church:

- *The Single-Adult Ministry Solution Leader Manual*
- *Start a Revolution: Nine World-Changing Strategies for Single Adults* (also sold separately)
- Set of six audiotapes

To gain the best results from these resources, follow these suggestions.

- Provide copies of toolboxes in this leader manual for leaders and groups in your church who would benefit from the issues addressed. You have permission to copy the toolboxes from this leader manual for use in your church.

- Lead your key single-adult ministry leaders through a study of this leader manual. A study guide is provided on pages 133–37.
- Enhance your reading of this manual by listening to the audiotapes for additional information and ideas.
- Provide duplicates of the audiotapes for leaders and groups needing guidance in specific areas. You have permission to duplicate these audiotapes for use in your church.
- Purchase additional copies of *Start a Revolution* for single adults and follow the study suggestions on pages 30–35 in this manual. This book can empower single adults to discover God's will for their lives and can motivate them to serve Him.

God's Purpose and Direction for Single-Adult Ministry

The ministry diagram on the following page is provided as a guide to help you keep your single-adult ministry on a biblical track. Based on our Lord's Great Commission in Matthew 28:19-20, this diagram outlines the basic tasks a leader performs in a multiplicity of ways again and again. Methodologies and vehicles of ministry may come and go, but these basic, biblically rooted truths remain constant. These truths are:

Go. Go into the world of single adults. It's a demographically documented fact that single adults are not automatically programmed to attend church. The majority of single adults, in fact, are unchurched. The word *go* implies that the church must go to them. The church's ministry must reach out and proclaim to the single adult, "We are a single-adult-friendly church!"

Speak. Speak the good news of the gospel. Single adults are looking for good news, not bad. A ministry based on the redemptive love, grace, and acceptance of our Lord Jesus—a single adult Himself—is a must!

Introduce. Introduce single adults to the person of Jesus Christ. Christ-centered single-adult ministry does not stop with social interaction and membership in an organization. It leads single adults to vital relationships with God through His Son, Jesus Christ!

Teach. Teach single adults everything in God's Word

about relationships with God, others, and self. The Bible is a relationships Book—a natural for single adults, who are a relational people!

Empower. Christian single adults are the church, too. The opportunities and privileges of church membership should be the same for single adults as for married adults. Single-adult ministry helps change church culture so that single adults are full, first-class citizens of faith!

Equip. Equipping means discipling! Help single adults acquire and develop the spiritual disciplines and life skills that bring fulfillment and wholeness in Christ. In turn, they will want to reach other single adults for the faith and the church!

Have no fear. Isn't single-adult ministry a fearful risk? Yes, it's complex and diverse. As with life, we do not have the promise of a neat, tidy, predictable ministry. However, we can have confidence in the promise of Christ's presence. So don't let fear keep you and your church from needed ministry with single adults!

Continue. You may have attempted single-adult ministry in the past and found that it did not work. Yet you have no alternative but to continue. Evaluate. Make a better plan the next time—but continue. To quit is to ignore that the single-adult ministry field is ready for harvest. And we pray that you will be a laborer!

The Single-Adult Ministry
Great Commission

Go into the world of the never married, the separated, the divorced, the widowed, and the single-parent family. Speak the good news of the gospel. Introduce them to Christ and empower them to be the church. Teach them to grow in relationship to God, others, and self. Equip them to go and reach other single adults. Have no fear, for Christ is present with you. Continue, for more than 75 million single adults, mostly unreached, await you.

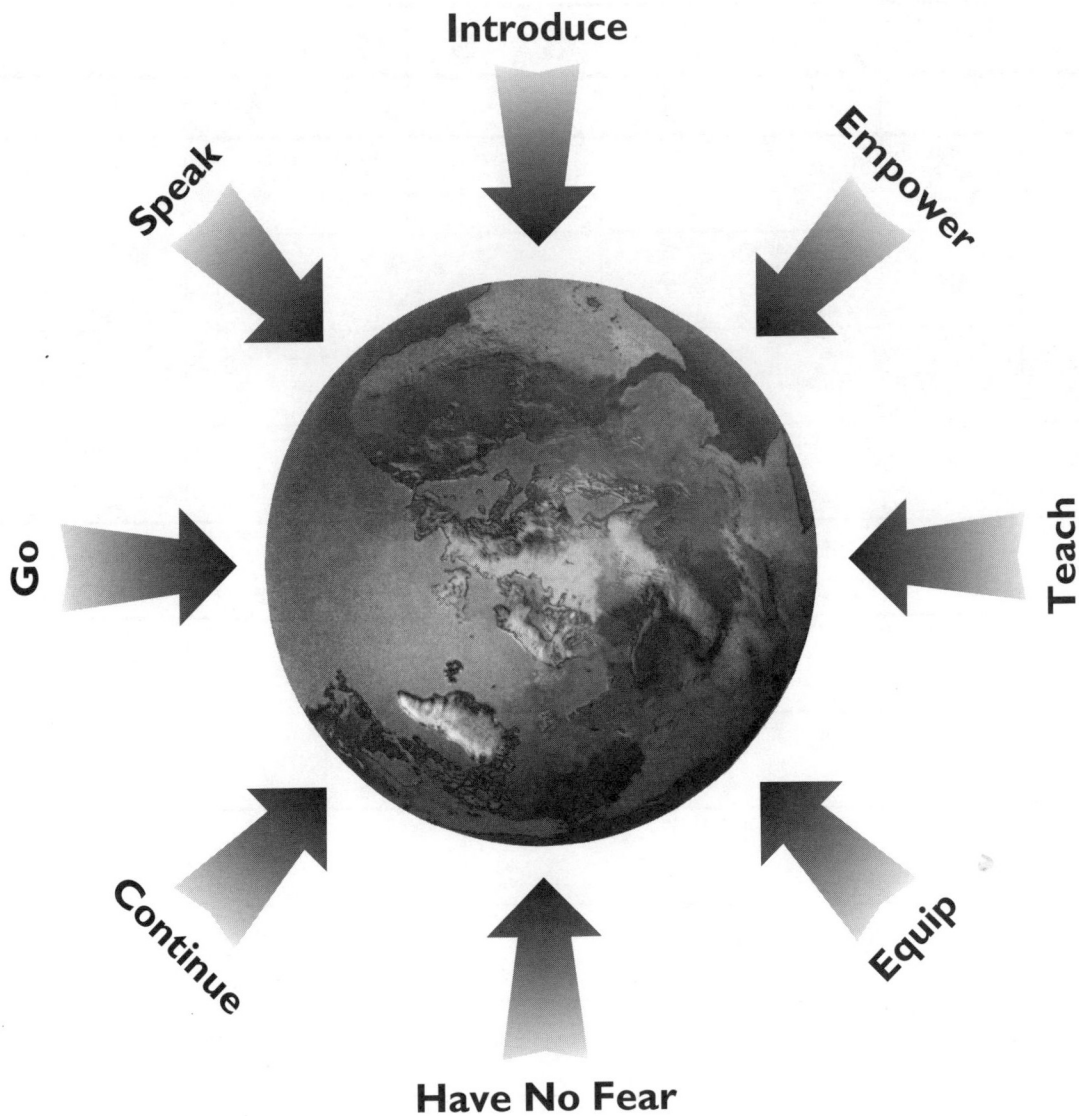

Introduce

Speak

Empower

Go

Teach

Continue

Equip

Have No Fear

use the single-adult
ministry toolbox

Tools for Planning Your Single-Adult Ministry

The Single-Adult Ministry Great Commission Sampler

This one-year sample planner illustrates a way ministry actions can be planned to address the eight issues in this manual. Note that each action includes in bold type a directive from the Single-Adult Ministry Great Commission that identifies the action's purpose (see the Great Commission diagram on the previous page). Make your own plans with the Single-Adult Ministry Great Commission Planner on the following page.

	ISSUE							
	1	**2**	**3**	**4**	**5**	**6**	**7**	**8**
Jan.	Survey the needs of single adults in your ministry. **Go.**				Organize a divorce-recovery or single-parent ministry. **Speak.**			
Feb.		Lead single adults in a study of *Start a Revolution*. **Empower.**						
Mar.			Organize a peer listeners' team. **Equip.**					
Apr.				Evaluate the user-friendliness of your church for single adults. **Go.**				
May					Invite leaders to an evaluation-and-planning day for the future. **Continue. Have no fear.**			
June								Sponsor a community volleyball tournament. **Go.**
July						Conduct a lay-counseling information seminar. **Continue. Have no fear.**		
Aug.								Plan a special outreach event. **Speak. Introduce.**
Sept.					Train leaders for the upcoming Sunday School/Bible-study year. **Equip. Introduce. Teach.**			
Oct.					Start a new Bible-study unit for single adults. **Introduce. Teach.**			
Nov.			Submit names of qualified single adults for church-leadership positions. **Empower.**					
Dec.								Share faith through a special holiday event. **Introduce.**

The Single-Adult Ministry Great Commission Planner
As you read this manual, select actions you can take to address the eight issues presented and determine appropriate months for taking these actions.
Record the Single-Adult Ministry Great Commission factor that relates to each action
you plan (see the Single-Adult Ministry Great Commission diagram on p. 9).

	ISSUE							
	1	2	3	4	5	6	7	8
Jan.								
Feb.								
Mar.								
Apr.								
May								
June								
July								
Aug.								
Sept.								
Oct.								
Nov.								
Dec.								

Issue ①
understanding today's
single adults

If you have recently read information about family structure, you have been confronted by the truth that the future of family ministry is also the future of single-adult ministry. Headlines like these consistently drive us to learn more about what the church can do to influence this population for Christ:

- The number of young people saying no to marriage has tripled in 25 years
- More single parents are never married
- The swinging single: fact or fiction?
- Percentage of two-parent families continues to decline
- National trend: older single women are choosing to have children on their own
- The virginity comeback
- How divorced people see the church
- Why Madison Avenue targets women who are single[1]

If these headlines have captured your attention, read on as you venture to understand single adults and to discover ways to minister with them. *—Tim Cleary*

---

[1] *Single Adult Ministries Journal,* issues 102, 99, 108, 111, 113, 106, 107, 105, 110.

Solution ①

Welcome to Single Land: Understand Single Adults' Demographics and Viewpoints[1]
George Barna

Between 1965 and 1991 the share of American adults who were not married grew from 27 percent of the population to 39 percent. Demographic trends show that unmarried America will continue to grow; some estimate that by the year 2000 half of American adults will be unmarried.

Within this block of nearly two of five American adults exists a variety of different marital statuses and living arrangements. In 1991 ¼ (26 percent) of American men and nearly ⅕ (19 percent) of American women had never been married. Almost ¹⁄₁₂ of men and ¹⁄₁₀ of women were currently divorced or separated. About 4 percent of Americans over 18 were cohabiting. Seven percent of American adults were widows or widowers. Finally, living with all of these adults were 28 percent of American children—more than one in four. One label, whether it is "single" or "unmarried," could never accurately describe all of these people. Never-married adults, cohabiting couples, divorced adults, and widows live

radically different lives. They have unique interests, pressures, and needs. Although they live side by side, they occupy different social and economic strata.

Therefore, there is no such thing as a one-size-fits-all single-adult ministry. Four distinct single-adult populations require special understanding and deserve unique ministry.

The Never Married

Six of every 10 single adults have never been married. In comparison to other single adults, they are young, sexually active, transient, cosmopolitan, independent, career-driven, concerned about their future, and in debt. Few believe in absolute moral truth. They are the least likely among single adults to read the Bible, to attend church services, or to view church as relevant.

Divorced Persons

Having experienced one of the most extreme life changes possible, divorced persons, especially women, struggle with emotional insecurity, relationships, cynicism, and economic displacement. Their marital problems typically cause them to become more spiritually inclined, but their spirituality is private. They appreciate Christianity but not Christian churches, often because they experience judgment in response to their divorces.

Single Parents

This hybrid segment (either never-married or divorced adults) is notable for high levels of stress, fatigue, and anger toward the opposite sex. They long for a return to lifestyle comfort and ample leisuretime. They are surprisingly optimistic about the future, often because of heightened attachment to their children—their source of stability and hope. Despite a heightened God-consciousness, they are inconsistently connected to church. The keys to their church involvement are time, energy, and outstanding youth and children's programs.

The Widowed

Today we have the healthiest, longest-living, and most financially comfortable segment of widowed adults in history. Their unique attributes are traditional moral values, the inclination to volunteer at churches, and relative disinterest in remarriage. Unlike in the past, today's widowed persons tend to be supporters rather than beneficiaries of church ministry.

Outreach to Single Adults

To be effective in ministry to single adults, be aware of certain facts and exercise certain cautions:

- Be sensitive to single adults' financial struggles. Funding appeals may receive negative reactions, while user fees may become limitations.
- Single adults need—and expect—ministry that is customized to their unique situations.
- Emphasize interpersonal relationships rather than the institutional church.
- Anticipate transience and inconsistent involvement.
- Some single adults may seem hypercritical of your ministry.
- Expect single adults, except the widowed, to reject moral absolutes.

On the other hand, be aware of these opportunities:

- Single adults respond well to persons who honestly care about their life change and who provide realistic guidance.
- Single adults appreciate low-pressure environments for establishing significant friendships.
- Biblical teaching that addresses single adults' life needs

and makes tangible application captures their attention.

- Single adults with children need help in providing balanced parenting.
- Single adults with time on their hands are seeking opportunities to serve and to be valued.

The following chart, which depicts the different sizes of age groups, shows how each age group's marital status is split among never marrieds, spouses, divorced persons, and widows and widowers. Very few Americans over the age of 35 have never been married, and very few Americans younger than 55 are currently widowed.

What makes this chart look different than it would have decades ago is the presence of vast numbers of divorced persons. The share of currently divorced Americans peaks between ages 35 and 44, reflecting the fact that widespread divorce is a fairly new trend. In several decades a graph like this may reveal a much greater share of divorced elderly and never-married middle-agers.

factoid

Some estimate that by the year 2000 half of American adults will be unmarried.
Source: George Barna

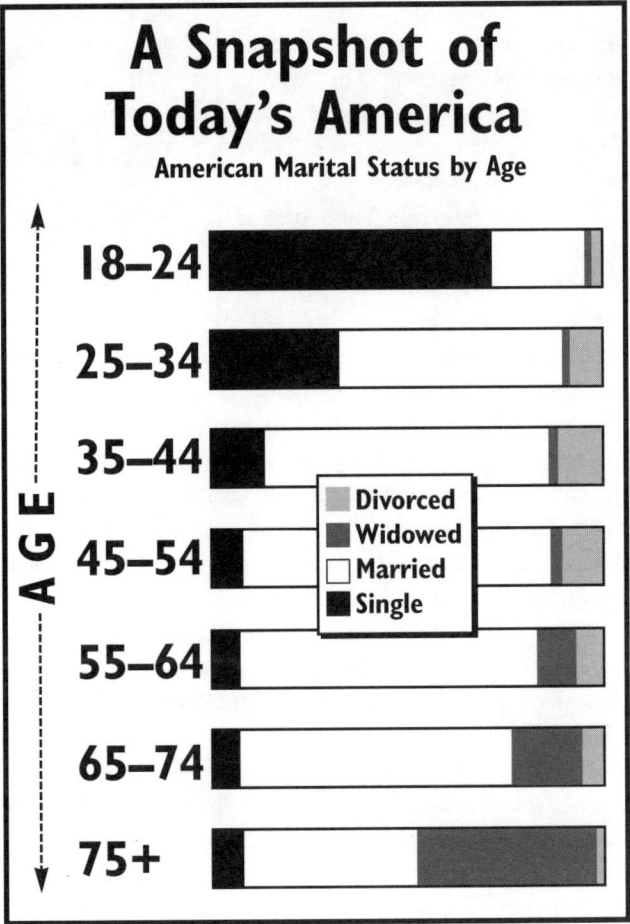

A Snapshot of Today's America
American Marital Status by Age

AGE

- 18–24
- 25–34
- 35–44
- 45–54
- 55–64
- 65–74
- 75+

Legend:
- ■ Divorced
- ■ Widowed
- □ Married
- ■ Single

[1]This section is based on George Barna, *Unmarried America: How Singles Are Changing and What It Means for the Church* (Glendale, Calif.: Barna Research Group, 1993), 5, 7, 19–20, 22–24.

Welcome to Single Land:
Understand Single Adults' Lifestyles
Harold Ivan Smith

What is it like to be a single adult today? One thing is certain: it is tougher to reach today's single adults than in our early years of ministry, and in the words of one mountain man, "It's a-fixin' to get even tougher."

The greatest threat to reaching single adults is attempting to minister without a knowledge of the culture. Often, like the Israelites pining for Egypt, we long for a bygone golden age of the family–likely the result of watching too many episodes of "The Waltons" and "Leave It to Beaver." Change, moral decay, violence, technological advances, stress, and isolation are all part of the raveling American social fabric. Every single adult is affected, directly or indirectly, by the cultural shaking and sifting. There's no place to hide!

Let's look at some of the hot buttons:

Angry males. "I am angry! Hear me roar!" Days after the 1994 Congressional elections a major newspaper published a front-page story about angry-male-voter backlash. Males are angry at the absence and security of good jobs; at feminists; at gays; at nonwhites; and apparently at one another, given the amount of male-on-male violence and spousal violence. The leading question of the decade may be, What does it really mean to be male? Some persons who are answering the question are not resolving but refueling the debate.

The loss of civility. Rudeness, vulgarity, crudeness, and the absence of manners are epidemic. Forget Mama's guidance, "Be nice." Call talk radio and get a few biases off your chest about "them" and "those people." What passes for dialogue in movies and television leaves little to the imagination; four-letter words and sexual double entendre make it more "realistic." The average American spends 28 hours a week ingesting such "entertainment," and some single adults watch twice the average.

The loss of trust. Whom do single adults trust–especially those who are relationally challenged or have been deeply wounded? Soon the answer will be "No one." In the "Whom do you respect?" poll, politicians are neck in neck for last place (with used-car salespersons). Politicians are about the business of getting elected, then reelected. *Family values* is a new code phrase grabbed by too many politicians who ditched their first families for more politically expedient or helpful mates. Can you trust the government? Social Security? a savings-and-loan association? your neighbor? a single-adult leader? Too often, the answer is "I don't think so."

> ## factoid
> The greatest threat to reaching single adults is attempting to minister without a knowledge of the culture.
> Source: Harold Ivan Smith

The loss of community. Despite the widespread philosophy that we all need others, most single adults want to do their own thing. Why do I need a single-adult group, much less the church? "Here today, gone tomorrow" is as true for church involvement as for an apartment lease. We have become a nation of strangers even where we worship. We may allow 2.6 minutes to be "friendly," and we may sing a chorus about fellowship with God's family, but after the final amen, reality supplants the implementation of the lyrics.

In spite of these bleak trends, there is good news. As Mordecai reminded Queen Esther, " 'Who knows but that you have come to royal position for such a time as this?' " (Esth. 4:14). Who knows but that you have come to ministry for such a time as this? Sure, it would have been easier to carry out ministry in the '50s and '60s, but today offers an incredible opportunity for authentic New Testament ministry with more than 75 million single adults. This is no time for hand-wringing! A leader should not resist change or even try to understand it but should regard it as an opportunity.

Remember when David fled from the menacing King Saul, who was determined to kill him? His friend Jonathan "went to David at Horesh and helped him find strength in God" (1 Sam. 23:16). Like Mordecai and Jonathan, we are creatively and redemptively to encourage single adults to "find strength in God" to deal with the issues, pressures, complexities, and challenges of singleness in the last years of this millennium. May God help us be faithful.

I recently saw a hopeful sign: an 87-year-old, never-married single adult named Oseola McCarty gave the University of Southern Mississippi $150,000 to endow a scholarship program. Her example should give all single adults a jolt upside the soul!

Check the statements with which you agree and discuss why with someone.
Ministry with today's single adults is about—
❑ **respecting their individuality;**
❑ **resourcing their responsible responsiveness to their culture;**
❑ **relinquishing our desires to squeeze them into our molds and expectations;**
❑ **resisting the pressure to make the teachings of the New Testament more palatable to the inhabitants of this highly secular culture;**
❑ **regularly remembering to ask, How would Jesus love today's single adults?**

How do we minister to single adults today?
• By listening to the ends of their sentences, especially

when they are telling us what it is like to be them
- By staying alert to the culture, breaking free of yesterday's mind-sets and assumptions
- By getting to know them so that we can pray specifically rather than generically for and with them
- By being there for them, particularly in the black-and-blue losses and the three-cheers celebrations of their lives

- By reminding them that the God who used Esther (and Mordecai to remind Esther) has a plan for each single adult today

And if you haven't run into a single adult recently, you ought to get on your knees and ask why. Today's single adults represent more than 75 million opportunities!

Solution ②

Meet Mr. and Ms. Single Adult: Understand Their Spiritual Needs
Carolyn Koons

As we move toward a new millennium, we will hear more about the spiritual aspect of life. The Christian faith is being challenged by New Age and spiritualism movements. An effective ministry with single adults must realize the tremendous opportunity presented by this interest in the spiritual side of life. The book *Single-Adult Passages* outlines considerations in meeting single adults' spiritual needs:

Because God designed people as spiritual creatures, we all possess a desire to explore and understand the supernatural. Some may deny the need for divine guidance, but few reject it altogether. Many Christian singles who have experienced divorce may drift back to the church seeking spiritual answers and growth. A sense of inner renewal may take place because they now have more freedom to explore their spiritual nature.

People searching for spiritual direction react more easily to a warm, positive presentation of the gospel than to a cold, judgmental approach. The spiritual teaching and personal counseling must be practical as well as inspirational. Leaders must convey warmth and friendship and be transparent enough in their teaching that listeners feel free to open up and discuss their concerns. The most successful leaders are those who share their own feelings in the process of instruction and counseling.

Teaching spiritual truths must be viewed as more than delivering biblical information. The portrait of Christ in the New Testament shows that He was genuinely concerned about the spiritual growth of His audience. He took into consideration their specific needs and adjusted His

methods to meet them. Those who teach single adults should not be afraid to adjust their lesson plan to accommodate a recent teachable moment or current issue.[1]

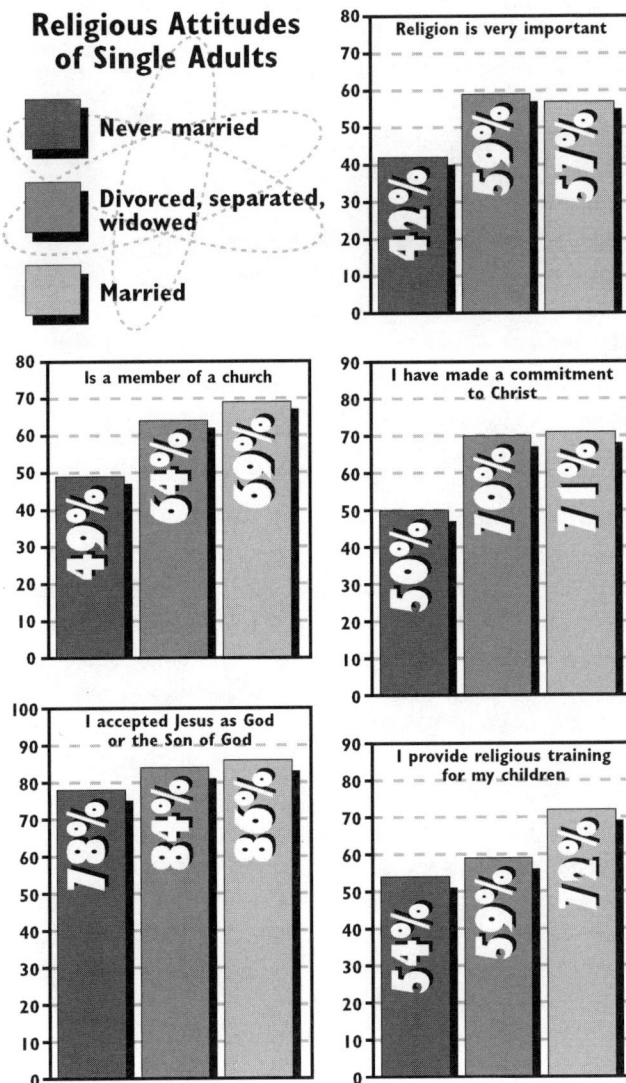

Religious Attitudes of Single Adults
- Never married
- Divorced, separated, widowed
- Married

Religion is very important: 42%, 59%, 57%

Is a member of a church: 49%, 64%, 69%

I have made a commitment to Christ: 50%, 70%, 71%

I accepted Jesus as God or the Son of God: 78%, 84%, 86%

I provide religious training for my children: 54%, 59%, 72%

[1]Carolyn A. Koons and Michael J. Anthony, *Single-Adult Passages: Uncharted Territories* (Grand Rapids: Baker, 1991), 175.

Meet Mr. and Ms. Single Adult: Understand Their Personal Needs
Norm Yukers

It is with design and purpose that we gather single adults around the concept of family. Every time we bring single adults together with one another and within the extended church family, we strengthen a single family. The challenge of meeting the needs of contemporary families includes the single-family unit.

Like other families, single adults should be guided to develop their relationships with God, self, and others. They are encouraged to seek personal relationships with God through Jesus Christ. They are urged to know themselves better, becoming aware of the many aspects of their person-hood. Finally, single adults can have successful relationships with significant others. Significant others include children if the single adult is a parent. They also include immediate family members, such as parents, grandparents, uncles, aunts, sisters, and brothers. Significant others are often found among acquaintances made in the workplace or friends made in all walks of life. Single adults are also part of God's family, the extended family of the church. Many single adults find their most significant family relationships within this context. For many single adults, the church is their family. So remember—single adults are single but not alone. Leaders have a responsibility to help this family develop and grow in Christ. Perhaps this Scripture says it best: "Let us not give up meeting together" (Heb. 10:25).

Identity Groupings

Before we can attempt to understand single adults, we must first discover who they are. Are they really different from married adults? If you have an effective ministry to couples, do you automatically have a successful single-adult ministry? The answers to these questions are yes and no!

Single adults can be categorized by status: never married, divorced, and widowed. They can also be divided by age as married persons are: Busters, Boomers, and the Silent Generation, for example. To this mix we could add married individuals who must function as single adults because they are separated. The divorced and widowed categories can be subdivided into those with children and those without. A further division could be made by grouping single parents with custody and those without.

Are you ready to give up? I hope not! Ministry with single adults is challenging but also very rewarding. Let's discover who single adults are so that we can better minister to and with them.

factoid

Eighty-one percent of men and 60 percent of women ages 20 to 24 have never married.
Source: U.S. Census Bureau

Never-Married Adults

Never-married adults are found in all age groups. The majority, however, are under age 35. Twenty-five percent of the U.S. population is in this category. These single adults, coupled with the Boomer or Buster age grouping, could be the largest mission field in the United States.

According to U.S. census data among women in their early 20s (20 to 24), 60 percent have never married. Among women 25 to 29 a full ⅓ have never married, and in the age group of 30 to 34, 19 percent have never married. Fifteen percent of women ages 35 to 39 have never married.

Of men ages 20 to 24, 81 percent have never married. Fifty percent of men ages 25 to 29 have never married. Thirty percent of men 30 to 34 and 20 percent of those 35 to 39 have never married. Obviously, the percentage decreases as age increases.

Ministry to never-married adults must include a balance of spiritual, social, and recreational activities. Open gym, volleyball leagues, weeknight Bible studies, and mission trips are the types of activities that must complement the traditional Sunday School/Bible-study ministry.

Strong male leadership is another must. After male leaders are developed, they in turn can help develop new male leaders.

Planning and programming for the never married must consider the number one myth they are battling. That myth is: to attain the American dream, you must have a successful career, be married, and have children (preferably one boy and one girl). Because many vocations require advanced education, many young adults delay marriage to obtain the required training. If marriage is seen as a goal for success, not to be married might be interpreted as failure.

Never-married adults live at home with their parents in greater numbers than ever because of unemployment, crises, or transitions. Although most of these periods are temporary, long-term situations result when a single adult wants to eliminate expense altogether or to avoid facing the real world. This circumstance often arrests single adults' sense of release from their parents. The need for relationships and skills for developing them are key needs for all single adults, especially never-married adults living with parents.

Divorced Adults

The United States is the home of 16.7 million divorced people. The ratio of the divorced to persons in intact marriages is 154 divorced per 1,000 married persons. The divorced compose almost 10 percent of the adult population but more than 22 percent of the single-adult population.

Today a strong divorce-recovery ministry is essential.

Because divorced persons entering a ministry are usually in pain, healing and reconciliation are major components of a ministry to them. Such a ministry might be divided into three distinct stages.

The first stage of a divorce-recovery ministry includes the early weeks and months after the realization that the divorce is imminent. This is crisis ministry that requires much support. All divorcing persons suffer blame and guilt to some degree. Anger is a huge obstacle, and overcoming it is emotionally and physically draining. If children are involved, any remaining energy is used to help them cope.

The second stage of a divorce-recovery ministry often extends from the early weeks into the first two years. A variety of issues may surface during this period, including these:

- Many divorced Christians search for forgiveness during this stage, even if they tried everything possible to save the marriage.
- The formerly married face the challenge of living on a changing budget.
- Divorced persons may need to confront the real or perceived stigma attached to divorce—the feeling that they wear a huge *D* on their foreheads.
- Formerly married persons must leave old relationships and make new ones.

The third stage begins in the second or third year beyond the divorce. At this point the formerly married are usually ready to begin setting new goals, which may include further education, a new vocation, or major purchases. Having left behind much of the hate and bitterness, the divorced have accepted singleness as a lifestyle, and many may have begun dating.

When offering a ministry to the formerly married, a church should focus on several key issues:

- Divorced persons need to have their identities and self-esteem affirmed in a healthy way. They need to recognize who they are in Christ, and the unsaved need to accept Christ and develop an identity in Him.
- Biblical teachings on forgiving self and others are essential as these single adults come to terms with their divorces. Teachings on marriage, divorce, and remarriage are often very helpful in this regard.
- Relational skills must be resurrected or taught as new skills. The divorced must learn how to deal with former spouses and in-laws. Those who date may face a new set of problems.
- Developing financial-management skills is crucial for divorced persons. In addition, financial stewardship needs to be modeled, and how-to seminars are important for persons without job skills.

- Sexual activity must be addressed. Formerly sexually active persons must be shown and taught the value of abstinence.
- Loneliness is an issue all single adults deal with but rarely want to discuss. Address this topic in discussions of companionship, fellowship, and community.
- More than any other group, the previously married need to find a place of stability. That's what your single-adult ministry needs to offer.

Widowed Adults

Widows and widowers share characteristics with divorced adults, although the results may be very different. A formerly married adult may direct anger or hatred toward the former spouse; the widowed may display anger or hatred toward God for "taking" a spouse. A widow or widower may display resentment because the spouse escaped difficult circumstances the surviving spouse must now confront alone.

Loneliness can be very intense. Often, a surviving spouse's self-worth suffers with the death of the spouse. During the expected time of grief, this new single adult is vulnerable and under great stress. Widowed persons often doubt their self-sufficiency and may avoid social activities. This time may be a period of disorganization and lack of personal care. Depression, self-pity, and a fear of rejection are other problems that may develop.

The church needs to minister to surviving spouses, and this ministry needs to extend beyond a few weeks after the death. The surviving spouse often needs help regaining self-acceptance and self-worth. Good friends are needed to listen, understand, and provide comfort during this difficult time.

Single Parents

Cutting across all of the previous categories are single parents. Census data reveal 10.9 million single parents. They account for 30 percent of the total number of families in which children are present. This same census showed an alarming statistic about single parents. More than half of the children of single parents resulted from out-of-wedlock pregnancies.

Single parents' needs are many. Current statistics show that female-headed single-parent families are the fastest-growing group of families in the United States. Women, in most cases, are the disciplinarians, cooks, nurses, teachers, counselors, maids, repair persons, and spiritual leaders of the home. More than 80 percent of mothers with custody have been granted child support, but less than 50 percent receive what is granted. The single-parent custodial father faces the

> **factoid**
>
> The church needs to minister to surviving spouses, and this ministry needs to extend beyond a few weeks after the death.
> Source: Norm Yukers

problem of providing for and nurturing his children. Providing comes naturally for most men, but nurturing is foreign to them. Noncustodial single parents experience an exaggerated sense of losing regular contact with their children.

Most often, single parents share or have dual custody of children. A church that tries to reach single-parent families must consider weekend-visitation circumstances.

Single parents are challenged to deal with issues like—
- understanding dual roles and responsibilities;
- financial problems;
- custody issues;
- effective discipline;
- communication between homes;
- stress overload.

Effective ministry to single parents must include ministry to their children. It must be a family ministry. The church needs to rethink its traditional view of the family to include children of single parents, at the same time equipping single parents to address grief, anger, rejection, fear, and their children's feelings of abandonment. Ministry to the children of single parents is more than child care.

Separated Adults

Separated persons live as single adults, although they are actually still married. Bud and Kathy Pearson have addressed three areas to consider when ministering to the separated:

- What we need to know about separated persons
- Attitudes about separated persons
- Goals for separated persons

The Pearsons state that the feeling of loss is an every-moment experience for the separated. Their guilt over their part in the separation and anger directed at self and spouse are also constant realities. The changes and uncertainties in their lives cause them to fear the future. If children are involved, explaining what is happening may be difficult.

The Pearsons also believe that it is important to know how others are treating the separated person. Often, parents do not understand and therefore add to the devastation. Friends, unable to cope with the situation, sometimes send signals of rejection. Co-workers display insensitivity and are unsupportive.[1]

Consequently, separated persons feel alone and alienated and are often open to caring ministry. A single-adult ministry must offer counseling and encouragement and can help the separated avoid quick romantic or emotional relationships. Emphasizing the need to wait can encourage the person to view reconciliation as an option.

factoid

Separated persons feel alone and alienated and are often open to caring ministry.
Source: Norm Yukers

Generational Groupings[2]

A look at the lives of Mr. and Ms. Single Adult would not be complete without a discussion of generational characteristics. Christian education is currently being reoriented to meet the needs of adults through generational groupings like the following.

- The GI Generation was born before 1930 and came of age during the Depression. Many fought in World War II. Frugal and patriotic, they make up 14 percent of the U.S. population. In the single-adult population these are now primarily older, widowed women.

- The Depression Generation was born between 1930 and 1939. Many Depression women married GI men and produced Baby Boomers; women from this generation had babies younger and went to work in greater numbers than any other generation. Having moved from difficult economic times as youngsters to prosperous times as young adults, they make up 8 percent of the population.

- War Babies were born between 1940 and 1945. Composing 6 percent of the population, this group is poorly defined and is often grouped with the generation preceding or following. This segment, including older Boomers, is on the forefront of the divorce epidemic. Many have remarried, creating a need for blended-family ministry. Others, moving through mid-life single again, search for meaning.

- Baby Boomers, born between 1946 and 1964, make up 30 percent of the population. Early Boomers, 1946 to 1959, are quite different from later Boomers. Early Boomers were greatly influenced by Vietnam, Woodstock, and the Kennedy and King assassinations.

- Seventeen percent of the population, born between 1965 and 1976, are often called Baby Busters. They are characterized by disillusionment, feelings of abandonment, independence, and defensiveness. They are also sensitive to people, pragmatic, and pluralistic. Seventy percent of Busters are single.

- The remaining 25 percent of the population, although not adults, compose the Baby Boomlet. Born between 1977 and 1995, this generation is a product of the Baby Boomers and is approaching Boom status in its size and scope.

The chart on the next page summarizes the single status of each generational grouping of adults.

---

[1]Bud and Kathy Pearson, "Singles—The Separated," in *Singles Ministry Handbook,* ed. Douglas L. Fagerstrom (Wheaton, Ill.: Victor, 1988), 54–56.
[2]Diane Crispell, "Where Generations Divide: A Guide," *American Demographics,* May 1993, 9–10.

GI GENERATION
Divorced - - - - - - - - - - - - - 5 percent
Never married - - - - - - - - 5 percent
Widowed - - - - - - - - - - - 35 percent

DEPRESSION GENERATION
Divorced - - - - - - - - - - - - 10 percent
Never married - - - - - - - - 5 percent
Widowed - - - - - - - - - - 10 percent
Separated - - - - - - - - - - - 3 percent

WAR BABIES
Divorced - - - - - - - - - - - - Almost 15 percent
Never married - - - - - - - - 6 percent
Widowed - - - - - - - - - - - 3 percent
Separated - - - - - - - - - - 3 percent

BABY BOOMERS
Divorced - - - - - - - - - - - - 11.5 percent
Never married - - - - - - - - 16 percent
Separated - - - - - - - - - - More than 3 percent
Widowed - - - - - - - - - - - Less than 1 percent

BABY BUSTERS
Never married - - - - - - - - 70 percent
Divorced - - - - - - - - - - - - 3 percent
Separated - - - - - - - - - - 2 percent

Meet Mr. and Ms. Single Adult: How to Respond in Ministry
Tim Cleary and Norm Yukers

You can meet single adults' needs through three major components of your single-adult ministry:

Ministry with Single Adults Through Relationships

Premise: A single adult is a family unit of one or more. Single adults are extended family to one another.

Ministry principle: Scripture admonishes us that it is not good for persons to be alone. We were created for relationships with God, self, and others. Helping single adults develop Christian community with others is vitally important to a successful single-adult ministry.

Response ideas:
- Organize prayer partners.
- Start men's and women's accountability groups.
- Sponsor activities encouraging fellowship among single adults.
- Plan dinner parties of fives.
- Encourage generational roles within the single-adult group, such as brothers, sisters, aunts, and uncles.

- Recognize areas of church life already involving single adults.
- Provide wholesome information and atmospheres for healthy male-female relationships to develop.

Ministry with Single Adults Through Peer Groups

Premise: Although all adults have similar needs, single adults do not always have the same support systems in place to meet those needs. Adults who are recently single again, for example, have crisis clusters of needs unique to their situations. Consider that the church often plans for twos, fours, and sixes—when single adults may come in ones, threes, and fives. For example, in Sunday School/Bible-study groups, peer families of single adults are needed for ministry growth to occur. Single adults thrust into couples-only groups often feel like fifth wheels. Men's and women's classes are often better integrators, as well as single-adult departments, classes, and groups.

Response ideas:
- Start peer Sunday School/Bible-study groups.
- Develop single-adult discipleship groups and opportunities.
- Provide opportunities to build friendships through outdoor outreach activities like hiking and camping.
- Organize ministry around peer needs, such as single parents, divorce, and recovery issues.
- Plan ministry around social opportunities that allow single adults to gather and make friends in safe environments.
- Formulate affinity groups around professions, hobbies, and personal interests.

Ministry with Single Adults Through Church-Integration Strategies

Premise: Many single adults have no need for a single-adult peer-group ministry. They want to be seen first as adults and then as single. Strategies are needed to integrate single adults throughout a church's life and leadership. Many areas of a church already minister with single adults who participate in those areas. Intentionally or unintentionally integrated Sunday School/Bible-study groups, sports teams, and other groups are needed to reach these individuals.

Response ideas:
- Encourage church members to serve as surrogate grandparents or parents for single-parent families.
- Invite another church organization to sponsor a single-adult activity. For example, the women's enrichment ministry could sponsor a single-mothers conference.
- Provide lists of qualified single adults for church-leadership positions.
- Develop intentionally mixed married and single-adult Sunday School/Bible-study alternatives.

Solution ③

Understand the Micro Viewpoint: Solutions for Smaller Churches
Karen Gibson

A church understands single adults when it takes time to know them not only by faces or names but also by talents and needs. A smaller church is often in a unique position to get to know its single adults. In fact, more ministry with single adults may take place in a smaller church simply because of its size.

Single adults need to be understood as individuals with specific emotional, physical, social, and spiritual needs. Jesus is our example. He met the woman at the well, understood her need for living Water, then met her need. Jesus saw Zacchaeus in a tree, understood his need for fellowship and love, then met that need. Jesus taught us to look at persons, listen to their hearts, accept them, love them, and meet their needs.

Most smaller churches are adept at dealing with the widowed, a category of singleness they know well. Healing in times of grief is an individual process and takes time. Be available to listen; writing on your calendar dates important to widowed friends and remembering them with cards and words of encouragement can be very meaningful.

One church family experienced loss by the death of a husband and father, and the church responded in a caring way. Because the widow was lonely, she remarried too soon, and a divorce resulted. One day shortly after the divorce, her six-year-old asked, "Where are all the people?" The woman asked, "What do you mean?" Her daughter replied: "When my first daddy went away, our friends at church brought food and came to play with me. No one came when my second daddy left." The need for this church to understand divorced persons was evident.

Following are ways leaders and members in smaller churches can get involved in ministry with single adults through relationships. Doing so is a potential church-growth opportunity, because demographics indicate that at least half of all single adults prefer smaller churches.

- Invite one or two single adults to be part of your life. Everyone will be blessed.
- Single adults enjoy having meals with others. An evening or weekend, Sunday after church, or a holiday would be a great time to involve single adults in your extended family.
- Intergenerational friendships can be very rewarding. Older or younger friends can often provide enlightening perspectives on life. The majority of single adults in our population are under the age of 35.
- Families can be one person or many. Include single-adult families in church activities.
- Another adult can volunteer to escort a single parent's child to church events when a parent is not available.
- Special adult friends are important to children. Meeting the needs of a single-parent family may include taking a child shopping for the parent before Christmas, Mother's Day, Father's Day, or a birthday.
- Bartering baby-sitting or a parents' night out can allow the single parent time to see a movie, shop, or rest, providing a much-needed break from the pressures of single parenting.
- Be a friend to a single parent. Sometimes just having a conversation with another adult over coffee or a soft drink is a treat.
- Single adults in your church have many of the same needs as married adults, such as the need for Christ, the need for acceptance, the need to serve, and the need for Christian friendship. Look for commonalities to draw you together and differences to help you learn about single persons.
- Invite single adults to serve as church leaders. Some may actually have time on their hands. In many smaller churches single adults can be an important part of the leadership infrastructure.

Whatever approaches you use to get to know your single adults, remember that they want to be understood and accepted for who they are and that they do not want to be stereotyped. Single adults want their needs met, but they also want to help meet others' needs. And single adults want acceptance and respect from the church in which they have chosen to worship and serve.

> **factoid**
>
> Half of single adults prefer smaller churches with fewer than one hundred members.[1]
> Source: George Barna

---

[1] George Barna, *Unmarried America: How Singles Are Changing and What It Means for the Church* (Glendale, Calif.: Barna Research Group, 1993), 55.

Solution ④
use the single-adult
ministry toolbox

Tools for Understanding Today's Single Adults

Identifying Single-Adult Needs and Interests

This tool, regularly used with leaders and participants, will help you constantly focus ministry actions on single adults' life needs and interests. Take a few moments to identify common needs and interests of single adults in your church and community, including your own needs and interests. Then suggest ideas for addressing these.

Category	In the Church	In the Community	Ideas for Meeting Needs
Spiritual Needs/ Interests			
Emotional Needs/ Interests			
Relational Needs/ Interests			
Material Needs/ Interests			
Physical Needs/ Interests			
Intellectual Needs/ Interests			
Recreational Needs/ Interests			
Crisis Needs/ Interests			
Other			

Single-Adult Needs Action Planner

Use this tool to help single adults communicate their needs and interests so that you can build ministry actions around their needs. On the worksheet identify the needs of a single adult or a single-adult group and plan simple or complex ministry actions. To identify needs, write above the circle the name of the person or group. Record obvious needs of the person or group illustrated by each concentric circle. Then write an action plan for each need.

Individual or group: _____

PHYSICAL/MATERIAL

RELATIONAL

EMOTIONAL

SPIRITUAL

PSYCHOLOGICAL

Needs

1. _____

2. _____

3. _____

4. _____

Ministry Action Plan

1. _____

2. _____

3. _____

4. _____

Adapted from Jerry and Lana Wilkinson, *Developing Ministries with Single-Parent Families* (Nashville: Convention, 1993), 29.

Needs-Focused Group Dynamics Planner

Single adults have the same basic needs as all adults:

Basic Needs

- Food, clothing, and shelter
- Sexual satisfaction
- Love and intimacy
- Intellectual stimulation
- Hope for the future
- Spiritual fulfillment
- Meaning and purpose

Within this context of basic adult needs, single adults in your church and community also have a diversity of their own needs, which the following categories will help you evaluate.

Identity Needs

Review the single-adult identity groupings and characteristics as a basis for learning how to meet their needs (see issue 1, solution 2). Determine the mix of identity groupings predominant in your ministry. Example: Those recently single again by divorce or by a spouse's death experience a cluster of needs, creating a crisis. Plan a loss-recovery workshop.

Generational Needs

As you examine the characteristics and needs of generational groupings, such as Busters, Boomers, and the GI Generation, apply these to your church's single-adult ministry. Example: Busters do not think of themselves as single adults. Therefore, consider addressing this group in your church by a name like 20-Something Ministry.

Felt Needs

Felt needs are conscious needs with which most single adults readily identify. Become familiar with these needs and interpret them for related church ministries to be developed. The Single-Adult Needs Action Planner on the previous page can assist you. Example: Most single adults desire social/relational connections, so allow time to socialize at your activities.

Discerned Needs

Discerned needs are those of which leaders may be aware but of which participants may not, such as spiritual, emotional, and psychological needs. God gives leaders insight and discernment to help single adults become aware of their deeper needs. Evaluate the single adults in your ministry arena and list their needs, realizing that one ministry goal may be to make them aware of these needs. Example: All single adults need to know Christ as Savior and Lord, so train single adults to share their faith with others.

The diagram on the next page will help you identify the needs of single adults in your church and community.

Dynamic energy is released as you plan and develop a balanced approach to meet single adults' needs. Identify and record on the illustration the needs represented in your group. When completed, the diagram will help you better understand your group's dynamics as you seek to meet its needs.

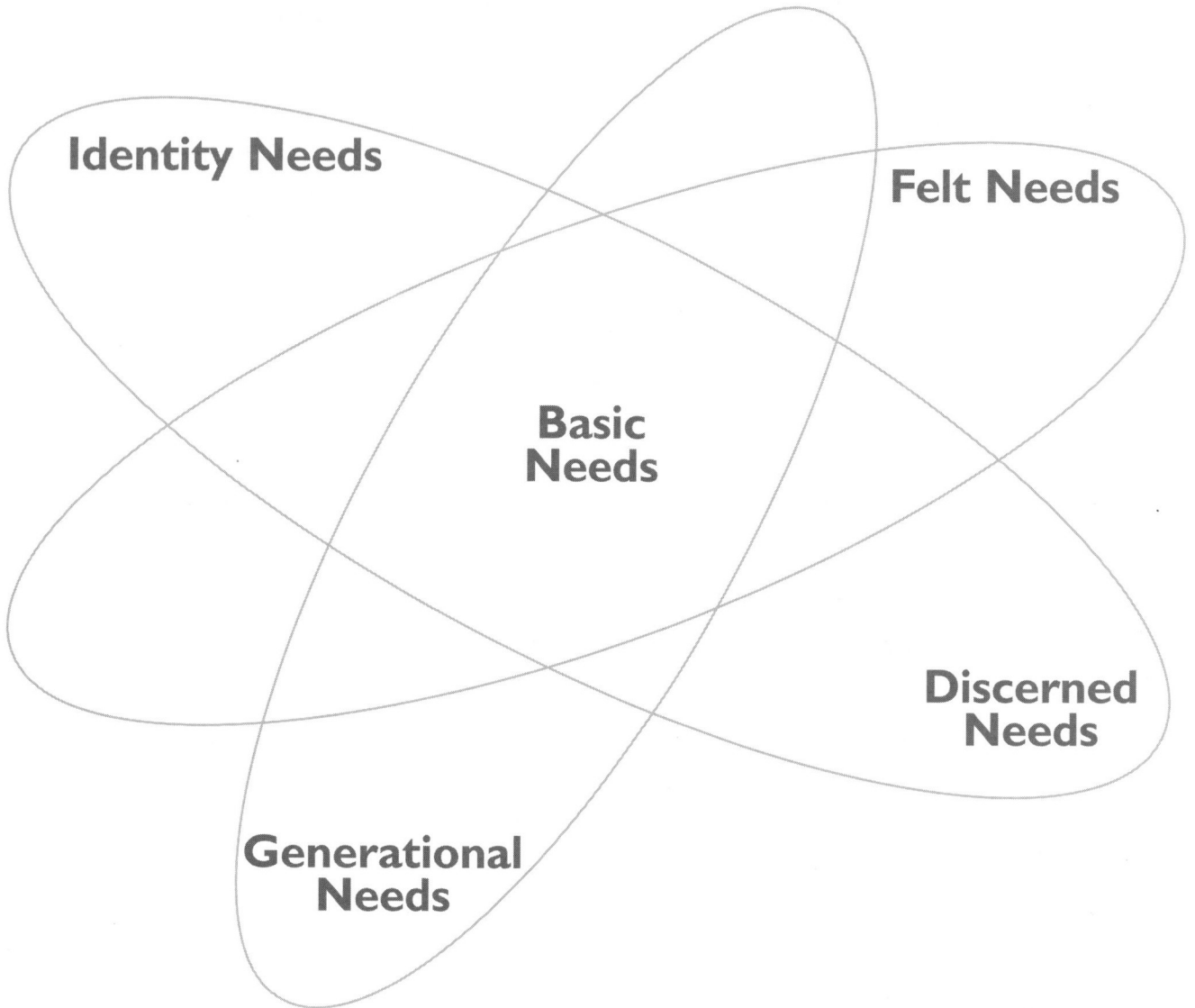

Identity Needs

Felt Needs

Basic Needs

Discerned Needs

Generational Needs

Issue ②
empowering single adults
for christian living

Empowerment is the difference between providing someone a meal and teaching him to grow his own food so that he can feed himself for a lifetime. Single-adult leader, are you doing ministry *for* single adults or *with* them? The material in issue 2, along with the book *Start a Revolution*, provides practical, hands-on ways to empower those you lead. —*Tim Cleary*

Solution ①

Determine the Primary Ministry Model to Meet Single Adults' Needs
Larry Garner

Single-adult ministry usually follows one or a combination of several ministry or leadership models. These are the entertainment model, the extended-youth model, the enabler model, the umbrella model, and the empowerment model. These are not exclusive of one another; rather, when one exists, all or some characteristics of the other models can also be found in the same single-adult group.

The Entertainment Model

The focus of an entertainment ministry model is social. Activities are used to attract single adults to a location or a function. Generally, this model differs very little from any number of other clubs or groups centered on social activities, sports, or interests. Single adults attracted by this model usually have low commitments to anything other than the quality of the event. When the fun runs out or another church or group offers a better time, the participants move on. Loyalty to the group is low. Little spiritual growth results, because the emphasis on spirituality is negligible.

> ## The Entertainment Model
> Focus is social
> Activity-oriented
> Low commitment level
> Limited spiritual growth

The Extended-Youth Model

Single adults are sometimes considered as no more than extended youth, regardless of their age or level of personal responsibility. Because they are not married, they are considered less than fully adult.

The extended-youth model is leader-centered. Low expectations are placed on single adults. Because they are treated as adolescents, they respond as adolescents. Rather than assume responsibilities for themselves and their ministry, they leave it up to the leader, who plans and conducts the activities.

Low expectations become self-fulfilling prophecies that lead to irresponsible behavior. Responsible single adults are not attracted to this type of ministry. If they find themselves in the situation, many leave or drop out. The group's nature becomes more and more adolescent as responsible single adults seek a ministry geared to adult needs.

> ## The Extended-Youth Model
> Leader-centered
> Low expectations
> Irresponsible behavior

The Enabler Model

Sometimes this model is thought of as a positive approach to single-adult ministry. *Enable*, however, is a psychological term meaning *one who allows or encourages another's inappro-*

priate or destructive behavior. This ministry model takes a soft-love approach. Rather than demanding progress toward healing, wholeness, and maturity, this model enables single adults to continue practicing arresting, if not destructive, behaviors.

The Enabler Model
Caring
Sympathetic
Soft love
Low expectations

The Umbrella Model

The umbrella model incorporates all single adults of all ages into one comprehensive unit. This model is generally characterized as small, unified, and loving but limited in its outreach, growth, and attractiveness to others beyond its existing membership.

Some, if not most, single-adult ministries necessarily begin with an umbrella model since the number of single adults in a particular congregation is usually small at the beginning of a ministry. If the single-adult population remains small, the group probably remains in an umbrella structure for an indefinite period. If the population of single adults is large, a structure must be developed beyond an individual unit for the ministry to be effective in reaching single adults from various segments of the population.

The umbrella model relates more to organizational structure than the previous three models do. The entertainment model, the extended-youth model, and the enabler model primarily concern philosophy and leadership styles.

The Umbrella Model
Small
Unified
All-inclusive
Limited

The Empowerment Model

The empowerment model is based on the ministry of Jesus. Jesus Christ was the most intentional person who ever lived. He said of Himself, " 'The Son of man did not come to be served, but to serve, and to give his life as a ransom for many' " (Mark 10:45). Ministry to single adults must be as intentional as Jesus' ministry.

In John 13 Jesus washed the feet of the twelve. When He finished, He asked the disciples, " 'Do you understand what I have done for you? … I have set you an example that you should do as I have done for you' " (vv. 12-15). In all areas of His life Jesus set the example for us. If we want to know how to relate to others, we look at the way Jesus related to persons. If we want to arrange our priorities, we look at Jesus' priorities. If we want to know how to treat our enemies, we look at the way Jesus treated His. If we want to be good teachers, we follow the example of the Master Teacher. If we want to know how to lead a person to faith, we look at the way Jesus led the Samaritan woman to ask for living Water. If we want to know how to lead, how to equip followers for effective ministry, how to take a group from unbelief to belief and responsible ministry, we look at the ministry of Jesus, the One who entrusted to a motley band of fishers the greatest work of all time.

Jesus often used interchangeably the terms *salvation, healing,* and *wholeness.* A ministry that follows Jesus' model must move persons toward these dimensions of full life.

An empowering ministry recognizes that every believer is a priest—a minister whom God has gifted with spiritual gifts. Placed in the body, the church, according to God's will, these gifted persons have places and ministries that only they can fulfill.

The empowerment model approaches single adults with the understanding that they are adults. The leader of single adults is an adult among other adults, a learner among other learners, a minister among other ministers. This type of ministry places expectations for commitment, conduct, and performance on participants.

Empowerment is a process. Moving a person from initial belief to maturity and responsible ministry takes time. Jesus called some of the twelve to belief in Him at the beginning of His ministry. A year into His ministry He formed the group of the twelve to follow Him in a different relationship. For the next year He taught them, modeled ministry before them, trained them, and sent them out. For another year, the last year of His earthly ministry, Jesus continued the process of preparing the disciples for the time when He would no longer be with them. Jesus' process in discipling the twelve is one we should emulate in our ministries with single adults.

The Empowerment Model
Salvation-healing-wholeness
Priesthood and giftedness
Expectations
A process

Solution ②

Choose the Empowerment Model
Larry Garner

Characteristics of the Empowerment Model

The empowerment model of single-adult leadership is based on several major ideas inherent in Jesus' ministry, in New Testament teachings on the nature of Christian ministry, and in the practice of adult education.

The Empowerment Model
Salvation-healing-wholeness
Priesthood and giftedness
Expectations
A process

Salvation-Healing-Wholeness

Jesus often used these terms almost interchangeably. For instance, He said to a man He had healed of blindness, " 'Receive your sight; your faith has healed you' " (Luke 18:42). To the woman healed of the hemorrhage Jesus said, " 'Daughter, your faith has healed you' " (Mark 5:34). The ideas of healing and salvation are linked, both containing the ideas of restoration and wholeness. In healing, the body is restored or made whole; in salvation the spirit is restored to a relationship with God—in a very real way, made whole. Single-adult ministry must have at its core the idea of wholeness.

The empowerment model accepts single adults' individual entry points but is not satisfied to allow them to remain in their situations. In this model those who need healing are encouraged to grow toward it.

The empowerment model is especially attractive to single adults who are healthy, well balanced, progressive, productive, and happy. When they enter groups with less-than-appropriate leadership models, they soon leave or limit their participation.

Priesthood and Giftedness

The doctrine of the priesthood of believers also empowers single adults for ministry. This teaching holds that each believer is a priest before God. Although our priesthood includes the dimensions of personal access and solely Christ-mediated forgiveness, another important aspect of priesthood is often overlooked: every believer is a minister.

The empowerment model of single-adult ministry highlights each believer's responsibility to engage in personal ministry. To equip each believer for that ministry, God gives

spiritual gifts (see 1 Cor. 12:7,11). These gifts of grace empower believers to build up the church (see 1 Cor. 14:5,12,26), to minister to one another (see 1 Pet. 4:10), and to glorify God (see 1 Pet. 4:11). This ministry is reciprocal: single adults are to minister as well as receive ministry.

Ministry is a two-way street.

Single adults
are to minister to others
as well as receive ministry
from others.

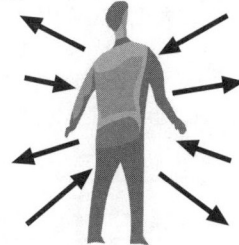

Expectations

When Jesus called His disciples to follow Him, He expected them to be His witnesses and to minister to others. When single-adult ministry is based on these principles, it establishes high expectations for participants and leaders, including mature responses, moral behavior, responsible ministry, and mutual love and care. Leaders' expectations for participants determine the nature and outcomes of a ministry to and with single adults.

A Process

The disciples enjoyed a special teaching relationship with Jesus for two years. From this example we learn that a key ingredient in the process of discipleship is relationships. Relationships allow for instruction, example, and apprenticeship—ingredients that empower single adults for ministry.

Ministry Models and Leadership

What tips the scales in terms of a positive or negative single-adult ministry model? The determining factor is means and end. For example, if entertainment is the dominant thrust of your ministry as an end in itself, it becomes a negative model.

**Freedom
and responsibility
must be balanced.**

The empowerment model never loses sight of the ultimate end: to take single adults from initial belief to responsible ministry. Activities and strategies are means to that end. This model addresses all areas of a person's life and development. Based on the areas of development suggested in Luke 2:52–"Jesus grew in wisdom and stature, and in favor with God and men"–a holistic ministry to single adults can be developed. Jesus developed in four dimensions:

• Intellectual/emotional
• Physical
• Spiritual
• Social

Although elements of various models can be reflected in a given ministry, one model probably predominates. One of the best ways to detect the dominant ministry model used in your single-adult ministry is to analyze your calendar and your budget.

WHAT IS YOUR MINISTRY MODEL?

On the following scale circle the number that indicates the degree to which each model is reflected in your single-adult ministry, with 5 being highly characteristic.

Entertainment model	1	2	3	4	5
Extended-youth model	1	2	3	4	5
Enabler model	1	2	3	4	5
Umbrella model	1	2	3	4	5
Empowerment model	1	2	3	4	5

Leadership: The Critical Link in Single-Adult Ministry

Leadership is the key element in determining the ministry model your single-adult ministry follows. The church's leadership team (pastor, deacons, minister of education, and so on) and single adults need to determine the priorities of your single-adult ministry in relationship to the church's ministry priorities. For instance, a church's priority might be evangelism, discipleship, fellowship, group building, or a number of priorities.

After your church's leadership team and single adults decide on the direction and type of single-adult ministry desired, the most important step is to find and empower leaders who are gifted to move the ministry in the chosen direction. These might be laypersons or a vocational minister working with laypersons, depending on the size of your church, single-adult ministry, and budget.

An important element in leadership is vision. The vision for your single-adult ministry determines the means chosen and, to a great extent, the end that will be achieved. Vision plays a major role in determining the model that shapes the outcome of your single-adult ministry.

Solution ③

Use These Principles of Empowerment

Larry Garner

The following principles of empowerment, which are at the core of Jesus' ministry with the twelve, provide a model for ministry with single adults.

Instruction

Jesus taught His followers. The Sermon on the Mount is actually teaching on the hillside; we are told that His disciples came to Him and that He taught them (see Matt. 5:1-2). Again and again Jesus is referred to as Rabbi or Teacher. In summary statements of His ministry, the Gospel writers always mentioned the teaching ministry first: He came teaching, preaching, and healing (see Matt. 4:23; 9:35). Jesus taught on a cognitive level, giving factual information, instruction, and direction. He taught persons about God's kingdom and instructed them in how to live as His followers.

Modeling

Jesus also taught persons on the affective level; that is, He sought to bring changes in their attitudes and feelings. One of the most effective ways to change attitudes is to model the attitude being taught. Jesus always provided an example for His disciples. He fleshed out His teachings. When He taught them to turn the other cheek, He did so too. When He taught them that service was the way to greatness in the Kingdom, He became the servant. When He warned of the dangers of material possessions, He had no place to call His own. When He taught them that the greatest love for one another is to lay down your life, He did.

Apprenticeship

Jesus was the preeminent teacher. He instructed, modeled, and required His hearers to put His teachings into practice or action. Today we know that learners retain–

- 10 percent of what we hear;
- 30 percent of what we see;
- 50 percent of what we hear and see;
- 70 percent of what we say;
- 90 percent of what we do.

Jesus set the lessons in life with assignments. He sent the disciples on tours of Galilee to proclaim, heal, and cast out demons (see Matt. 10:2-42; Luke 10:1-24). Jesus put them in situations that would test, stretch, and strengthen them.

This work was part of the discipleship process Jesus used to prepare His disciples for the Kingdom work ahead of them. This apprenticeship demanded risk, allowed failure, practiced patience, and required follow-up that included both public praise and private correction. Much of our discipleship is limited to instruction in group settings. Like Jesus, as part of discipleship we need to provide opportunities to practice in ministry what is learned.

Authority

The twelve were given authority before they were sent out. *Authority* means *mastery or dominion over persons, things, or situations—dominion granted by or derived from one with power.* Jesus was given authority by the Father, and the twelve were given authority by Jesus. On Jesus' authority we proclaim the gospel and baptize.

We must support single adults in their ministry endeavors with our authority and power, although our support is minor compared to that which God has already given to each believer.

Stewardship

Jesus gave the disciples responsibility and held them ac-

countable for completing their assignments. When the 72 returned, they reported to Jesus the results of their ministry (see Luke 10:17). The ministry teams were given responsibility but were also held accountable. They were expected to give accounts of their stewardship.

In too many instances our discipleship efforts focus on drawing a crowd, conducting a study, or leading a group. For our discipleship to be complete, it must find expression in ministry. God requires much more than presence. He demands performance.

Rewards

Empowerment brings rewards. Jesus addressed rewards in discussions with the twelve. When Peter mentioned to Jesus what they had abandoned to follow Him, Jesus said that whatever they had left would be restored a hundredfold (see Mark 10:28-31). In the parables Jesus often told of rewards. In the parable of the talents (see Matt. 25:14-30), the faithful servants were rewarded with a commendation from the master and increased responsibility. To the twelve, following Jesus brought the rewards of—

- maturity;
- trust;
- responsibility;
- relationship.

These principles undergird a model of ministry that leads single adults from initial belief to responsible ministry. The empowerment model can be used effectively in single-adult ministry to achieve the type of results Jesus had with the twelve.

factoid

The empowerment model leads single adults from initial belief to responsible ministry.
Source: Larry Garner

Solution ④
use the single-adult
ministry toolbox

Tools for Studying *Start a Revolution*

Larry Garner

The key to single-adult ministry is empowerment. *The Single-Adult Ministry Solution* not only talks about empowering single adults for Christian living and ministry but also provides you the tool for doing so. The book *Start a Revolution: Nine World-Changing Strategies for Single Adults,* included in your resource pack, was written by a single adult for single adults. It may be utilized for personal reading or group interaction. Provide a copy for each single adult in your ministry to use as a resource for living a Christian lifestyle. Use it to help single adults discover individual and group-building insights into their personality styles and spiritual gifts. Use it to challenge and equip them to minister as well as receive ministry.

Opportunities to use *Start a Revolution* include—
- a short-term group study on Sunday or on a weeknight;
- a weekend retreat study;
- a guidebook for leadership team building;
- gifts for new group members to help them discover God's place for them in your church's ministry.

In most cases single adults should be asked to pay all or part of the book's cost. Order additional copies (item 7200-59) by contacting the Customer Service Center; 127 Ninth Avenue, North; Nashville, TN 37234; 1-800-458-2772.

This introduction provides general guidelines needed to conduct each study session. Although they are listed only once, the study leader needs to review them when preparing for each session.

Following these general guidelines are specific suggestions for facilitating six group study sessions based on the content of *Start a Revolution.* You will need to adapt these suggestions for your specific situation, leadership style, and group of single adults.

General Guidelines

1. Become thoroughly familiar with the content of *Start a Revolution* and the suggestions in this guide for leading the study sessions. As the leader, you will help members process the material in *Start a Revolution.* You will bring life to this study. Questions will be directed to you. Members will engage you in discussion, so be as well prepared as possible.

2. Arrange the room to provide the best environment for teaching and learning. The setting and group size have a significant impact on how you lead the study. Generally, a group of 30 or fewer allows for more discussion and questions. The larger the group, the more leader-centered it is. This does not prevent your using methods and activities that encourage interpersonal exchange, but it becomes more difficult in a larger group. If you want a high level of interaction from participants, keep the group under 30 and seat them at tables in a large room. The more informal the setting, the better.

3. Prepare visual aids, including posters, overhead transparencies, and video or computer-generated presentations, to enhance the retention of learning. Learner retention scales are roughly as follows. We retain—
   - 10 percent of what we hear;
   - 30 percent of what we see;
   - 50 percent of what we hear and see;
   - 70 percent of what we say;
   - 90 percent of what we do.

   The greater learners' participation, the greater their learning retention. Utilize visuals to communicate ideas and content. Utilize questions and answers and small-group assignments to involve participants in the learning process.

4. Check all equipment to ensure proper operation. Prepare it for use.

5. Arrive early to greet participants as they enter. Much of the spirit of the study sessions depends on your de-

meanor. A friendly, open, tolerant spirit in the leader will encourage the same spirit in group members.

6. Provide name tags to encourage participants to become acquainted. Name tags will also enable you to call persons by name during the sessions.

7. Have available supplies such as paper, pencils, large sheets of paper, felt-tip markers, masking tape, Bibles, and a copy of *Start a Revolution* for each participant.

8. Depending on the allotted time and the setting, you might plan for refreshments.

9. Prior to session 1 distribute copies of *Start a Revolution* to participants. Ask them to read strategies 1 and 2 and to complete the spiritual-gifts inventory and personality profile in strategy 2 before group session 1.

10. Study sessions are designed to last one hour, with 50 minutes for learning activities and 10 minutes for fellowship, prayer, and housekeeping agendas such as taking roll. Start and stop the sessions on time.

11. The six sessions cover the content of *Start a Revolution* in the following manner.
   • Session 1: strategies 1–2
   • Session 2: strategy 3
   • Session 3: strategy 4
   • Session 4: strategy 5
   • Session 5: strategy 6
   • Session 6: strategies 7–9
   You may wish to extend the number of sessions to explore the content more fully.

12. When you give an assignment, place a time limit on it. This will galvanize the group into action.

13. Single adults who complete the study are eligible to receive Christian Growth Study Plan credit. Complete form 725, provided in the current *Christian Growth Study Plan Catalog*, and mail to the Christian Growth Study Plan Office; 127 Ninth Avenue, North; MSN 117; Nashville, TN 37234-0117; fax (615) 251-5067. Request credit for *Start a Revolution*, course CG-0183.

Study Sessions

Session 1
Learning goal: After this session participants will be able to define *total integrity*, identify the results of total integrity, describe major avenues for identifying their purposes in life, and name their spiritual gifts and personality types.

1. Ask participants to form small groups of between three and five persons. Provide each group a large sheet of paper and a felt-tip marker. Ask each group to develop a clear definition of *total integrity* from the introductory remarks in strategy 1 of *Start a Revolution*. After groups have finished their work, ask them to share their definitions with the large group.

2. Ask members to think of examples of persons who live with total integrity. Instruct them to identify the persons and to describe some of their qualities.

3. Direct participants to the section "The Results of Total Integrity" in strategy 1 and ask them to identify results of living with total integrity (identification of purpose, focus of energies, increased impact, discovery of direction). Be prepared to discuss or emphasize the importance of these.

4. Present a brief lecture on the four avenues for identifying your purpose in life, listed in "Identifying Your Purpose in Life" (identify early clues, commit to accountability, listen to your heart, listen to the Holy Spirit). A visual presentation of these ideas would be helpful.

5. Ask participants to share in their small groups the results of their spiritual-gifts inventories and personality profiles. Ask them also to share their sense of purpose in life as they presently understand it. If they do not have a clear understanding of their purposes, that's all right. Discuss commonalities found in the group. If possible, identify a specific group style based on individuals' assessments.

6. Suggest that the small groups conclude by praying that each participant will discover a clear direction and purpose for life, by celebrating the variety of their gifts and personalities, and by praying for God's direction as they consider their purposes in life and in ministry.

Session 2
Learning goal: After this session participants will be able to list a church's contributions and limitations, identify primary leadership models found in the church, and summarize the biblical foundation for self-directed ministry teams.

1. State: We all have strengths—spiritual gifts, talents, and skills. What role do other Christians play in developing a ministry strategy?

2. Read this statement from strategy 3 of *Start a Revolution*: "Working from your strengths … does not mean working within your comfort zone." Ask participants to form small groups of between three and five persons and to identify and discuss persons in Scripture whom God called out of their comfort zones (Moses, David, Amos, Jonah, Paul, Peter, Esther, Mary, Sarah, Leah, Elizabeth, Ruth).

3. Ask participants to remain in small groups and give each group a large sheet of paper and a felt-tip marker. Ask the groups to read Acts 2:42-47 and to identify the various roles the church body plays in our lives. Direct the groups to list these on large sheets of paper, to post them on the wall, and to discuss and compare the lists. Suggest that they compare their lists with the information in the section "The Role of Your Church" in strategy 3.

4. Prepare a brief lecture on a church's limitations (methodology, purpose, process). Under "Methodology" note that the church needs to devise ways to practice being the church in the world. The church needs to provide case studies, examples, models, and practice opportunities that

facilitate preparation for ministry and witness in the real world. Under "Purpose" note that the primary role of vocational ministers is to equip God's people for the various ministries to which God has called them. The church must structure what it does to focus on the church's purpose: to prepare people to witness and minister in the world. Each Christian then becomes a minister in the world. Fulfillment in the Christian life comes as a person integrates all of life's experiences, creating a Christian lifestyle under Christ's lordship.

5. Give each small group a large sheet of paper and assign each one of the four leadership styles outlined in the sections "Process" and "Self-directed Ministry Teams: A Better Approach" in strategy 3. Ask each group to define its assigned style and to develop a diagram that illustrates it. Have the groups rank the styles 1 to 4, with 1 most nearly like the leadership style in your single-adult ministry. Allow time for each group to share its conclusions. Discuss appropriate ideas, especially the leadership styles reflected in your group.

6. Briefly explain the origin of self-directed teams in business. Emphasize the true origin of self-directed teams by exploring the imagery of the body presented in Romans 12 and 1 Corinthians 12.

7. Ask participants to find the section "Self-directed Ministry Teams: A Better Approach" in strategy 3. Tell them to rate your single-adult ministry on each characteristic listed on page 110, using a scale of 1–10, 1 being low and 10 being high. Ask them to share their conclusions in their small groups. Then ask volunteers to share their responses with the large group. Lead members to discuss how these characteristics can be developed in your single-adult ministry.

8. Conclude the session by praying for God's continuing leadership in developing a team ministry with all single adults in your church.

Session 3

Learning goal: After this session participants will be able to identify the common phases that occur in the formation of a ministry team and to outline the sequential process for developing a ministry team.

1. Introduce this session by reviewing the four prevalent ministry leadership styles examined in session 2.

2. Ask participants to form small groups of between three and five persons. Provide large sheets of paper and felt-tip markers. Assign each group to develop a chart that lists the flight dynamics of geese. These are described in the section "The Need for a Change: The Self-directed Team Concept" in strategy 4 of *Start a Revolution*. Also direct the groups to list leadership parallels for ministry teams. After the groups have finished, ask them to share their work with the large group. To save time, after the first group shares, you might wish to deal only with differences that

are reported. Be prepared to discuss the implications for ministry.

3. Prepare a brief lecture to explore two misconceptions about ministry teams, described in the section "Ministry Teams in the Church" in strategy 4. Emphasize the importance of each believer's having a personal ministry to others and participating in group ministry opportunities based on spiritual gifts and personality style.

4. Ask participants to return to their small groups and to share their experiences participating on or observing a team of any type—work or sports, for example. Ask them to discuss what made the team a dynamic force.

5. Direct participants to read Romans 12:4-6a, Ephesians 4:11-16, and 1 Corinthians 12:4-31a and to discuss how the images used in these passages relate to the work of ministry teams. As you lead participants to discuss their ideas, include material from the section "How a Ministry Team Works" in strategy 4 as needed.

6. Prepare and deliver a lecture about the common phases that occur in the formation of a ministry team. Use the section "Transitional Phases of a Ministry Team" in strategy 4. Create a visual like the one below to help you communicate these ideas.

> ## Transitional Phases of a Ministry Team
>
> **An enthusiastic beginning**
>
> ▼
>
> **A state of confusion**
>
> ▼
>
> **A coach-centered team**
>
> ▼
>
> **A conceptually tight team**
>
> ▼
>
> **A self-directed team**

7. Direct participants to return to their small groups and give each group a large sheet of paper and a felt-tip marker. Ask the groups to use the section "How to Begin a Ministry Team" in strategy 4 to outline a sequential process for beginning a ministry team. After the groups complete their work, ask them to report to the large group and to identify where they are in the process.

8. Ask volunteers to share their visions for ministry. Explain that participants' visions do not have to be specific; generalities are expected at this point.

9. Present the following three characteristics required for those adopting a ministry-team model.
   - I am willing to change.
   - I like trying new things.
   - I am willing to take risks.

   Ask participants to complete a personal evaluation like the one below. You can write these statements on a chalkboard or on a large sheet of paper to present for the group's consideration, or you can duplicate them on small sheets of paper for individual distribution.

PERSONAL EVALUATION

To what extent do you meet the challenge of being part of a ministry team? Rate yourself on a scale of 1 to 10, with being 1 low and 10 being high.

_____ I am willing to change.
_____ I like trying new things.
_____ I am willing to take risks.

---

10. Dismiss by praying the following prayer or a similar one: "Father, I pray that You will work in our lives to give each of us a vision and a sense of calling for ministry. Create in us a willingness to change the things You would have us change and to embrace new ideas and ways of doing ministry that You give us. Amen."

Session 4

Learning goal: After this session participants will be able to identify elements that unite a team, problems a team faces, and stages of a team's learning process.

1. The first learning activity, though rather involved, is designed to help participants process the material in strategy 5 of *Start a Revolution*. This activity will consume most of the session time. Create small groups of between three and five persons and make the following assignments. You might wish to provide these in written form on sheets of paper, a chalkboard, or a large sheet of paper. Instruct groups to base their work on the section "Elements That Unite a Team" in strategy 5.
   - Assignment 1: Formulate a statement of common cause—a purpose statement for your single-adult group or team (if you have already developed a team).
   - Assignment 2: Read Mark 10:35-45 and Philippians 2:5-11. Explain why the world's hierarchical model is not a biblical model of leadership.
   - Assignment 3: Identify from the Book of Philemon the elements of common ground that Paul emphasized in his letter to and relationship with Philemon.
   - Assignment 4: Explain how being a team player leads to

or highlights personal success.
   - Assignment 5: Explain the phrase *intelligent failure*.
   - Assignment 6: List internal motivators.
   - Assignment 7: Identify personal sacrifices a person might be asked to make for the success of the team.
   - Assignment 8: Develop a sample group covenant.

   After the groups have completed their work, ask them to share the results with the large group. Allow opportunities for discussion.

2. Prepare a lecture based on the section "Common Problems on Teams" in strategy 5. Before delivering it, ask participants to suggest possible problems a team might encounter. Make a list on a chalkboard or on a large sheet of paper. Highlight problems participants do not mention or focus attention on the dimensions of the problems in strategy 5 as you present your lecture.

3. Prepare a lecture that presents the four stages of learning that a team must progress through on the way to success. At the beginning of your presentation, make this or a similar statement: Just because five gifted basketball players wear the same uniform, show up at the same time, and play ball together doesn't mean that you have a team! That team must share a common vision, practice together, and share enough experiences to mold itself into a team. A team progresses through several stages of learning as it works to become successful.

4. Dismiss the session with prayer, asking God to guide participants to grow in love, care, and respect for one another as team ministry develops in your single-adult group.

Session 5

Learning goal: After this session participants will be able to explain the difference between a dream and a vision, write goals for their lives, and evaluate their present activities in light of their stated goals and dreams.

1. Prepare and deliver a brief lecture on the relationships among dreams, visions, and goals, using the ideas in the opening pages of strategy 6 in *Start a Revolution*.

2. State: When we seek a vision for our lives that is within God's will, we need to be aware of certain necessary ingredients of success. Draw these diagrams:

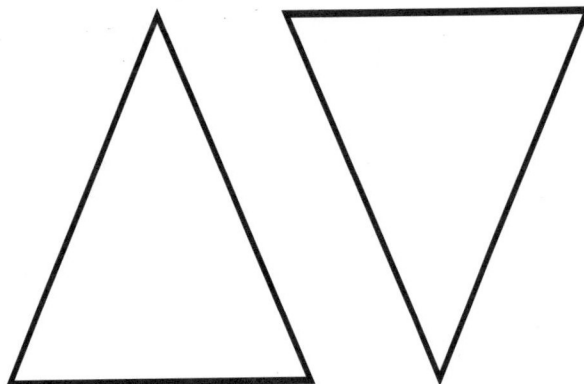

Ask participants to read Mark 10:35-45. Then ask them to form small groups and to discuss the concepts of success represented by these triangles or pyramids. Instruct participants to search strategy 6 to identify the four ingredients of success (personal relationship, responsive action, active faith, quality). Then direct the groups to rank these ideas in their order of importance to them and to be prepared to explain why they ranked them as they did. Allow time for small groups to work; then call for their responses.

3. Develop a brief lecture on the value of goals and the characteristics of good goals, based on the material in strategy 6. Stress the importance of each person's establishing goals for his or her life.

4. Direct participants to the section "Practical Guidelines for Setting Goals" in strategy 6. Suggest that they use this section to help them complete the following activities. You might wish to provide these activities in written form on sheets of paper, a chalkboard, or a large sheet of paper.
   • Write a statement of your life goal as a Christian single adult.
   • Write an objective for each of the four areas of your life: mental, physical, spiritual, and social.
   • Under the four categories list the activities that engage your time and energy. If you have difficulty categorizing a particular activity, list it under miscellaneous.
   • Prioritize the top 10 activities you listed in each of the four areas.
   • List your dreams and aspirations. If you had unlimited resources, what would you want to do?
   • Look at your lists of activities. Based on the activities that consume your time and energy, what are your values? Are your current activities leading you toward your dreams? What changes need to be made to move you toward achieving your dreams and aspirations?
Allow enough time for participants to formulate responses. Then ask that they form small groups of between three and five persons and share responses. If some members do not wish to share, honor their wishes. After time for sharing, remind participants of the suggestion in strategy 6 for using their goals and dreams in team ministry:

Setting goals in light of your personality and spiritual gifts is a great start toward the dream of being greatly used by God. When you establish your spiritual goals, you can then find others who share them. Together you can form a ministry team whose work is based on each member's personality strengths and spiritual gifts. You will create a formidable team that has a clear vision and the means to accomplish your incremental goals, broader visions, and life dreams. Your unity will come from the common vision each of you shares for ministry.

5. Ask participants to remain in their small groups and to conclude by praying that they will be able to achieve their dreams and God's purposes for their lives, individually and together.

Session 6
Learning goal: After this session participants will be able to outline the process for starting a new ministry.

1. Direct participants to read Matthew 25:31-46 and Luke 16:10-12. After a few moments ask them what these passages reveal about the importance of details. To illustrate the principle, ask members to follow the formula suggested in the section "The Potential of Small Starts" in strategy 7 to discover the huge difference little things make.

2. Direct participants to form small groups of between three and five persons. Provide each group a large sheet of paper and a felt-tip marker. Ask each group to select one of the following ministries.
   • Divorce-recovery support group
   • Addiction support group
   • Bible-study fellowship
Instruct the groups to develop ministry plans to launch their new ministries. Ask them to refer to the section "Determine What Needs to Be Learned" in strategy 7 for actions that need to be taken and to list these in a logical sequence for their particular ministries, from the first step to the last. After allowing time for the groups to complete their work, call for reports. Ask the other groups to critique the suggested sequences and to offer suggestions. Follow this procedure with two or three ministries to help participants understand the elements and actions required to begin a new ministry.

3. Highlight the explanation of *innovation* on the opening pages of strategy 8. Develop and present a lecture on the seven character traits of a person who is open to innovation, based on the section "The Characteristics of an Innovator."

4. Ask participants to complete the rating scale on the next page to evaluate their openness to innovation. Make individual copies of the scale or prepare a chart large enough for participants to read.

5. Instruct participants to read the passages detailing Jesus' temptations (Matt. 4:1-11), the feeding of the five thousand (John 6:1-15), and Jesus' receiving word of Lazarus's death (John 11:1-6). After they have read these passages, note that in every instance Jesus said no—to the tempter, to the crowd who wanted to make Him a king, and to the immediate demand to go to Lazarus. In each case Jesus did the Father's will and glorified Him. Jesus knew how to say no.

6. Prepare a brief lecture on the two ways we can run too fast, based on the section "Spiritual Opposition" in strategy 9. Be sure to emphasize the three methods of saying

no: Do we have the time? Do we have the skills? Is this God's will for us at this time?

7. Ask participants to read 2 Timothy 2:2. State, Paul's instruction to Timothy offers a key idea in discipleship: what we have received, we are to pass along to others, who in turn can pass it along to others. Ask participants to form small groups of between three and five persons. Give each group a large sheet of paper and a felt-tip marker. Instruct the groups to list ways they can pass the torch of ministry to others. After they have made their lists, ask them to share their suggestions with the large group. Ask participants to think of persons they might enlist as ministry apprentices. If they cannot think of anyone, suggest that they begin praying that God will direct them to others with similar gifts with whom they can team to duplicate ministry for the Kingdom.

8. Conclude the study with a time of prayer, committing your single-adult ministry to God. Allow a time of open group prayer in which any volunteer can pray. Conclude by leading a prayer of commitment for the group to start a revolution.

INNOVATION RATING SCALE

Rate yourself from 1 to 10 to indicate your openness to innovation and change, with 1 being low and 10 being high.

_____ 1. I have a high tolerance for the ambiguous, unclear, and uncertain.

_____ 2. I keep an open mind to consider all opinions on a subject before making a decision.

_____ 3. I *always* avoid entrenching my language in terms that close the door on *anybody, everybody,* and *nobody!*

_____ 4. I maintain a positive attitude.

_____ 5. Generally, I can laugh at myself and at situations.

_____ 6. I remain open to new learning experiences.

_____ 7. I am open to various expressions of worship and ministry that do not violate biblical principles.

What is your score?

0–30	The thought of change makes you break out in a rash.
30–50	You think about changing—sometimes.
50–70	You are a genuine innovator.

Issue ③

developing your single-adult
ministry leadership team

Team: a number of persons working together to minister to others. The best leaders know how to share leadership with others, and they weave a beautiful tapestry of participation and ownership. Be a leader! *—Tim Cleary*

Solution ①

Cultivate a Passion for God
Bruce Moore

The question of how to know God and to make Him known has been Christians' quest for centuries. The problem is that most Christian leaders view their faith as mundane, uneventful, and unheroic. We look at sports events and think: *I want to go big-time like that! I want to live passionately, too!* You can go big-time! Your arena is bigger than a sports arena; it is all heaven and earth. Your stakes are much higher: the eternal souls of humankind. The applause you crave is the applause of heaven.

A leader without a passion to know God and to make Him known is like a pen without ink or a car without gasoline. Knowing God was the magnificent obsession of the apostle Paul and the penetrating power behind great Old Testament leaders like Isaiah, Jeremiah, and Moses. How can a leader have the ability and consistency to go the distance—to stay on course with an enthusiasm that motivates others to follow Christ? How do you develop a passion for God?

How to Get It

You develop a passion for God by spending time with Him. We often spend time with a book or a tape describing someone else's time with God, but we also need to spend time with Him ourselves. God wants to spend time with you. To be like Him, you must spend time with Him.

Someone once challenged me to spend at least five minutes alone with God each day in His Word and prayer. With few exceptions I have done so every day for 11 years. Genesis 39 says four times that the Lord was with Joseph. The Lord was with Joseph because Joseph was with the Lord!

Let me suggest that you adopt the following practice to spend time in the Word. Select a Scripture that you believe would benefit you and follow these steps:

1. *Perimeter.* Read the verse(s) before and after to understand the context.
2. *Paraphrase.* Write the verse(s) in your own words.
3. *Pulverize.* Select two key words that seem to be the heart or the central theme of the verse(s). Apply the following questions to each word: Who? What? When? Where? Why? How?
4. *Personalize.* Write one action you will take as a result of the Scripture. Be specific. Generality kills application.
5. *Pray.* Pray the verse(s) to God as a commitment.

Practicing this procedure will ensure that you have a power-packed time with God and a renewed passion for Him.

How to Keep It

The secret to longevity in having a passion for God is spending time with persons who have the same passion. It takes more than desire to stay on course. First Corinthians 15:58 challenges us to "stand firm. Let nothing move you. Always give yourselves fully to the work of the Lord, because you know that your labor in the Lord is not in vain." Standing firm is best achieved when you're part of a team that is seeking the same goal. To be a spiritual

> **f a c t o i d**
> You develop a passion for God by spending time with Him.
> Source: Bruce Moore

leader, you must find others who are like-minded, or you will perish.

How to Pass It On

Paul challenges us to entrust the important things to "reliable men who will also be qualified to teach others" (2 Tim. 2:2). If you want the people around you to catch a passion for God, you must spend time with these people. These four ingredients are essential to influential relationships with others:

- Time in prayer
- Talks about their problems and God's solutions
- Ministry projects together
- Discussions of principles from God's Word

Don't let the details of everyday living keep you from investing time in people who have potential for the Kingdom. Developing other warriors for Christ must be intentional.

Set an aggressive pace. You must live with extraordinary passion and commitment if you want others to catch the same spirit. You must love God in a way that makes others want to do the same.

Solution ②

Develop a Leader's Heart for Single Adults
Ben Young

Today's most popular television shows have one feature in common: they address the art of living single. Hollywood recognizes that by the year 2000, the majority of people who will be channel-surfing and sitting in our pews will not be married couples with 2.5 children but single adults.

Although contemporary culture and the Bible affirm the single life as a viable, healthy status, many churches shun this ever-expanding population as if it had the plague. A church's advertising, programming, and sermons can make single persons feel like second-class citizens. The single-adult revolution is here, and if your church wants to be on the cutting edge, relevant, and seeker-sensitive, you must develop leaders who have a heart for reaching single adults.

For two decades our church has reached and equipped thousands of single adults by applying what we call the fabulous *E* factor. The *E* stands for—

- exploding;
- examining;
- equipping;
- empowering.

Exploding. To develop church leaders with a heart for single adults, you must first explode existing stereotypes about the single lifestyle. Many congregations view single adults as lonely lounge-lizards who fear commitment. From a biblical and cultural perspective, nothing could be farther from the truth. Jesus was single. Paul was single. Timothy was single. The majority of the apostles were single. We must

proclaim the message loudly and clearly: "It's OK to be single!" Marriage is wonderful. Children are blessings from the Lord. Yet God equally affirms both single and married persons in His Word. Leaders must view single adults as a viable part of the church.

Examining. To help leaders develop a heart for single adults, encourage them to examine the felt needs of single adults. Most churches fail to reach single adults because they do not tailor their ministries to meet the real needs of single persons in their communities. Married leaders should build friendships with individual single adults and should begin to learn more about their needs. Leaders who are single should not assume that because they are single, they automatically know the needs of other single adults. As leaders ask single adults what their needs are, they discover the niche market their church can reach, such as Busters, 30-somethings, single parents, widowed persons, or divorced persons. Always view single adults in niches because of their diversity of needs. If you are starting a group or trying to revitalize an existing one, know and listen to single adults. Then focus on one segment of the single-adult community at a time. Use a laser, not a shotgun.

Equipping. A critical *E* factor in developing leaders with a heart for single adults is equipping single adults to minister. Our SingleLife University on Thursday nights offers classes on prayer, spiritual disciplines, self-image, God's will, and people skills. Our emphasis on equipping reminds single adults that their primary functions in the body of Christ

> **factoid**
>
> The single-adult revolution is here, and if your church wants to be on the cutting edge, relevant, and seeker-sensitive, you must develop leaders who have a heart for reaching single adults.
> Source: Ben Young

are to discover their spiritual gifts and to use them to serve others. Our mission statement makes clear that our purposes are to reach lost single adults in Houston and to help them grow to their full potential in Christ. We equip single adults to fulfill the Great Commission, teaching them to reach others and helping them become authentic followers of Jesus.

Empowering. If you explode myths, examine needs, equip for ministry, but fail to implement the final *E,* your ministry will fall short. Single adults must be empowered by church-staff members. Empowerment comes by placing single adults in major leadership positions. At our church there is no glass ceiling. Single adults serve on the paid staff as deacons, as Sunday School teachers, and as committee members. If you placed only married adults in leadership roles, Jesus and Paul would not even qualify. Recognize and appoint persons as equal members of the body, not according to marital status.

Pray that God will give your leaders a heart for single-adult ministry in your community.

Solution ③

Learn the Dynamics of Team Building

Rich Hurst

Those who want to build a ministry team must make a very basic decision. They must choose between program ministry and people ministry. Jesus never asked us to build programs; He asked us to build disciples—that means people. Furthermore, Jesus encouraged us to work in teams, as He demonstrated when He sent out the 72 in pairs (see Luke 10).

Let's look at five principles for developing effective ministry teams.

The leader is committed to team building and starts by discovering the dreams of the team members. Take time to ask team members what their dreams are for ministry and for their relationships with God. Remember what God told the prophet:

> "Your old men will dream dreams,
> your young men will see visions" (Joel 2:28).

Ask team members what they would like to do in ministry if money and time were not barriers.

The leader is committed to weaving these personal dreams into a shared dream. A shared dream creates a sense of commonality that permeates the ministry and gives coherence to all of the diverse activities. God said this about shared dreams:

> "Write down the revelation
> and make it plain on tablets
> so that a herald may run with it" (Hab. 2:2).

> ### factoid
>
> Those who want to build a ministry team must choose between program ministry and people ministry.
> Source: Rich Hurst

A team committed to a common dream is an awesome force. It can accomplish the seemingly impossible. Many ministries that result from one person's dream are limited, but ministries based on shared dreams can accomplish amazing results because they reflect the individual dreams of many persons. And those dreams fuel a passion for ministry.

Weave your team members' dreams together by creating a vision statement and then by agreeing on an action plan that will best carry out each member's dream. When a new person joins the ministry team, incorporate his or her dreams into the corporate dream. Keep asking yourselves: *What does God want us to do? What kind of persons does God want us to produce?* Be willing to be flexible, to change directions when you need to, based on the team's leading.

The team is committed to communicating expectations clearly. Job descriptions, team guidelines, and ways to resolve conflict are extremely helpful.

The leader is committed to trusting team members. Sometimes leaders enlist talented, capable laypersons for ministry teams and then suddenly treat them as incompetent. A great way to create a team is to trust team members to create an effective, healthy ministry.

The team is committed to something bigger than itself. The purpose of your ministry extends beyond simply meeting the needs of the persons who attend each week. A mission—not just activities—must exist to serve persons where they live. This happens when the team invests itself in training others so that the ministry reaches beyond the church walls. God's presence is realized whenever His will is being done.

Solution ④

Build Your Single-Adult Ministry Leadership Team: Peer Listeners

Ken Brumley

Single adults share two needs that emerged the moment Adam and Eve ate from the forbidden tree in the garden. With the first sin the young couple lost their identity and purpose. The Bible records humans' efforts to meet these needs and ways God sought to help them. The ultimate solution, of course, came in God's Son, Jesus Christ. Jesus repeatedly emphasized who we were created to be and why we were placed on this earth.

A church's ability to minister to and with its members depends primarily on how well it helps them understand and experience their new identity and purpose in Christ. To help persons meet these needs, most churches have three basic objectives:

- spiritual growth
- fellowship
- ministry

Churches define and articulate these objectives in a variety of ways. All three are equally important, and they all need focused attention and development. All three must function properly for the church's ministry to develop strength and effectiveness.

Most single-adult ministries provide their single adults opportunities to grow spiritually and to have fellowship, but few understand the great need to give them opportunities to minister to others. Single adults may have Bible studies and creative fellowship activities that are well attended, but if they are not given opportunities to serve and express their God-given purpose in this world, the ministry will soon become tasteless and will lose its appeal. A church's ability to create strong leadership and to influence its community corresponds directly to its desire to minister.

With this understanding in mind, 14 years ago our single-adult ministry began to seek safe ministry opportunities for single adults—ministries that were nonthreatening, were service-oriented, and required few relational skills. The opportunity was realized when we recognized the need in our world for caring listeners and encouragers—safe, nonthreatening persons, willing to listen and encourage. A ministry opportunity was born.

We began our preparation and training two months prior to launching the ministry. Training focused on three basic areas: the eyes, ears, and heart of an encourager.

The eyes of an encourager. We emphasized awareness of everyone's basic need for strong identity and purpose and of the often destructive ways we seek to satisfy these needs. We also taught single adults to understand the dynamics of body language and to recognize barriers of fear.

The ears of an encourager. We taught single adults to listen at a deeper level to what others say. Many single adults struggle with identity and purpose in the areas of acceptance, significance, confidence, and relationships with God and others. These are a person's four greatest longings; unfortunately, they are also the sources of many persons' problems. When single adults listen to others' problems, they need to be able to discern any messages being communicated beneath the surface.

The heart of an encourager. We also gave listeners an opportunity to share their life stories in a concise form. We carefully distinguished between counseling and sharing only in areas of mutual identification. Single adults learned to use encouraging Scripture verses that emphasized viewing ourselves from God's perspective. They also learned how to ask questions that would reveal a person's relationship with the Lord and how to lead someone in a prayer to receive Christ.

After the training we launched the ministry at a national single-adult Labor Day conference. At strategic points around the campus we stationed single adults wearing badges that read, "Professional Listener" and instructed them to give smiles, directions, and encouragement. Each night they met together and described their experiences listening to and sharing with others.

The result was greater than we had imagined. When our single adults returned home, they wore their badges to church the next Sunday morning. They enjoyed this new identity and purpose as encouragers and wanted to continue. The greatest benefits were the confidence and courage they felt to minister to other church members. A peer ministry of encouragement through listening was begun and continues today.

Use the following guidelines to organize a peer listeners' ministry.

1. Make sure that participants understand their responsibilities. They are to—
   - provide information about the single-adult ministry;
   - serve as an extension of the ministry's personality, exhibiting a warm smile and an open heart;
   - be available to listen to any who want to share their stories;
   - help persons see beyond their problems by identifying

> **factoid**
>
> A church's ability to create strong leadership and to influence its community corresponds directly to its desire to minister.
>
> Source: Ken Brumley

their positive attributes;

• close each encounter with prayer.

2. Conduct five preparatory meetings at which you do the following.

• Ask individuals to write and share their testimonies with one another. Provide guidelines in outline form for preparing the testimonies.

• Discuss the first three chapters of *The Gift of Encouragement* by Larry Crabb.

• Teach participants how to spend quality time each week in prayer for those they encouraged. Ask them to share encouraging Scriptures and to memorize the verses.

• Have participants begin prayer journals for at least two persons they have consciously encouraged every day during the past week.

• Have participants select accountability partners in the group to encourage them.

3. Conduct a monthly sharing meeting to follow up on the peer listeners' ministry process.

4. Encourage participants to study courses like *Search for Significance* and *In God's Presence* (see "Resources for Single Adults and Their Leaders," p. 138). They should be continually involved in Bible studies and discipleship studies.

5. A key leader or minister should meet with and encourage any peer listeners who express difficulty in carrying out their tasks.

Build Your Single-Adult Ministry Leadership Team: Single Adults Are Leaders, Too

Candy Smith

"Let me tell you about our exciting ministry!" exclaimed a single adult as he phoned a recent Sunday visitor. These are thrilling words to overhear during outreach night, especially when this same person was on the receiving end of the phone line only one year before.

Many single-adult visitors or new members are potential single-adult leaders. Creating an environment to support the transformation is deliberately and skillfully moderated. The process of building single-adult leadership is the steel frame in a vibrant, solid, and growing single-adult ministry. Take a look at a few reinforcement tips for building and equipping leaders.

Demonstrate Love for Single Adults

If single adults are to see themselves as leaders, this idea should be reflected by the church, the pastor, and the staff. Single adults must have the church's authentic respect and support not only in words but also in actions. Mainstreaming single adults into churchwide leadership positions such as steering committees and deacons should be an ongoing strategy. A negative statement is made when single adults serve only within the walls of the single-adult area. Bringing single adults to the forefront as worthy church leaders and contributors communicates value and acceptance.

Build Ownership in the Single-Adult Ministry

Single adults need to feel that a ministry belongs to them. Planning and propelling a ministry should come from the leadership; then ownership should spread throughout the membership. Every member needs an invitation to participate. One suggestion is to create a "What's my job?" sign-up to provide a way every single person can volunteer for a responsibility. Photographer, birthday brigade, to-do team, and greeter suggest only a few necessary jobs.

Building ownership must include a regular leadership-team huddle. Nothing surpasses the effectiveness of rallying the troops to promote accountability, encouragement, and vision. This can be the most valuable hour of the week.

Equip Leaders

Every teacher, director, outreach coordinator, care-group coordinator, or council coordinator should be trained to recruit and train new leaders. They should learn to recognize and nurture leadership potential in visitors, new members, and inactive members. Keeping the resource pool growing is essential to long-term ministry.

Training rallies and special training conferences are staples in a healthy ministry. Breakdowns occur when leaders are recruited but later fail and resign because they were not trained to do their jobs.

Develop a Vision

"No vision, no people" is true for every level of ministry. All leaders should understand why they do what they do and should know the goals and visions of the church and the single-adult ministry. To reach the single adults of your area, create an environment of hunger that penetrates planning meetings, prayer times, retreats, and special events. The foundation will crumble if the vision is anything less.

List several ways your church's single-adult ministry incorporates one or more of these principles for involving single adults in leadership.

Use the book *Start a Revolution: Nine World-Changing Strategies for Single Adults* and the toolbox in issue 2 in this manual to plan ways to equip your leaders.

> ## factoid
> Bringing single adults to the forefront as worthy church leaders and contributors communicates value and acceptance.
> Source: Candy Smith

Build Your Single-Adult Ministry Leadership Team: The Role of Married Leaders in Single-Adult Ministry

Bill Morgan

For many years fishers have constructed and used nets to catch fish. They build the nets by weaving and joining together lengths of cord until the net has the necessary size, strength, and endurance to support the weight of many fish.

Developing a single-adult leadership team can be compared to constructing a fishing net. The leadership team becomes a net that is woven and joined together with faith, hope, and love:

- Faith that the net is large enough to reach out to the single-adult community with the gospel of Jesus Christ
- Hope that when single adults are exposed to the truth of God's Word, their lives will change
- Love for Jesus Christ, which provides the specific care and encouragement single adults need

Interweaving married and single leaders into this net adds strength, consistency, and longevity to the single-adult leadership team.

Most single adults are more concerned about a leader's character than about his or her marital status. The strength added to the team with married leaders is evident as the single adults observe their Christ-centered marriages. Because 90 percent of single adults desire eventually to marry or remarry, these couples play a significant mentoring role in single-adult ministry leadership. They have opportunities to instruct and guide single adults to make choices that lead to healthy relationships.

Another benefit of having married leaders on the team is the consistency they bring. Many times when single leaders become involved in a relationship that ends, one or both of them leave the ministry. This is not an issue with married leaders. Married leaders also eliminate the male-female issues in the care-group ministry, since a married couple can minister to both men and women—he with the men and she with the women.

Another reason to have a combination of married leaders and single leaders is longevity. Single adults in leadership often have an attrition rate higher than that of married adults. Married leaders add longevity to the team. This reduction in turnover of leadership helps create stability in the entire single-adult ministry.

The ratio of married leaders to single leaders is important. If you have too many married leaders, your ministry could become a ministry *for* single adults instead of *with* them. However, don't overreact to single adults' negative comments about the ratio. If you have a majority of single-adult leaders, you run the risk of a higher rate of turnover.

It is important for each married couple you enlist to be spiritually mature and emotionally secure. This will alleviate any insecurities that could develop as they build relationships with single adults.

Pray to " 'the Lord of the harvest … to send out workers' " (Matt. 9:38) for your single-adult ministry. Watch with expectation as He provides opportunities to enlist married and single leaders. Use these opportunities to interweave and join together a leadership net that catches the lost single adults in your area.

List married couples in your church who would make good single-adult leaders by the criteria that have been presented. Pray for them by name daily for one week prior to enlistment efforts.

Build Your Single-Adult Ministry Leadership Team: Resolving Conflicts Among Leaders

Doug Fagerstrom

Developing a single-adult leadership team can be the greatest joy or the worst nightmare imagined. Joy comes when everyone works harmoniously toward the stated goals and objectives that grow from your vision statement. Joy results when lives are changed and persons commit their lives to Christ. Joy can come even in the midst of difficulties when in unity the team works long and hard to solve problems.

Ministry nightmares begin when conflict arises—when team members compete, complain, and dispute, destroying the ministry they first fought so hard with faith to develop.

Conflict resolution is never easy. But it must be done, and it must be done according to biblical principles. Let's look at three principles in the Books of Ephesians and James.

Honesty

When conflict arises, we need to talk. Almost everyone in Christian ministry has heard Paul's advice about "speaking the truth in love" (Eph. 4:15). Ephesians 4 describes an atmosphere in which believers work in harmony, but that doesn't always happen. Some volunteers get tossed around like small boats on a tempestuous sea. But as we submit to Christ, the Head of the church, we must lovingly speak the truth.

Truth and love go hand in hand. In the midst of conflict, truth without love often stings and hurts, leaving others with the wind knocked out of them (see Jas. 3). Love without the truth leads to an emotional struggle that causes

> **factoid**
> Most single adults are more concerned about a leader's character than about his or her marital status.
> Source: Bill Morgan

someone to wonder if what he or she says or does will ever meet the other's expectations. Love alone is built on results and emotions, and often the end is claimed to justify the means.

So we need to learn how to be lovingly honest with one another. It is hard to love the unlovely or the irritating, but the liberating truth is that we must love one another and thereby cover the multitudes of sins and wrongs done to one another (see 1 Pet. 4:8).

This truth is expressed as members of the leadership team come together for honest sharing and evaluation. As rules of confidentiality are established, the leader bravely stands in the midst of conflict. He or she lovingly and truthfully moderates open, honest sharing through the differences and dissensions. It is important to bring leaders together to talk.

Forgiveness

James asks a tough question: "What causes fights and quarrels among you?" He answers: "Don't they come from your desires that battle within you? … You quarrel and fight … because you do not ask God" (Jas. 4:1-2). Prior to chapter 4, James rebukes believers for harboring bitterness and selfish ambition (see Jas. 3:14-16). In Ephesians 4:31-32 Paul charges us to get rid of all selfish bitterness; to let go of all pettiness; and to move on to kindness, forgiving one another as Christ forgave us.

Again, the leader stands in the balance. He or she brings together embittered team members in conflict and reminds them of three essential ministry ingredients:

- This ministry is not ours; it belongs to the Lord. Let's put our self-seeking agendas away. So discard all bitterness, anger, complaining, and gossip.
- This ministry must be built on kindness and love, or those outside our group will be repulsed by our infighting. So be kind and love one another.
- This ministry needs to be marked by forgiveness. So cancel all the debts of hurt feelings and petty issues; then move on to love God and one another.

It is important to bring leaders together to let go and forgive.

Prayer

We must pray with one another. Members in conflict need to show selfless kindness and love as they forgive and literally put their arms around one another, pray with one another, and pray for one another. And the prayer of righteous men and women is powerful and effective (see Jas. 5:16). It is important to bring leaders together to pray.

Solution ⑤

Develop Your Church's Pastoral-Leadership Team
Steve Smith

As a child I was fascinated by maze puzzles. My eyes would rapidly search for the words *Start here.* Those words gave me permission to begin the task of finding the hidden treasure.

In single-adult ministry a good start with your church's pastoral-leadership team is vital. Persons employed by your church provide leadership for the congregation. In a small church this may be one person: a pastor. In a multistaff church many ministers may be employed, each specializing in a specific area of ministry, such as music, education, youth, or single adults.

Today an estimated 1,600 churches in America employ a staff member with major or partial responsibility for ministry with single adults. As more churches of all sizes discover single adults as a viable church-growth audience, the number of staff positions will increase. Your church may be in the process of adding a single-adult staff person. You'll need several tools to assist you, such as a simple job description to build on and help in locating qualified candidates. You'll also need an idea of how the single-adult ministry position integrates with and relates to the pastoral-leadership team. Staff relationships are very important to a full- or part-time single-adult minister or director.

Your church may not have the luxury of employing someone to work with single adults. If you enlist a volunteer leader, the pastor needs to understand single adults and single-adult ministry in order to provide guidance and support to this volunteer. Likewise, the volunteer leader needs to know how to represent single adults and the single-adult ministry vision to the pastor and staff.

The following material will address these issues. For additional assistance consult your peers from churches doing single-adult ministry, a denominational consultant with responsibilities in this area, or experienced leaders in single-adult ministry. Examine "Resources for Single Adults and Their Leaders," beginning on page 138, for individuals and groups that can assist you.

> **factoid**
> An estimated 1,600 churches in America employ a staff member with major or partial responsibility for ministry with single adults.
> Source: Steve Smith

A Vision for Ministry

A single-adult leader should have a biblical vision for ministry. The apostle Paul provided a checklist for effective ministry in 2 Corinthians 4:1-6. Three major standards are identified:

A right philosophy. "Since through God's mercy we have this ministry, we do not lose heart" (2 Cor. 4:1). Ministry without a clear, simple vision causes people to lose heart. A lofty, well-written vision statement can make an impressive wall hanging, but it doesn't translate into applicable leadership. A simple statement like "Reach, teach, and grow" brings clarity and direction to persons who want to serve. A simplified vision includes an abundance of mercy and creates an atmosphere that is marked by consistency and stability.

An inspired methodology.

> We have renounced secret and shameful ways; we do not use deception, nor do we distort the word of God. On the contrary, by setting forth the truth plainly we commend ourselves to every man's conscience in the sight of God. And even if our gospel is veiled, it is veiled to those who are perishing. The god of this age has blinded the minds of unbelievers, so that they cannot see the light of the gospel of the glory of Christ, who is the image of God (2 Cor. 4:2-4).

Something you can be certain of in single-adult ministry is change. Most people struggle with change. To be nudged constantly from a comfort zone without being adequately prepared can become unnerving. Therefore, continuing education is needed for leaders to be prepared for positive change. Positive change should reject all forms of human deceit and should refuse to rely on all human cleverness. Although a godly ministry is flexible, it holds truth in the highest regard and does not mishandle the Scripture or give way to fads that do not appeal to the conscience. At the same time, those extolling Christ-centered outreach must understand that some persons will not believe.

A model of authenticity. "We do not preach ourselves, but Jesus Christ as Lord, and ourselves as your servants for Jesus' sake. For God, who said, 'Let light shine out of darkness,' made his light shine in our hearts to give us the light of the knowledge of the glory of God in the face of Christ" (2 Cor. 4:5-6). The creativity of the ministry activates personal and organizational learning that results in the transformation of people's lives. As you give yourself to servanthood, you become the kind of leader who can give direction to dreams.

Efficiency is heightened when the ministry moves in a positive direction. A biblically revitalized ministry ignites growth by helping all involved visualize where they are going, then to communicate and transfer the right vision.

When are leaders at their best? Leaders shine when they practice commitment to exemplary biblical leadership. Without credibility it is impossible to lead. For the leader to mobilize and involve people in the process of ministry, the people must see these practices in those who lead.

The Single-Adult Minister Providing Leadership as a Church-Staff Member

To encourage people to unite in a common purpose, a single-adult minister as key leader must communicate the vision in a way that attracts, excites, and invites the support of your church's professional staff and lay leaders.

Single-adult ministers must have the courage to confront and change the status quo. A young shepherd boy named David saw Israel's army cowering to a giant Philistine. David was not content to be afraid like the others. He moved against the status quo by assaulting the giant himself. True leadership makes people look beyond their fears and find constructive ways to challenge the process. Leaders experiment and take risks, learning from mistakes and successes. Peter warmed himself by a fire just a few feet from the place where Jesus endured a mock trial. He denied Jesus three times because of his fear. After the resurrection, however, Peter was the great preacher at Pentecost. Later, he would die the death of a martyr rather than renounce his faith in Christ.

Single-adult ministers should have a dream for the future and believe that no dream is too bold to attempt. By focusing on the vision, not the encumbrances, they stay on track. They guide and inspire others to share the vision. John the Baptist envisioned Christ's coming and, like a voice crying in the wilderness, entreated all to follow the one true God. Leaders enlist others and attract people to a common purpose. They develop a sense of destiny that assists people in discovering their common purpose. These leaders clearly understand that to enlist others in a common vision, they must win their trust and call forth their values, hopes, and dreams. Because of Moses' humble faith, he was able to convince the entire nation of Israel to escape from the pharaoh's domination in Egypt and to remain focused on the vision of their promised land.

Single-adult ministers need to foster collaboration by promoting cooperative goals and mutual trust. They help the players understand that ministry is a team effort. The great apostle Paul, in his letters to the churches he had planted, continually fostered a partnership of love. He was supportive and

> **factoid**
>
> Single-adult ministers should have a dream for the future and believe that no dream is too bold to attempt.
> Source: Steve Smith

went to great lengths to sustain an ongoing interaction. Paul worked to build relationships by communicating openly and by showing his vulnerability.

Single-adult ministers must set an example in order to be role models for others. Leaders should not ask others to do what they wouldn't be willing to do. They clarify values and guide choices and actions. Choosing their words deliberately, they can use life's stories as a timely way to teach virtue. Jesus, like no other leader, modeled the way, the truth, and the life. His substitutionary death for humanity on the cross will stand for all time as the ultimate act of love by a leader.

Single-adult ministers must recognize contributions. People value being appreciated for their contributions. Recognition does not have to be elaborate, just genuine. Being positive and hopeful liberates people to succeed. The real commitment to the challenge of leadership is to love those who follow.

Single-adult ministers are effective leaders when their blueprint for character is Scripture and their continual source of power is prayer. Start here!

Guidelines for Finding a Single-Adult Minister

As I prayed about my call to single-adult ministry, I felt insecure and doubted my ability. My pastor, recognizing my struggle, shared this truth with me: "God does not always call the equipped, but He always equips the called."

The called can be found in numerous places:

- Look within. The quality minister may be serving in your fellowship as a godly layperson. God may be calling someone who has already proved to be faithful and committed to ministry.
- Consider those who are already involved in or trained for pastoral ministry. A single-adult ministry requires someone who understands how to pastor.
- Youth ministers have years of valuable experience that can be utilized in single-adult ministry.
- Denominational and religious groups and associations can provide the names of talented, well-trained ministers who are qualified for this important work.
- Seminaries often help place students.
- Other churches with mature single-adult ministries are great sources for networking and finding qualified ministers.

When searching for a single-adult minister, understand that gender or marital status is not as critical as it may be for other staff positions. Many times a single or single-again person is a positive choice for this job.

A Sample Job Description

A single-adult minister's job summary should encompass all actions needed to plan, conduct, and evaluate a comprehensive ministry with single adults. Responsibilities may include the following.

- Select, enlist, train, and supervise workers in the single-adult ministry.
- Develop and direct outreach programs for single adults.
- Lead in setting, attaining, and reporting on growth and ministry goals for the single-adult ministry.
- Prepare and administer the budget.
- Work with the other education staff in coordinating the total church ministry.
- Direct evangelism and discipleship training with single adults.
- Serve as staff leader for churchwide projects as assigned.
- Conduct regular single-adult leaders' meetings for communication and planning.
- Develop and train interns.
- Visit single adults in the hospital.
- Teach single adults how to become church members.
- Contact visitors, new members, and prospects weekly.
- Lead a weekly single-adult Bible study.
- Be available for counseling with single adults.
- Perform weddings and funerals for single adults.

Integrating Single-Adult Ministry Leaders with the Church Staff

Part of the single-adult staff's job is to educate the church staff about the importance of the single-adult ministry. It is critical that single-adult programming be churchwide in scope. The single-adult ministry must also be proactive in doing all it can to help the church's other ministries. Practical applications include the following.

- Encourage other ministries to recruit single adults for ministry roles such as preschool, children's, and youth workers; choir members; and churchwide committees.
- Provide single volunteers for special churchwide events and service projects.
- Encourage and equip other areas of church life and minister with single adults through those areas.

Ways the Pastor Can Support Single-Adult Ministry Leaders

- Remain aware of who single adults are.
- Affirm from the pulpit the value of single-adult ministry and of single adults.
- Refer to single adults as adults and not as older youth.
- Spend time in fellowship with single adults, perhaps

factoid

The single-adult ministry must be proactive in doing all it can to help the church's other ministries.
Source: Steve Smith

hosting a question-and-answer session about faith and church life.
- Participate in evangelistic visits to single adults.
- Be available for speaking engagements or Bible studies with single adults.
- Support single adults in churchwide leadership roles.

Supporting Your Pastor
- Teach your pastor how to make positive statements about singleness from the pulpit.
- Talk with the pastor when he uses too many illustrations irrelevant to single adults.
- Regularly give the pastor articles on single-adult issues.
- Encourage the pastor to be positive about placing single adults in all levels of church leadership.
- Demonstrate support for all areas of church life through your finances and presence.

Solution ⑥

Understand the Micro Viewpoint: Solutions for Smaller Churches
Karen Gibson

A church's single-adult ministry leadership team must first determine why a specific ministry is necessary. A verse that gives us a reason, a purpose, and encouragement for a ministry with single adults is John 10:10, in which Jesus said, " 'I have come that they may have life, and have it to the full.' " The church's duty is to provide a place where all individuals can experience the abundant life Jesus Christ came to give.

After determining the ministry's purpose, you must decide who will serve on the single-adult leadership team. Initially, the team may be only one person, a coordinator. Single adults should take the lead in ministries that meet their specific needs and interests. Married adults who feel called to minister with single adults should be encouraged to serve on the leadership team, as well. Also seek the involvement of your pastor and staff, deacons, and other church leaders.

All good teams have a game plan. Single-adult ministry leadership teams should also have a specific plan. The team needs to determine—

- what the church can do with available human and financial resources;
- which group(s) of single adults will be targeted for the ministry;
- how the church can meet the needs of single adults in the church and community;
- what the team will not be able to do.

It is very important that the leadership team be realistic about the possibilities, at the same time allowing God to work beyond its expectations.

Teams that are successful in executing their plans train properly for their jobs. Individuals who serve on the leadership team should be well-grounded, growing Christians. They should take the time and effort to train, and the church should encourage their training. State and national denominational events provide specific training for persons involved in single-adult ministry. If it is not possible to attend a training conference, take advantage of the many excellent resources for single-adult ministry available in Christian book stores.

Smaller churches often work together in clusters or associations to provide ministry with single adults. The opportunity to enlist leaders from a larger resource pool of churches can broaden the ministry base of all.

List the names of married and single adults who are potential single-adult leaders in your church.

Name other churches in your area with which you could team for single-adult ministry.

Whether yours is a new or developing ministry, always seek the support of your pastor and the church body. Single-adult ministry must be a church ministry, not a one-person project. Not everyone in the church must be directly involved, but the ministry needs the support of the church body through prayer; encouragement; and, when possible, finances. The pastor's influence should promote a positive atmosphere in the church body for building a single-adult ministry. The pastor should include single adults in sermon illustrations and remarks. He must also be willing to allow single adults to minister and be ministered to. The church will follow the pastor's lead in creating a fellowship in which single adults can experience the abundant life Jesus offers.

> **f a c t o i d**
>
> Smaller churches often work together in clusters or associations to provide ministry with single adults.
> Source: Karen Gibson

Solution ⑦
use the single-adult
ministry toolbox

Tools for Developing Leaders

**Leadership-Assessment Profile for Recruiting a
Single-Adult Ministry Team**

Circle the numbers representing your opinions about the prospective leader.

Characteristic	Evaluation	Strongly Agree				Strongly Disagree
➲ Spiritual	Demonstrates an interest in knowing God and His will for life	1	2	3	4	5
➲ Creative	Shows the ability to be creative in performing ministry tasks	1	2	3	4	5
➲ Team player	Is dedicated to achieving the ministry team's goals	1	2	3	4	5
➲ Humor	Maintains a sense of humor in times of pressure and difficulty	1	2	3	4	5
➲ Responsible	Accepts responsibility for assigned ministry tasks and follows through until a project is completed	1	2	3	4	5
➲ Respect	Receives support and respect from peers and coworkers	1	2	3	4	5
➲ Skills	Expresses a desire to learn and develop new skills to complete the ministry task ahead	1	2	3	4	5
➲ Cooperative	Demonstrates a cooperative spirit in working with others	1	2	3	4	5
➲ Faithful	Is dedicated to the church's mission and is faithful to Jesus Christ	1	2	3	4	5
➲ Decision making	Demonstrates sound judgment when facing decisions	1	2	3	4	5
➲ Group participation	Expresses a desire to participate in special ministry projects, events, and retreats	1	2	3	4	5
➲ Compassion	Cares about others and is sensitive to their needs	1	2	3	4	5
➲ Risk taker	Demonstrates the courage to try something new by moving out of his or her comfort zone	1	2	3	4	5

Name of prospective leader: _____

Contact information: _____

Leadership role for consideration: _____

Key leadership characteristics/strengths needed: _____

_____

Is there a match between these strengths and this individual's assessment?

❑ Yes ❑ No ❑ Possibly, with instruction and support

Staffing the Single-Adult Ministry Leadership Team

Copy and provide this information for single-adult ministry leaders.

Single-Adult Ministry Volunteer Coordinator

- Enlists and works with leaders to equip and coordinate the church's single-adult ministry
- Develops and manages the single-adult ministry budget
- Advises the church on single-adult ministry directions
- Works with leadership and church staff to develop ongoing, comprehensive single-adult ministry plans
- Works with leadership to select and order appropriate materials
- Works with pastor or staff assigned to single-adult ministry
- Coordinates work for and assists with enlistment of the single-adult leadership team

Sample Single-Adult Ministry Leadership

Promotion-and-Publicity Team
Markets the single-adult ministry and its activities in the church and community

Special-Events Team
Envisions and coordinates retreats, conferences, seminars, and other special activities for single adults

Newsletter Team
Produces quarterly or monthly updates of activities and news to inform single adults about the single-adult ministry

Outdoor-Outreach Team
Connects single adults in relationships with God, self, and others through nature

Friends-Ministry Team
Helps single adults discover relationships with Christ and other Christian brothers and sisters

Community-Service-Projects Team
Provides opportunities for single adults to give their time and service to others outside the church (examples: Room in the Inn, citywide and nationwide opportunities, and ministry-team opportunities)

Personal-Profile Team
Involves single adults in identifying their spiritual gifts and personality styles and in assessing their experiences and interests to find their places in the Christian community

Small-Groups Team
Develops small-group learning experiences at a variety of times and in a variety of settings to disciple Christians and to create Christian community

Review and place check marks beside the essential tasks that need attention in your single-adult ministry. Using the suggested descriptions as guidelines, write your own job descriptions to match the tasks you have identified.

Coordinator

_____

_____

_____

_____

_____

_____

_____

_____

_____

Teams

_____

_____

_____

_____

_____

_____

_____

_____

**Leadership Enlistment and Development
Planning Tool**

Based on the content of issue 3, list actions for developing leaders for your church's single-adult ministry. Beside each action list the insight or principle to apply. The first is provided as an example.

ACTION	INSIGHT/PRINCIPLE
1. Search for a single-adult minister.	Use guidelines for finding a single-adult minister and job description on page 44.
2.	
3.	
4.	
5.	
6.	
7.	
8.	
9.	
10.	

Issue ④
incorporating single adults into
the body of Christ

In 1 Corinthians 12 Paul, a single adult, states that each member of the body of Christ has a function and must carry out that function for the church to be complete. Does your church or single-adult ministry have any body parts missing? Many Christian leaders bemoan the fact that their churches don't have enough doers and givers. You've probably heard that in most churches 20 percent of the members contribute 80 percent of the work and resources. This issue will challenge you to involve single adults so that the whole church body can be complete. —*Tim Cleary*

Solution ①

Understand the Biblical Foundation for Single-Adult Ministry
Ron Hill

God Relates to Each of Us

" 'God so loved the world that he gave his one and only Son, that whoever believes in him shall not perish but have eternal life.' " John 3:16, often called the gospel in one verse, is probably the most widely known and memorized verse in the Bible. This glorious verse reveals God's plan of reconciliation. Through its simplicity we see God's inclusive nature. Whoever believes is included. In fact, the next verse states that God's purpose in relating to us is not to condemn but to embrace us: " 'God did not send his Son into the world to condemn the world, but to save the world through him' " (John 3:17). This verse reminds us of God's openness to each one of us.

Jesus' Model of Ministry

This marvelous relationship God offers each of us is revealed through Jesus Christ. Jesus preached great messages of hope and encouragement to multitudes, but He related and ministered to individuals. In the middle of a crowd He turned to confront the woman who had faith that she would be healed if she touched His garment (see Mark 5:25-34). She was healed by this personal encounter, and He responded to her fear by proclaiming, " 'Go in peace and be freed from your suffering' " (v. 34). Such faith is paramount for our healing and peace. Jesus' approach to personal ministry is exemplary for us today.

The Scripture preceding John 3:16 relates Jesus' nighttime encounter with Nicodemus. Nicodemus was an intelligent member of the Jewish ruling council who had questions, as well as a longing to know God. Jesus ministered to Nicodemus as he was, connecting with him through his heritage (see John 3:1-15). Jesus taught us how to reach out to others.

In John 4 we see Jesus walking through Samaria, contrary to Jewish custom, and resting at Jacob's well. Jesus needed a drink, but the lonely single adult who had come to the well in the heat of the day needed the living water of eternal life. The encounter in John 4:7-42 focuses on a single adult who had seemingly given up on relationships. Her religious talk was of history. She seemed to have no friends. After five failed marriages she had given up on marriage and was living with a man. When Jesus gave her living water, He modeled for us a ministry to persons, meeting them where they are, not where we think they ought to be spiritually. Christ gave compassion rather than judgment and established a sacred trust between the Savior and the individual.

Jesus' encounter with this dysfunctional single adult caused a spiritual resurrection and renewal. She immediately wanted to share her faith and her new life. The Scripture says that she left the water pot to go tell others about her new relationship with Christ. This still happens today when the church leads others to Christ. He still sees us as we are and loves us, for He knows what we can become through a living, loving relationship with Him.

John 11 reveals a continuing relationship Jesus had with an exceptional single-adult family, the brother and sisters from Bethany. This special relationship prompted the request by Mary and Martha: "The sisters sent word to Jesus, 'Lord, the one you love is sick' " (v. 3). Jesus, a single adult, ministered to this single-adult family of siblings. Through their grief He showed the power of the resurrection. Through their sorrow He revealed Himself as " 'the resurrection and the life' " (v. 25). Through their tears He identified with their pain and wept. In this relationship we see friendship, fellowship, and a strong faith in Jesus as Savior and Lord.

Once again, Jesus modeled our pattern of ministry to others. Although He responded in friendship, He encouraged their faith: " 'I am the resurrection and the life. He who believes in me will live, even though he dies; and whoever lives and believes in me will never die. Do you believe this?' " asked Jesus (vv. 25-26). Martha not only said yes but also communicated her faith: " 'I believe that you are the Christ, the Son of God, who was to come into the world.' " Jesus helped her see, in her weakest moment, that she could be strong because of her faith and her personal relationship with Christ.

The Bible gives many examples of mass evangelism, worship, and ministry. Jesus chose to perform personal ministry in small groups or one-to-one. He is our model for ministry to and with others—meeting persons at their point of need, building their faith, encouraging their personal growth, and giving them hope. When Jesus discerned the faith of the woman who touched His garment, the whole world stopped while He turned and acknowledged her faith. When the Light of the world shone on Nicodemus in his darkest night, Jesus spoke with eternal understanding. Jesus met a broken woman at the well and gave her new life. When Lazarus came forth from the tomb, tightly wrapped in death garments, Jesus said, " 'Take off the grave clothes and let him go' " (John 11:44).

Our call to ministry with single adults is no less specific and powerful. We should help single adults remove the grave clothes of death and set them free to walk in the fresh path of God's grace, love, and eternal direction. That is freedom, and that is our mandate for ministry.

A Ministry to and With

We can identify three stages of the Christian life: being fed by others, feeding ourselves, and feeding others. As in any developmental process in life, a person can get stuck in one stage. A primary ministry of the church is to encourage per-

sons on their journey—individually and collectively. For example, a seeker of God needs to be around persons who witness of their faith in God's power. After the person accepts Christ personally and becomes a believer, we should provide the prayer, support, and encouragement necessary for growth. Paul said that leaders should use their gifts "to prepare God's people for works of service, so that the body of Christ may be built up until we all reach unity in the faith and in the knowledge of the Son of God and become mature, attaining to the whole measure of the fullness of Christ" (Eph. 4:12-13). This edict for ministry directs us to be involved in the lives of Christ's people and to help them mature in their spiritual development. This maturity is not linear; it is cyclical. Ministry should be involved not in addition but in multiplication. A seeker who becomes a believer who becomes a servant establishes a personal ministry that, in turn, helps others.

Today nearly half of the adults in the United States are single. We cannot spiritually afford to ignore this giant resource. Many of these people need our help and encouragement. The church is the only body God gave us to accomplish this ministry of spiritual touch, encouragement, renewal, and restoration. An ever-growing percentage of single adults, however, needs to help and serve. These people need to be the church in action. John the Baptist proclaimed the coming of Christ's earthly ministry as a single adult. Paul, another single adult and the apostle of Christ, was the chief architect of the New Testament church by the power of the Holy Spirit. This giant of faith and action stated that single adults, through their undivided loyalty to Christ, can make a significant difference for the Kingdom's sake (see 1 Cor. 7). Single adults are called to invest their hearts and lives in Christ and His church. The Bible gives examples of ministries to as well as ministries with single adults. Our mandate today is no less.

Our Challenge

As we minister to and with single adults in the inexorable and upward journey of God's kingdom, Jesus is our example and guide in modeling ministry. His words in Matthew 28:19-20 guide our mission as a church. We are to go, make disciples, and teach obedience to God. He gives us the power, reason, and motivation to accomplish this awesome task through His presence with us always. His abiding presence is assurance beyond measure.

The message is clear: we must minister to those around us, including single adults. The methods vary according to the situations, but the abiding presence of our compassion-

> **factoid**
>
> Jesus is our model for ministry to and with others—meeting persons at their point of need, building their faith, encouraging their personal growth, and giving them hope.
> Source: Ron Hill

ate, living Lord is a foundation to each of us—never changing, always steady and anchored. Christ's presence prompts us to grow in our service, His grace propels us to new heights and riches in Him, and His love holds us secure.

The growing population of single adults should motivate us to reach out and share, include others in our fellowship, and serve together in His army of faith. While there is day, let us renew ourselves to the example of Christ in reaching single adults so that they can reach others. What a great challenge! What a great opportunity!

Solution ②

Integrate Single Adults into Your Church's Ministry and Leadership
Ralph Starling

A common need all humans share, whether married or single, children or senior adults, is the need to belong. The church, the body of Christ, can meet this need because it includes all people. As the apostle Paul said, "There is neither Jew nor Greek, slave nor free, male nor female, for you are all one in Christ Jesus" (Gal. 3:28).

In many ways the church is like a team, made up of persons who come in a wide range of ages, abilities, and experiences. Just as a team requires players with different talents, the church needs a variety of persons with different gifts to complete the body of Christ. A team would not be successful if it consisted of players who could field only one position. For instance, a baseball team of only infielders and outfielders but no pitcher or catcher would be incomplete.

Traditionally, the church has revolved around the married culture. A church that fails to include single adults in its ministry and leadership limits its effectiveness for ministry in the community. The challenge for the church of the future is to integrate the growing single-adult population into its life and leadership.

Many myths about single adults exist. One common myth is that single adults lack commitment. This misconception occurs in part because of the transitional nature of single adults, particularly those in their 20s and early 30s. Young single adults are busy establishing their financial independence and making career choices. Their time is valuable. They invest heavily in their vocations and in their available leisuretime. The church of the future will find ways to challenge young single adults in balancing their vocational, recreational, and spiritual lives. Many young single adults continue to place high priority on their commitment to Christ and His church, regardless of the many other demands in their lives.

As single adults move into their 30s and beyond, they put down roots and reassess personal priorities and values. Spiritual values and Christian community become increasingly important, as demonstrated by their desire to attend and support the church. The church of the future will recognize the vitality and readiness of these single adults and will seek to integrate them into the church's life and service.

Another common misconception is that all single adults are lonely. The truth is that no one is immune to loneliness. All of us experience feelings of isolation and discouragement. Even Jesus felt times of loneliness and discouragement: " 'Father, if you are willing, take this cup from me; yet not my will, but yours be done' " (Luke 22:42). Especially during times of loneliness we are reminded of the importance of God and people in our lives.

Also during times of loneliness we learn to be comfortable with ourselves. God is able to transform our times of isolation and discouragement and to renew our faith and hope, to "be transformed by the renewing of your mind" (Rom. 12:2).

The church of the future will be aware that single adults are hungry for relationships and community, just as all people are. By acknowledging them as an important part of the church, the body of Christ is strengthened.

Single adults want to be an integral part of the church. They represent one of the greatest untapped resources in our churches today. The church of the future will demonstrate its care and concern for single persons by affirming and utilizing their spiritual gifts. They will create avenues through which single adults can serve Christ. If the church is to reach the world for Christ, single adults will help lead the way. They desire to be on the most exciting team our Lord has created—the church, the body of Christ.

Four basic elements are essential to the life and vitality of the church: worship, caregiving, equipping, and missions. You can use these four important areas to integrate single adults into your church's life and leadership.

factoid

Single adults want to be an integral part of the church. They represent one of the greatest untapped resources in our churches today.
Source: Ralph Starling

Worship

Worship is offering ourselves to God–our attitudes, actions, and talents. When we worship, we declare God's worth and glory. All of God's children are called to worship the Lord. Single adults need an opportunity not only to experience worship within the Christian community but also to facilitate and lead in worship as members of the body of Christ. Use the following suggestions to integrate single adults into your worship services.

- Invite single adults to lead in prayer and to read Scripture.
- Give single adults opportunities to share their faith through testimonies.
- Involve single adults in creative worship, such as drama and mime.
- Encourage single adults to use their musical abilities by singing in the choir, playing musical instruments, and so on.
- Enlist single adults to participate in holidays and celebrations. For example, when selecting families to light Advent candles, include a single-parent family.
- Ask single adults to plan a worship service as part of Single-Adult Day.
- Invite single adults to serve on the church's worship committee.

Caregiving

A significant ministry of the church is caring for those who are emotionally, physically, and spiritually wounded. The church can be a place of healing and wholeness for hurting persons. Everyone needs a loving, supportive community in times of crisis. Ministry to persons in transition not only demonstrates the church's care and compassion but also grows single adults in the ministry of caregiving. Those who are single-again due to the loss of a spouse through death or divorce can become some of the best caregivers in the church. The church of the future will integrate single adults into the ministry of caregiving by taking steps like the following.

- Design church programs to minister to the whole person.
- Recruit those who have experienced crises or transitions in life to become caregivers to others.
- Enlist single adults to start small groups at church such as divorce-recovery groups, LIFE Support groups, and prayer-and-sharing groups.

Equipping

Every believer is a minister, and every believer has been given a gift by God. Single adults are some of the most gifted members of the church. Major tasks of the church are to help persons discover their gifts and to encourage them to share their gifts through the church's ministry. The pastor and other ministers have been called to equip believers for ministry. The church's ministry is to be shared by all believers.

Single adults want to be equipped to serve in the ministries God has given them. Pastors and ministers know that the best preparation for ministry is performing ministry. The church of the future will focus on developing, nurturing, and equipping single adults for ministry in and through the body of Christ. Here are some ways your church can integrate single adults into the body of Christ as it equips them for ministry.

- Seek qualified single adults to serve in all areas of church leadership.
- Enlist single adults to serve on church committees.
- Seek single adults to work with other ministries in the church, such as the children's or youth ministry.
- Recruit qualified single adults to serve as deacons.
- Seek single adults to teach Sunday School/Bible study and to facilitate small groups.

Missions

God has called us to cooperate with Him in His work in the world. His mission is our mission. Jesus, Himself a single adult, ministered in a variety of ways. He provided emotional and spiritual nourishment to all who would trust Him. He also ministered to persons' physical needs.

The challenge of the Christian life is to meet persons' needs. Deploying single adults on mission is an important way the church can fulfill the Great Commission. The church of the future will not only integrate single adults into the church's mission, but it will also challenge them to be on mission for Christ wherever they are. Here are some ways your church can involve single adults in missions and ministry.

factoid

Deploying single adults on mission is an important way the church can fulfill the Great Commission.
Source: Ralph Starling

- Appoint single adults to serve on the missions committee.
- Create missions opportunities for those who are often overlooked because they are single again.
- Encourage single adults to participate in volunteer missions through their denomination's missions agencies.
- Offer local missions projects through which single adults can serve Christ, such as Habitat for Humanity, Backyard Bible Clubs, and nursing homes.

Solution ③

Make Your Church User-Friendly for Single Adults

Hazel Bell

Daunting, overwhelming, fearsome, assuming, unfamiliar, negative, cliquish, pious, or user-friendly? Which describes how your church relates to single adults? Single adults need a church that provides support, encouragement, and guidance. They need a church that is user-friendly.

A user-friendly church is highly visible. Residents of the community know where it is located and know about its activities. The church building is easy to enter. Greeters at the doors help visitors find their places. Upon arriving, visitors receive warmth, smiles, and acceptance from each member. A user-friendly church does not embarrass visitors but provides a warm greeting and a sincere Christian welcome. Members of Bible-study groups wear nametags to help visitors and new members get acquainted.

A user-friendly church provides varying levels of involvement for single members and visitors. Some want to be involved immediately in every single-adult activity, study, and group. Others want to sit quietly, observe, and enter group activities according to their own timing.

A user-friendly church is in touch with the needs of single adults, enables them to know and serve the living God, has a strong spiritual character, and maintains a holistic perspective on ministry. A user-friendly church develops a quality ministry that has integrity because it is consistent, credible, and reliable.

A user-friendly church has a positive attitude that shows in members' smiles, words, and behaviors and in its publications. This church has a vision for ministry. Bible teaching instills uplifting attitudes in the group. Single adults attend because they are excited about going to church. Members feel that they are an important part of the ministry team. Most people devote time, money, and energy to matters they consider important.

In a user-friendly church, ministry is not about programs but about people. Ministry happens when needs are met. Programs develop around ongoing ministries.

A user-friendly church encourages spiritual growth through prayer, Bible reading, and sharing faith. It encourages, equips, and commends members for ministry. This church reminds members to be the church, not just attend it.

A user-friendly church continually evaluates its programs and is not afraid to change. This church has well-defined goals and plans for ministry. A user-friendly church seeks God's vision for the church, and every member knows what that vision is. Members of a user-friendly church feel that they are associated with a body that is moving forward to accomplish something worthwhile.

Because members believe that the church has helped them and that it is relevant, they consistently invite others to attend. They accompany their guests to church and personally follow up. Advertising in newspapers, on the radio, through direct mail, and through other forms of mass communication informs people about the church, making it easier for members to invite others.

Single adults attend church events and services because they believe that their attendance will bear fruit in their lives, that they will emerge as better persons. Single adults feel that the church ministers to their needs. The user-friendly church conducts needs-based outreach, knowing that people want meaningful solutions to their deepest needs. The user-friendly church points to these solutions by providing resources through libraries, book stores, audiotape and videotape distribution, and literature.

Members of user-friendly churches give money as well as time to missions. They believe that prayer is an important opportunity to be in God's presence and to be filled with His mind.

The pastor and single-adult leaders understand single adults and provide necessary vision and spiritual guidance. Leaders delegate without reservation and empower members to do ministry. Leaders have frequent, meaningful interaction with members who are taking responsibility.

A user-friendly church is responsible for identifying gifts in single adults, refining those gifts, providing opportunities to use gifts, and supporting individuals in their ministries. It values its volunteers and gives recognition in their peers' presence.

A user-friendly church is not insulated from the community, does not alienate those who are different, does not avoid confrontation, does not apologize for seeking opinions and help, does not merely take the safe route, and does not operate solely on the basis of precedent.

> **f a c t o i d**
>
> A user-friendly church is in touch with the needs of single adults, enables them to know and serve the living God, has a strong spiritual character, and maintains a holistic perspective on ministry.
> Source: Hazel Bell

Solution ④

Understand the Micro Viewpoint: Solutions for Smaller Churches
Karen Gibson

"I am a member of this church because I know it is where God has called me to serve. He has shown me that this is the place where I can best use the gifts He has given me and where I will grow in my walk with Him."

Single adults who choose to be a part of a smaller church usually do so because they are confident that God has called them to minister in that place. Many single adults choose a smaller church rather than a larger church with a multifaceted ministry that reaches many single adults. The ability to be actively involved in the life of the church is a key reason why.

As you seek to incorporate adults into a smaller church, realize that marital status is only one part of who an individual is. All adults appreciate being included and treated as equals; marital status does not determine emotional or spiritual maturity. Single adults need to be allowed and encouraged to use their gifts in all areas of the church as teachers, musicians, committee members, and other workers.

Although a smaller church may not be able to offer a Sunday School/Bible-study group just for single adults, its groups should be age-appropriate, accepting, caring, and inclusive. The trend to put all single adults in one group, regardless of age, can be frustrating for all involved. In some instances a multiage group works, but many times it does not. Listen to your single adults. What would they like to do for Sunday School/Bible study? Because each church is different, it needs to make the best decision for its situation.

The process for incorporating single adults into a church should be the same as for married adults:
- Does your church use a spiritual-gifts inventory to help determine appropriate places of service?
- Does your church require a waiting period before a person can serve or teach?
- Is special training required for those who wish to serve?

Whatever the answers to these questions, the process should be the same for all adults. A church should not enlist someone to teach Sunday School/Bible study just because it does not have a group for the person to attend.

Someone in the church—the pastor, a Sunday School/Bible-study director, a Sunday School/Bible-study teacher, a deacon, or a layperson—needs to know the specific needs of the single adults in your ministry. The church can provide resources through the church media library that address pertinent single-adult issues. *Christian Single* magazine can be made available to church members and prospects. If your church cannot provide activities for single adults, encourage your single adults to be involved in area, associational, state, and/or national single-adult conferences and events. The church may want to help with child care or expenses.

As your church body begins to include single adults in activities, make them feel wanted and welcome. A church that focuses all adult activities on couples or parents ignores the needs of some of its members. Do not expect single adults to be baby-sitters. Do not expect single adults to have more time than anyone else. Do not expect single adults to do nothing. Allow and encourage them to use their gifts.

A church incorporates persons into the fellowship by being open, loving, and uplifting. This should be true for all members of the body of Christ, regardless of marital status.

factoid

Many single adults choose a smaller church. The ability to be actively involved in the life of the church is a key reason why.
Source: Karen Gibson

Identify single adults who are already involved in your church, ways they are ministered to, and by whom. Examples:

Single Adults	Areas	Who Ministers
Sally Jones	Sings in church choir	Our church organist
Bill Smith	Attends a men's Bible-study group	Men's Bible-study teacher

Solution ⑤
use the single-adult
ministry toolbox

Tools for Incorporating Single Adults

Making Your Church User-Friendly for Single Adults
To what degree do you incorporate single adults into your church? Beside each statement write the term from the thermometer that best describes your church's response in meeting single adults' needs.

_____ 1. Our church is highly visible in the community.

_____ 2. Single adults in this area know where to find our church.

_____ 3. Our pastor understands single adults' needs.

_____ 4. Single visitors are greeted and treated with dignity.

_____ 5. Church publications are positive and exciting and include information that interests single adults.

_____ 6. Information is readily available to single adults about all church programs.

_____ 7. We have regular socials for single adults at which visitors are welcome.

_____ 8. We offer support groups for divorced persons, widowed persons, never-married persons, single parents, and children.

_____ 9. We provide Bible-study literature and *Christian Single* magazine for all single visitors and members.

_____ 10. We have a library or a book store with resources about single-adult issues and needs.

_____ 11. We provide child care during all activities for single parents.

_____ 12. Our church plans short and long trips for single adults.

_____ 13. We promote weekday single-adult Bible-study groups.

_____ 14. We encourage Sunday lunch together for single adults.

_____ 15. We encourage Friday-evening and/or Saturday-evening activities for single adults.

_____ 16. We plan occasional seminars for single adults.

_____ 17. Activities are planned for various age and identity groups of single adults.

_____ 18. Single adults are asked to evaluate programs and activities of the single-adult ministry and of the church.

_____ 19. Single visitors are greeted at church entrances and are escorted to the single-adult area for Sunday School/Bible study.

_____ 20. The single-adult meeting area is easy to find.

_____ 21. Every Bible lesson, sermon, or devotional speaks to specific needs of single persons.

_____ 22. We provide a printed calendar of single-adult activities.

_____ 23. Single adults invite guests to come with them.

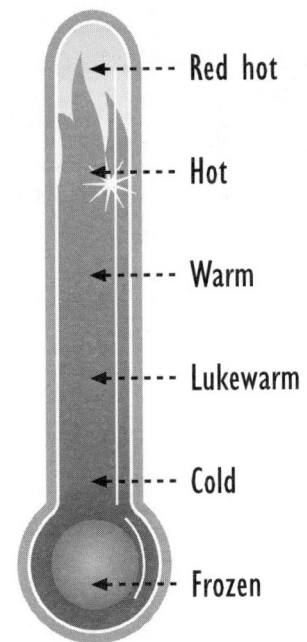

← ---- Red hot

← ---- Hot

← ---- Warm

← ---- Lukewarm

← ---- Cold

← ---- Frozen

_____ 24. Our members follow up on single visitors who attend with them.
_____ 25. We know single adults' needs.
_____ 26. We are meeting single adults' needs.
_____ 27. We give leadership responsibilities to single adults in the church and in the single-adult ministry.
_____ 28. Single adults are involved in missions projects, opportunities, and offerings.
_____ 29. We regularly pray for and with single adults.
_____ 30. We meet with group leaders to help them with their responsibilities and to encourage them.
_____ 31. We help single adults identify and use their spiritual gifts.
_____ 32. We recognize the contributions of single persons to our church.
_____ 33. We can list the short- and long-term goals for our single-adult ministry.

What is your church's overall temperature? Place a check mark beside one designation on the thermometer. Now circle the point at which your ministry needs to be. Make plans to raise the level of user-friendliness with single adults in your church. Begin developing a strategy by completing the following.

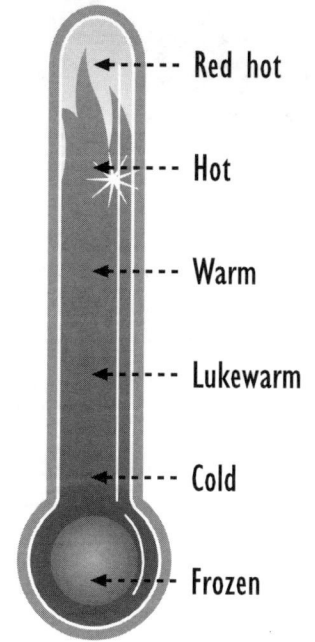

-- Red hot
-- Hot
-- Warm
-- Lukewarm
-- Cold
-- Frozen

1. List the major strengths that make your church user-friendly for single adults.

_____
_____
_____
_____

2. List five areas that could be improved to make your church more user-friendly.

_____
_____
_____
_____
_____

3. List goals for the next two months that can help make your church more user-friendly for single adults.

_____
_____
_____
_____

Who's on First?

The U.S. Census Bureau estimates that by the year 2000, 50 percent of all adults in the United States will be unmarried! Christian churches have exciting opportunities to involve single adults in their ministries. How effectively does your church recruit, integrate, and equip single adults to serve in your church's ministry?

In the left column score your church's present effectiveness in its ministry with single adults. In the right column score your goal for your church's ministry with single adults five years from now. Affirm what you are doing well. Use weaknesses to generate ideas for improving in other areas.

S = strikeout (poor), 1 = single (fair), 2 = double (good), 3 = triple (great), 4 = home run (outstanding)

Present						Future				
S	1	2	3	4	Single adults are an integral part of our church's ministry.	S	1	2	3	4
S	1	2	3	4	Single adults are actively involved in Bible study.	S	1	2	3	4
S	1	2	3	4	Single adults currently serve as deacons.	S	1	2	3	4
S	1	2	3	4	Our church budget includes allocations for a single-adult ministry.	S	1	2	3	4
S	1	2	3	4	Our church provides meeting space for single adults.	S	1	2	3	4
S	1	2	3	4	Our church observes Single-Adult Day each year.	S	1	2	3	4
S	1	2	3	4	Single adults are encouraged to participate in Sunday worship services (praying, reading Scripture, giving testimonies).	S	1	2	3	4
S	1	2	3	4	Single adults are included in holiday celebrations and special events.	S	1	2	3	4
S	1	2	3	4	Single adults are recruited for involvement in missions locally and internationally.	S	1	2	3	4
S	1	2	3	4	Divorced persons are encouraged to be active in our church's ministry.	S	1	2	3	4
S	1	2	3	4	Single adults are encouraged to teach, lead, or facilitate small groups.	S	1	2	3	4
S	1	2	3	4	Single adults are sought to serve on all church committees.	S	1	2	3	4
S	1	2	3	4	Single adults are challenged to serve in all areas of ministry (children, youth, music groups, and so forth).	S	1	2	3	4
S	1	2	3	4	The pastor and the church staff support single adults.	S	1	2	3	4
S	1	2	3	4	Our church offers seminars and workshops to meet the special needs of single parents, the divorced, the widowed, and never-married single adults.	S	1	2	3	4

Issue ⑤
organizing for effective
single-adult ministry

Organization should serve people and purpose. People and purpose should not serve organization. Organization, then, is simply a way of carrying out your purpose and of meeting people's needs. You may need a lot of organization or very little. This issue's agenda will present possibilities to help you evaluate your ministry's organizational needs and become the unique ministry God intends.
—Tim Cleary

Solution ①

Use the Paper-Clip-and-Pipe-Cleaner Principles
Tim Cleary

Traditionally, organizational and leadership styles were conceived, tested, and then placed in concrete, having proved to be tried and true, for numerous generations. Changes were minimal and occurred rarely, because the dynamics remained the same. It was assumed that program organizations met the needs of constituents because they had done so in the past.

These assumptions are no longer true. Today we are challenged to look at organization and leadership differently. While old organizational and leadership models were based on control, new dynamics are moving us to develop new models based on life needs and the empowerment of individuals for ministry.

The apostle Paul, himself a single adult, had a unique outlook on how to do ministry. At first glance these two principles seem to contradict each other. Put in the contexts of present reality and trends for the future, however, they make a great deal of sense.

- Principle 1: flexibility: "I have become all things to all men so that by all possible means I might save some" (1 Cor. 9:22).
- Principle 2: orderliness: "Everything should be done in a fitting and orderly way" (1 Cor. 14:40).

Developing organizational and leadership styles that can flex like a pipe cleaner allows for shaping to meet single adults' life needs. If you are aware of a need that is not being met, you must ask this question: If we changed our approach, our organization, our style, could this need be met? If you can answer yes to that question, then you must make that change.

Also strive to be the kind of leader who knows when things should be organized or "clipped together," increasing effectiveness and producing results. Ask the question, Is what we are doing to meet needs being done in a timely and orderly fashion? If not, get better organized.

Such an approach encourages leaders to be open to change and to think for themselves, discovering solutions that work. The paper-clip-and-pipe-cleaner approach is not an absence of organization but a facilitator of organization that is able to solve problems and get results.

In the following discussion of organizing effectively for single-adult ministry, you are called on to evaluate and choose approaches that will be effective for your church. You will choose from a variety of principles and examples representing a diversity of single-adult ministry organizational and leadership styles. Our research into successful ministries, volunteer or staff-led and of various sizes, will give you a composite picture of what single-adult ministries look like today and how they are evolving toward the future. Keep in mind the two preceding organizational and leadership principles as you determine the best organization for your ministry with single adults. The toolbox at the end of issue 5 gives practical help for organizing effectively.

John 12:24 says: " 'Unless a kernel of wheat falls to the ground and dies, it remains only a single seed. But if it dies, it produces many seeds.' " This verse summarizes the responsibilities of leaders who develop ministry:

- Prepare the ground.
- Plant the seeds of change.
- Nurture individuals and respond to their needs.
- Bring along your organization to the point that it is willing to change.

- Expect to die a little, to pay a price as a leader. Not everyone will immediately envision where you are leading.
- Watch for fruit. Note that the fruit stage often comes after the death stage, when the situation seems most discouraging.

Single-Adult Ministry Paradigms That Work

Ways to organize yourself and your church for ministry are numerous. No matter what approaches you choose, operating from these five paradigms will help you maintain flexibility and orderliness. They can help you prepare the ground and plant the right seed that will bear appropriate fruit.

Paradigm 1: Every church can minister with single adults. Although not every church can have a single-adult ministry, complete with budget, program, and staff, every church can minister to and with single adults; that is, it can build Christian community and relationships and can lead single adults to Christ.

Not enough large churches exist to reach the increasing single-adult population, which will grow to more than 50 percent of adults by the year 2010. Single-adult leaders in Dallas, Texas, estimate that they reach only 1 percent of the single adults in that vast metroplex. A Barna survey reveals that at least half of the single adults surveyed prefer smaller churches. Therefore, it is important to realize that smaller churches can minister with single adults, too! If they don't, churches will increasingly miss opportunities to share the gospel with over half of the adults in most communities. Wake up, smaller church! Here's how:

- Find one interested person to serve as the single-adult ministry coordinator. (Don't try to enlist the pastor. He already has enough to do.)
- Start a single-adult Sunday School/Bible-study group.
- The coordinator should begin building relationships with single adults—in the parking lot and church foyer, over lunch or coffee, and by phone.
- Plan and conduct one fellowship activity each quarter.
- Adopt a theme that focuses on family. Promote actions that encourage single adults to serve as extended family to one another and to the church.
- Contact and work with other churches to bring together small groups of single adults to form larger clusters or associations for fellowship and ministry.
- Pastors can use sermon illustrations that speak to unmarried as well as married participants in worship. An excellent resource is *Famous Singles of the Bible* (see "Resources for Single Adults and Their Leaders," p. 138).

Paradigm 2: Single-adult ministry involves networking relationships. See the networking cycle below.

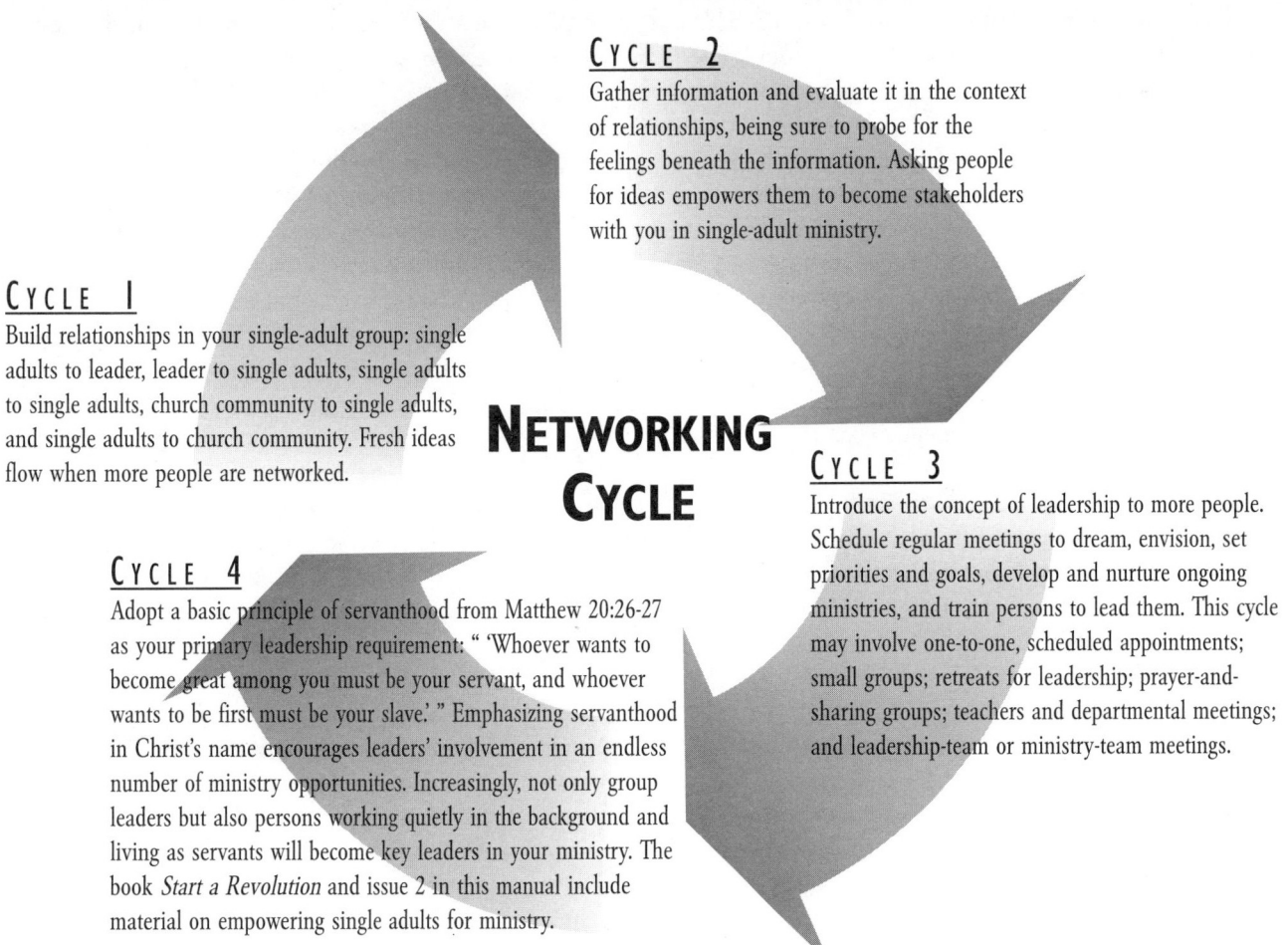

NETWORKING CYCLE

CYCLE 1
Build relationships in your single-adult group: single adults to leader, leader to single adults, single adults to single adults, church community to single adults, and single adults to church community. Fresh ideas flow when more people are networked.

CYCLE 2
Gather information and evaluate it in the context of relationships, being sure to probe for the feelings beneath the information. Asking people for ideas empowers them to become stakeholders with you in single-adult ministry.

CYCLE 3
Introduce the concept of leadership to more people. Schedule regular meetings to dream, envision, set priorities and goals, develop and nurture ongoing ministries, and train persons to lead them. This cycle may involve one-to-one, scheduled appointments; small groups; retreats for leadership; prayer-and-sharing groups; teachers and departmental meetings; and leadership-team or ministry-team meetings.

CYCLE 4
Adopt a basic principle of servanthood from Matthew 20:26-27 as your primary leadership requirement: " 'Whoever wants to become great among you must be your servant, and whoever wants to be first must be your slave.' " Emphasizing servanthood in Christ's name encourages leaders' involvement in an endless number of ministry opportunities. Increasingly, not only group leaders but also persons working quietly in the background and living as servants will become key leaders in your ministry. The book *Start a Revolution* and issue 2 in this manual include material on empowering single adults for ministry.

Paradigm 3: Get back to the basics. Here are 12 tried-and-true basics in single-adult ministry. They can help you start a ministry, or if you're experienced but perplexed, they can help you get back to the basics.

1. Identify yourself as a key to building or revitalizing single-adult ministry in your church. Whether you're single or married, prayerfully seek God's leadership and respond to the burden He lays on your heart.

2. Evaluate current resources for single-adult ministry. Review resources and select those that best meet your ministry needs. An annual mediagraphy is published by Christian Single Resources, MSN 151; the Sunday School Board; 127 Ninth Avenue, North; Nashville, TN 37234-0151. Also see "Resources for Single Adults and Their Leaders," beginning on page 138 in this manual.

3. Enlist the support of your pastor, key leaders, and single adults. Following the guidance of your resources, secure the support of key leaders and of single adults themselves. Such support will directly affect your ministry's immediate and long-term success.

4. Convene a task force, appointed by your pastor or another key leader, to research, assess, and plan to address the needs for starting or revitalizing your single-adult ministry. Include both single and married persons on the task force.

5. Determine the single-adult demographics in your church and community. Work with your task force to delineate age groupings. Define single-adult identity groupings: never married, divorced, widowed, single parents, young unmarried adults, and senior single adults. Church records and information from local censuses, available at public libraries or courthouses, can assist you. Survey single adults to discover their needs and interests. Use the toolbox in issue 1 for ideas. Begin your ministry by targeting the age and identity groupings your church style and consistency will most likely reach first; then expand your ministry to reach others.

6. Compile a maximal-potential list from your church records; church members' referrals; and community sources such as surveys, a newcomers organization, legal notices for deaths and divorces, businesses' mailing lists, and cross-reference directories.

7. Determine the purpose and objectives of your ministry with single adults. For help with writing a purpose statement, see issue 5, solution 2.

8. Start and develop a Bible-teaching ministry with single adults. Plan for Sunday School and weekday Bible-study opportunities. Secure attractive space inside or outside the church property, depending on where you can best reach single persons. In fact, starting a Sunday School/Bible-study group may be your church's initial step in beginning to minister with single adults.

9. Select qualified leaders. Consider these priorities in prospective leaders:
   • Spiritual maturity in Christ
   • A receptive attitude toward all single adults
   • An ability to relate to a variety of single adults
   • Commitment, time availability, and motivation

10. Plan a comprehensive ministry strategy. A successful, long-lasting ministry with single adults is characterized by balance. Balance Sunday School/Bible study and worship with weekday ministry activities to meet the needs and concerns of various age and identity groups of single adults. Balance inreach ministry (ministry directed to those presently involved) and outreach ministry (ministry directed to prospects in the community).

11. Promote and publicize your ministry with single adults. Some effective ways include:
   • The church newsletter
   • The Sunday-morning worship bulletin, inserts, direct mail, and brochures
   • *Christian Single* magazine with your church's name attached
   • Public-service announcements on radio and television
   • News releases and personal ads in local newspapers
   • Customized ads in newspapers' entertainment pages
   • Telephone contacts
   • Business cards

12. Provide for regular evaluation and assessment. In balanced ministries single adults readily move out of the role of taker into the role of giver.

Paradigm 4: Empowering people expands the possibilities. Have you noticed that leaders often stockpile single adults, not in warehouses and storage tanks but in groups, departments, classes, or auditoriums? Rather than hoarding single adults' increased numbers, let them loose. Equip them to serve in your church and send them out to help other churches reach single adults, too.

Paradigm 5: Learn from the past. Credible single-adult ministry has been around for almost 20 years. Many persons who have gone before can help you avoid making the mistakes they made. Avoid these single-adult ministry traps:

• Single-adult ministry is not youth ministry. The goal is not to have a homogeneous group dressed in look-alike theme shirts and cheering for Jesus. Single-adult ministry is for adults.

• The handy-dandy, superinflatable, one-size-fits-all, instant single-adult ministry program from the Single-

factoid

A successful, long-lasting ministry with single adults is characterized by balance.

Source: Tim Cleary

Adult Ministry Church of America won't work where you are. You can't be everything to everyone. Instead, find your church's niche. For example, does your church primarily consist of young, unmarried adults? Is your church considered a redemptive community that ministers with many persons who are single again? Pray about your church's strength and character and focus on them.

• Brother Harold and Sister Sue, the always-married couple chosen to lead the single adults out of the wilderness of the single life into the promised land of the married, don't have a clue about what it means to live life as a single adult, although they think they do. Planning activities based on their own needs and perspectives, they build a ministry *for* single adults rather than *with* single adults. It does not focus on single-adult needs. When all else fails, ask a single adult.

• The single-adult ministry can't live a healthy life in the church's isolation ward. Single adults may have their own worship, Sunday School/Bible study, and other activities. This peer interaction is needed, but so is integration into the church's life and leadership.

• Many single adults attend three churches—one for social activities, one for Bible study, and another for worship. And they do this in spite of your church's having the best, most expensive, and most spectacular single-adult activities in town. This is a Baby Boomer characteristic, not just a single-adult characteristic. Learn that hyperactivity is not enough. You must have a strategy to lead single adults to know Christ personally and to grow in commitment to Him and to the church.

Solution ②

Choose an Organizational Style to Meet Your Unique Needs
Larry Garner

Single-adult ministry is the most complex area of ministry in the church for many reasons. Single adults include all ages of adults—from 18 to the grave. Single adults encompass a number of identities, including never married, divorced, and widowed. Economics, interests, status as parents, psychological well-being, and spiritual states all add to the complexity of ministry to and with single adults. Because of this complexity, organizing single-adult ministry is also a complex process.

Several concerns must be addressed before the organizational structure of the single-adult ministry can be determined:

• Purpose
• Needs of audience
• Strategies
• Leadership
• Organization
• Resources
• Budget

These factors are illustrated in the diagram at right.

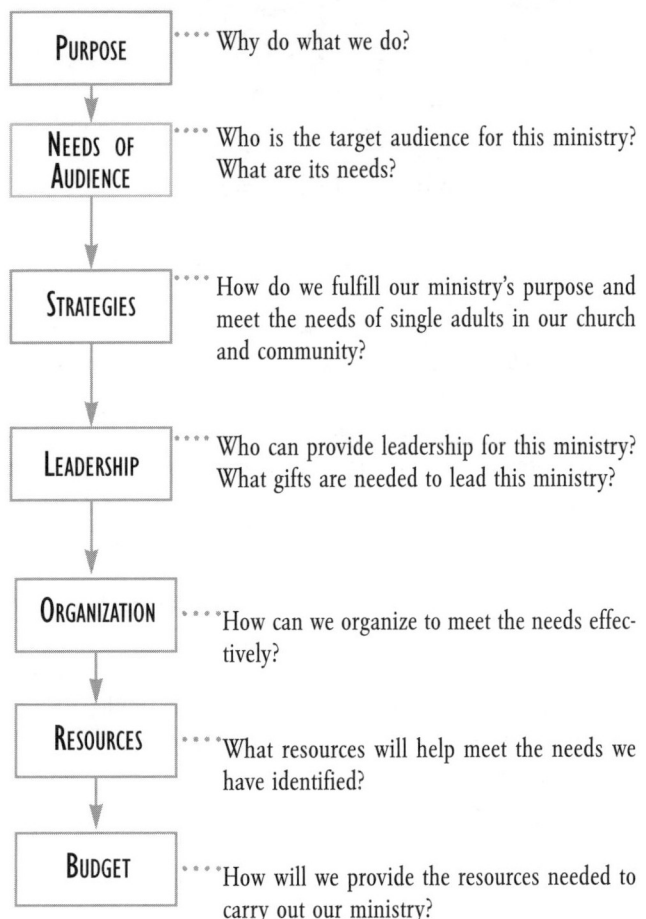

PURPOSE	Why do what we do?
NEEDS OF AUDIENCE	Who is the target audience for this ministry? What are its needs?
STRATEGIES	How do we fulfill our ministry's purpose and meet the needs of single adults in our church and community?
LEADERSHIP	Who can provide leadership for this ministry? What gifts are needed to lead this ministry?
ORGANIZATION	How can we organize to meet the needs effectively?
RESOURCES	What resources will help meet the needs we have identified?
BUDGET	How will we provide the resources needed to carry out our ministry?

Purpose

A purpose (mission/vision) statement is one of the most important requirements for any single-adult ministry. A clear understanding of purpose provides direction.

Look at the following symbols and select the one that most nearly reflects your single-adult ministry.

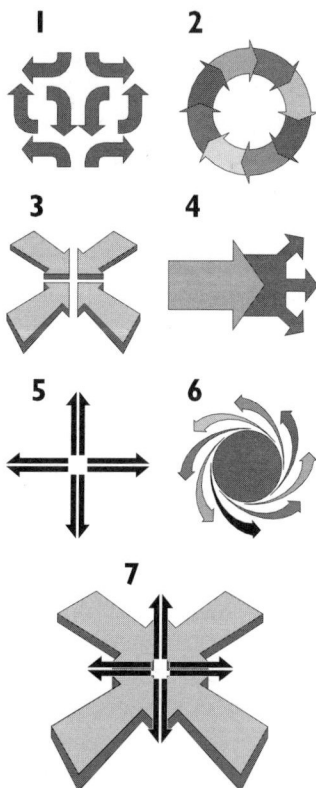

1   **2**

3   **4**

5   **6**

7

Which symbol did you choose? Why?

The symbol you selected indicates in some ways the purpose of your single-adult ministry. For example:

- Symbol 3 might represent a ministry that focuses on bringing single adults into the church or the group.
- Symbol 5 might reflect an outward focus on your group's ministry to single adults outside your group.
- Symbol 6 might represent a ministry with the core purpose of helping single adults discover their spiritual gifts and express those gifts in ministry.
- Symbol 7 might represent a group that focuses on a spiritual journey inward and on an outward journey of ministry to others.

The purpose of your single-adult ministry can be expressed as a directional symbol because purpose determines direction. A purpose statement identifies your ministry's goal. Having a definite ministry goal narrows the scope of study, equipping, and ministry to and with single adults. Ministry with single adults should be intentional, directed, and purposeful. A clear understanding of purpose provides direction for a single-adult ministry.

Draw a symbol that expresses the direction or purpose of your single-adult ministry.

Jesus was the most intentional person who ever lived. In speaking of the necessity of service for greatness in God's kingdom, Jesus said that He came not to be served but to serve and to give His life a ransom for many (see Mark 10:45). Because He knew who He was and why He was, He was able to live intentionally.

When tempted, Jesus could resist (see Matt. 4:1-11). When the crowd tried to make Him an earthly king (see John 6:15), He was able to resist because that was not in keeping with His mission. When told by Peter that He could not die (see Matt. 16:22), Jesus heard the voice of the tempter and resisted the temptation to go in a different direction. Luke revealed Jesus' intentionality when he stated, "As the time approached for him to be taken up to heaven, Jesus resolutely set out for Jerusalem" (Luke 9:51). He went to Jerusalem to achieve His destiny.

The apostle Paul succinctly stated his purpose in his letter to the Colossians:

> I rejoice in what was suffered for you, and I fill up in my flesh what is still lacking in regard to Christ's afflictions, for the sake of his body, which is the church. I have become its servant by the commission God gave me to present to you the word of God in its fullness—the mystery that has been kept hidden for ages and generations, but is now disclosed to the saints. To them God has chosen to make known among the Gentiles the glorious riches of this mystery, which is Christ in you, the hope of glory.
>
> We proclaim him, admonishing and teaching everyone with all wisdom, so that we may present everyone perfect in Christ. To this end I labor, struggling with all his energy, which so powerfully works in me (Col. 1:24-29).

Paul had a very clear understanding of his purpose: to present everyone perfect (complete) in Christ. The decisions he made and the actions he chose took him step-by-step toward that goal. What if your single-adult ministry adopted this as its purpose statement? What areas of ministry would be developed to present every person complete in Christ?

Without a clear sense of destination, any direction will do.

In a purpose statement we could use the areas of ministry suggested by Jesus' development: "Jesus grew in wisdom and stature, and in favor with God and men" (Luke 2:52). Jesus developed in four dimensions: intellectual/emotional, physical, spiritual, and social. These four dimensions of life contribute to a person's holistic development. A single-adult ministry should incorporate all four areas.

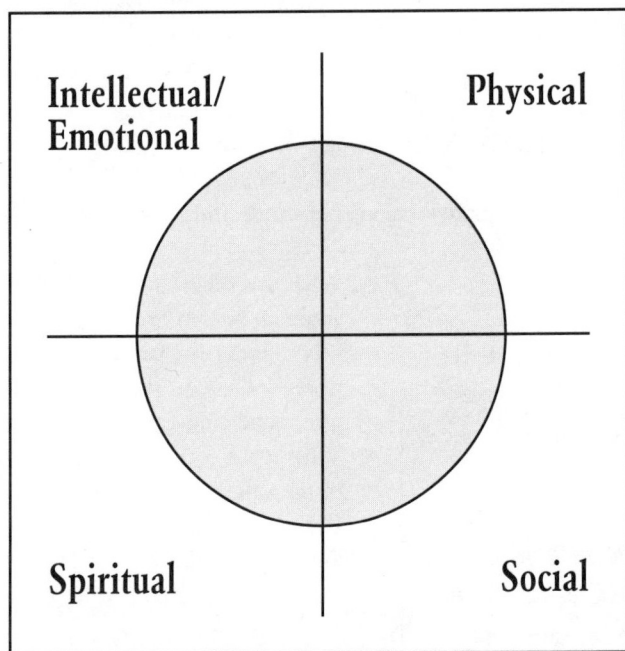

Although this diagram depicts a balanced view of single-adult ministry, real-life ministry is usually not so nice and neat. Single-adult ministry should be balanced—that is, the ministry addresses all of the needs persons have—but it does not necessarily give the same amount of time and attention to all areas of persons' lives.

Analyze your ministry activities from the past year by looking at your calendar and budget expenditures. Write the purpose of your single-adult ministry as reflected by your priorities.

Perhaps your church has a purpose statement. If your single-adult ministry develops a purpose statement, be sure it is compatible with your church's purpose.

Following are some examples of purpose statements from a variety of single-adult ministries.

Every single adult in our area will have the opportunity to hear the gospel of Jesus Christ and to respond by inviting Christ into his or her life (see Phil. 2:9-11). Christian single adults will be encouraged and given the opportunity to develop intimate relationships with Jesus Christ. These relationships include—
• daily communication through prayer and

Bible study (see Col. 2:6-7);
• support by and for other believers through worship and fellowship in the local church (see Heb. 10:25);
• sharing with others through word and ministry (see Matt. 28:19).

Our programs, ministries, and activities will have this philosophy as their basis. All events and activities will provide fellowship that supports and encourages a growing relationship with Jesus.

To instill a sense of urgency for sharing Jesus Christ, to equip for service through Bible-based teaching, and to develop personal relationships in a nurturing environment.

The purpose of our single-adult ministry is to honor God by—
• attracting persons to belief in Jesus Christ;
• encouraging them in every phase of life to grow in faith;
• equipping them to make a positive impact through ministry in the church and mission in the world.

The purpose of our single-adult ministry is to introduce as many single adults to Christ as possible, to perfect the saints to do the work of ministry, and to be a role model for other single-adult ministries.

• We will love God.
• We will love one another.
• We will learn and obey God's Word.
• We will use our lives, our talents, and our resources to tell as many as we can about God's love in Christ.

Purpose statements focus time, energy, thought, and resources. They clear away the clutter, providing a sense of being, defining who you are, and giving direction for your ministry. A purpose statement also provides a standard against which you can measure your ministry and stewardship.

Steve Smith, the minister with single adults at Prestonwood Baptist Church in Dallas, Texas, condensed the purpose statement to three key phrases so that it can be remembered and communicated: "Our purpose is to reach, to teach, and to grow." Steve said, "Instead of trying to be all things to all people, we have used our purpose statement to identify our particular niche of ministry." He explained:

At one point our single-adult ministry was conducting a wide range of social functions. Over a period of time the social emphasis lessened. As our leaders began evaluating why the transition had occurred, we went to our purpose statement. They concluded that while social activities were part of our ministry, they were not the focal point. We determined that what we want to do is to reach people for Christ, teach them the Bible, and help them grow in their faith.

The purpose statement shaped the ministry Prestonwood wanted to provide for single adults. It provided definition and direction for the ministry, as well as a standard for evaluating plans and actions.

Take a moment to think about and write a purpose statement for your single-adult ministry. It doesn't have to be fully developed, only a first draft at this time. If you need help getting started, read passages like Matthew 28:18-20; Luke 2:52; Ephesians 4:11-13; and Colossians 1:28. You may wish to incorporate some of the foundational concepts in these verses.

Audience

After you establish a purpose for your single-adult ministry, you need to consider the persons you want to target for ministry. Your target audience is unmarried persons in the church or community who are above age 18. This population segment now accounts for almost half of the adult population in the United States.

It is not enough to give such a general, sweeping definition, because the single-adult audience is varied. To identify the audience for your single-adult ministry, think about the individuals in your church or community who are single.

The composition of the audience for a single-adult ministry varies from church to church and from community to community. Each community differs in the number of single adults; their ages and stages; and their emotional, social, financial, and spiritual states.

For instance, if you are in a town or city that has a college or university, the primary single-adult target group might be college students. If your area attracts a large number of young professionals, single adults in their 20s and 30s might be the primary target group. Besides the primary target group, you will probably find single adults in other life

stations or situations—single parents, recently divorced persons, median-adult singles, or senior single adults. A church must develop a broad spectrum of ministry to reach as many single adults as possible. Although you may need to focus your ministry on one group of single adults, do not ignore other segments of the population.

The following questions will help you identify prospects for your single-adult ministry. A worksheet is provided in the toolbox at the end of this issue to help you process these questions. In answering each question, include single adults in both your church and community.

- Who is your primary single-adult ministry target group?
- How many persons constitute the potential ministry group?
- What are the identities of single adults in your church or community? Identify percentages of never married, divorced, widowed, and single parents.
- What is the socioeconomic status of the single adults in your target audience?
- What is the educational level of the single adults in your target audience?
- What vocations are represented in your single-adult audience?
- What is the spiritual level of the single adults in your target group?
- What are the generational groupings of most of your single adults?

These questions reveal the complexity of single-adult ministry and suggest that a variety of strategies is necessary to meet the needs of single adults in your church and community.

Strategies

A strategy is a plan of action for achieving an objective or a specific goal. Strategies for single-adult ministry arise from two primary sources: your purpose statement and the needs of your audience.

factoid

Strategies for single-adult ministry arise from two primary sources: your purpose statement and the needs of your audience. Source: Larry Garner

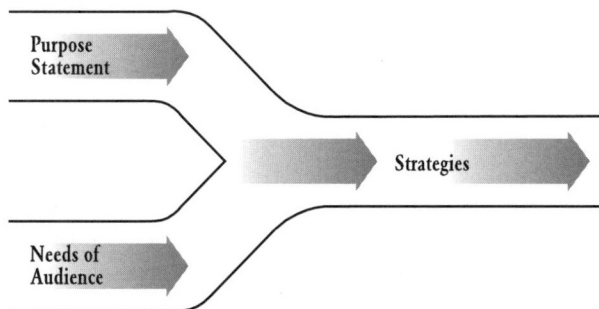

Purpose Statement

Needs of Audience

Strategies

The scope of your ministry will be dictated by the breadth of your purpose statement. Just as the purpose statement includes certain things, it also excludes certain things. For example, one single-adult group sponsored a line dance as a purely social function. When the leaders began formulating a purpose statement, they decided that the distinctive ministry they wanted to perform was single-adult Bible study. They decided that other opportunities were offered in their community for social events such as dancing. Their purpose statement led them to reconsider the nature of their ministry and the functions they performed.

The other element that determines your strategies is the needs of your audience. Part of the complexity of single-adult ministry arises from single adults' diverse needs. Their ages, identities, and life experiences are so varied that they create niches of ministry need.

Feasibility Factors

Your ministry cannot or should not address all of the many needs you discover in the single-adult community. Certain feasibility factors can help you determine the needs your single-adult ministry can address.

Malcolm Knowles, a leading adult educator of the 20th century, has done great work on developing programs to meet adult needs. Knowles created the following diagram to help institutions visualize the flow of a program or ministry's development process.

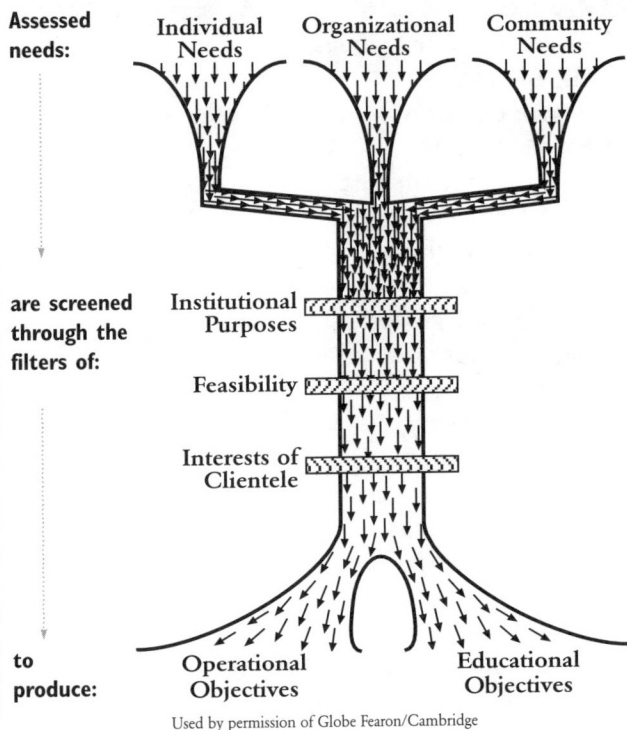

Assessed needs:	Individual Needs	Organizational Needs	Community Needs

are screened through the filters of:	Institutional Purposes
	Feasibility
	Interests of Clientele

| to produce: | Operational Objectives | Educational Objectives |

Used by permission of Globe Fearon/Cambridge

Operational objectives:	Educational objectives:
1.	1.
2.	2.
3.	3.
4.	4.

The process begins with assessing the needs of the community, individuals, and the organization. In this case the organization is the church. The church's needs should not be overlooked. We often assess the needs of the individual and the community while forgetting that the church has needs, as well. For example, the church needs members who know what they believe, who can be viable witnesses in the world, and who live by the moral standards espoused by the church.

After all areas of need have been assessed, the needs flow through a series of filters or grids—much like objects sorted by a series of screens. The needs that get through the grids become the basis of ministry development.[1]

Some needs that arise in the single-adult population may not be covered by your purpose statement. The purpose statement becomes the control agent for structuring ministry strategies. Only strategies meeting needs that fit within the scope of your purpose statement need to be developed. For instance, some single adults in your area of ministry might have a real need to borrow $10,000. It's a real need but probably doesn't fit within the scope of your ministry's purpose statement.

The availability of resources and leadership restricts some ministry endeavors. Resources include space, money, time, and church support. Sometimes trained, appropriate leadership is unavailable. The lack of resources and leadership limits ministry to single adults.

The interest of the clientele is a major factor in ministry with single adults. Sometimes ministry is planned and presented, but nobody participates. An accurate assessment of need is critical to the success of any ministry effort. But need alone is not enough. If it is not wanted, success is limited at the outset.

Offer courses of study or ministries that address some of the perceived needs of persons in your church and community. For example, one church offers divorce-recovery, parenting, and marriage-enrichment courses. By advertising these in the local newspaper, the church not only draws from its membership but also reaches into the community. Participants are made aware of additional ministries available through the church. Many times participants in these events begin to attend regularly.

> ## NEEDS OF PERSONS CAN BE IDENTIFIED IN SEVERAL WAYS:
> *Observation:* Become a people watcher. Observing can tell you much about people's needs.
> *Research:* Studies are available to help you understand many specific needs of various population segments.
> *Surveys:* A simple survey of church members reveals many areas of need.
> *Personal reflection:* Think about the needs in your own life. Many of your needs are felt by others.

When a ministry has come through the planning grid, it has great potential for success.

What are needs in the lives of your members?
❏ **Coping with stress**
❏ **Relationships**
❏ **Managing money**
❏ **Learning to pray**
❏ **Bible-study skills**
❏ **Leadership skills**
❏ **Teaching skills**
❏ **Doctrinal studies**
❏ **New-member orientation**
❏ **Knowing God's will**
❏ **Making moral choices**
❏ **Discovering spiritual gifts**
❏ **Understanding the beliefs of cults**
❏ **Learning to share their faith**
❏ **Parenting skills**
❏ **Divorce recovery**
❏ **Other:** _____

Possible Pitfalls
Developing strategies to reach single adults has pitfalls. One pitfall commonly encountered in contemporary expressions of Christianity is how we measure success. Successful ministry is often defined in numerical terms. If an event or a strategy draws a large crowd, it is considered a success. To reach a larger number of single adults, we might be tempted to take shortcuts or compromise our mission.

Many strategies can be developed that draw a crowd, but a crowd may or may not be desirable. Two events in Jesus' life address this issue. In the temptations at the beginning of His public ministry, Jesus faced a temptation to jump from the pinnacle of the temple (see Matt. 4:5-6). Seeing this amazing feat, the crowd would be drawn to Him. If Jesus had surrendered to this temptation, His ministry would have been short-lived. The next person claiming to be the Messiah with a let-me-entertain-you program would have drawn away those kinds of followers.

The other event occurred the day after the feeding of the five thousand. When the crowd started to make Jesus king by force, He left the crowd and went to a mountain to pray. Jesus and the disciples had been on the east side of the Sea of Galilee when He fed the crowd. During the night Jesus and the disciples went back across the sea to the region around Capernaum. The next day the crowds looked for Jesus. When they found Him, they didn't get the reception they had expected. He said to them, " 'You are looking for me, not because you saw miraculous signs but because you ate the loaves and had your fill' " (John 6:26). He repelled them by telling them that if they wanted something to eat, they could eat His flesh and drink His blood (see John 6:53).

When they heard that, many turned away from Him.

That was a crisis moment in Jesus' ministry at the peak of His popularity. Jesus forced the crowds to make a hard choice if they were to follow Him. He was unwilling to allow people to set His agenda. If they could not accept what He had to say, they had to live with the choice. This is not to say He didn't care. We know that He cared enough to die on the cross. But this same Jesus who died on the cross also told the rich, young ruler that he must sell all he had and give it to the poor (see Luke 18:18-24). Jesus watched with regret as the young man walked away; yet He did not compromise the call by lowering the standard.

Many strategies could be developed to draw a crowd of single adults. You must ask whether they are coming because of a let-me-entertain-you approach. Are they coming because they are getting bread and fish or because they really believe and want to follow Jesus? The strategies chosen to reach single adults must conform to your purpose statement.

What are some strategies you currently have or could develop that are consistent with your purpose statement and that could meet needs of the single adults in your church and community? Place an X beside the ones you currently have. Place a check mark beside those you need to develop.
❏ **Sunday School/Bible study**
❏ **Retreats**
❏ **Divorce-recovery groups**
❏ **Athletic teams**
❏ **Dinner groups**
❏ **Prayer groups**
❏ **Single-parent support groups**
❏ **Grief-recovery groups**
❏ **Discipleship groups**
❏ **Music groups**
❏ **Dependency groups**
❏ **Men's groups**
❏ **Women's groups**
❏ **Drama groups**
❏ **Purpose groups**
❏ **Ministry/care groups**
❏ **Fellowship groups**
❏ **Weeknight Bible-study groups**
❏ **Other:** _____

The Central Role of Ongoing Sunday School/Bible Study
The key organization in many churches' single-adult ministries is a Sunday School/Bible-study group or department. This is the proven, ongoing rallying point for single adults to gather on a regular, weekly basis. Sunday School/Bible study gives you an organization and a strategy for reaching, teaching, and caring.

Many Christian single adults attend church only once a week or less, and Sunday-morning worship is usually the time chosen. Scheduling Sunday School/Bible study before or after the worship service can be an important strategy in developing your church's single-adult ministry. For those who cannot or will not prioritize time on Sunday morning, weekday opportunities for Bible study should be explored.

Refer to issue 6 in this manual for detailed assistance in establishing an ongoing Sunday School/Bible-study organization for single adults. An organization may consist of only one group that targets a specific age or peer group. Or it may be targeted to many specific age and peer identities with multiple groups or departments.

Often, the target group you reach may be the group that is most compatible with your entire church culture. Since Barna research on single adults indicates that at least half of all single adults prefer smaller churches, the Sunday-morning Sunday School/Bible-study organization may be the single best way to do single-adult ministry in a smaller church.

Leadership

Leadership in the empowerment model focuses on equipping single adults for ministry. A primary task of leadership in the New Testament is to equip believers for the ministries to which God has called them. In Ephesians 4:11-12 Paul makes clear the task of church leadership: "It was he who gave some to be apostles, some to be prophets, some to be evangelists, and some to be pastors and teachers, to prepare God's people for works of service, so that the body of Christ may be built up."

The question we face is, What must be done to take single adults from initial belief or their present point of spiritual development to responsible personal ministry? Issue 2 in this manual describes an empowerment model for equipping leaders. Here we will focus on leadership concepts that empower an organization.

Jesus is our model for leadership in an empowerment model. He said that to be great in the Kingdom, we should become servants. The ideas of leadership and greatness that Jesus espoused run contrary to the world's ideas.

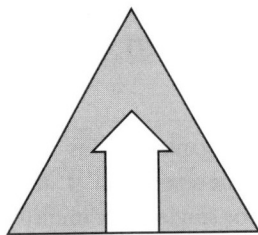

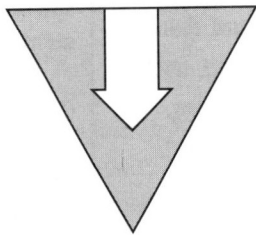

The World's View of Greatness   God's View of Greatness
See Mark 10:35-45.
Jesus was a servant leader (see John 13:13-17; Phil. 2:5-11).
We are not above our Master.
As He was a servant, so should we be.

The world's view of greatness is to rise to the pinnacle of the pyramid. Get to the top any way you can. The objective is to have as many as possible under you who are servants to you. Jesus' view of greatness is to get to the bottom of an inverted pyramid. The objective is to have as many people as possible above you to whom you are a servant. Become a servant—the servant of all—if you want to become great in the Kingdom. God turns all of our standards of greatness, importance, and ministry upside down.

Jesus embodied servant leadership for us. Leaders should find ways to support and serve those doing ministry. This means running interference, protecting the schedule from conflicts, finding resources—whatever it takes to ensure that necessary resources are available to get the ministry done.

Most leadership structures are diagrammed from the top to the bottom.

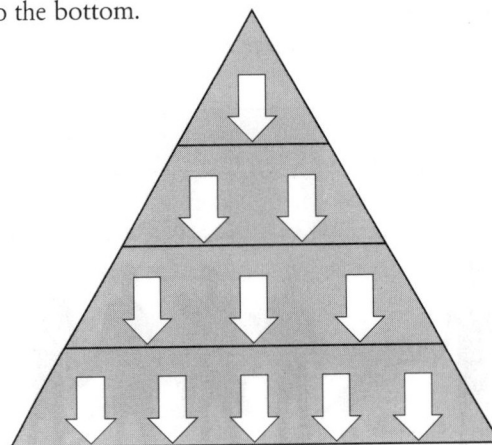

The higher the level of leadership on the chart, the higher the level of authority and power. This model is a line-management structure often found in the business world. Directives come down to lower levels, which act on those directives. Christian leadership turns the chart upside down.

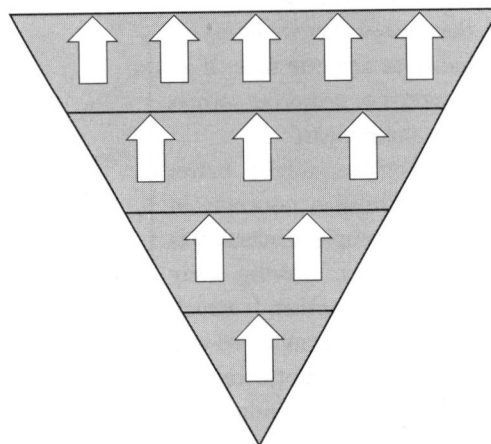

Christian leaders are servant-leaders. At every level, leaders support those around them with authority, teaching, training, modeling, protection, support, and cheerleading. This is exactly what Jesus did with the twelve. After a year of

Smaller and Simpler

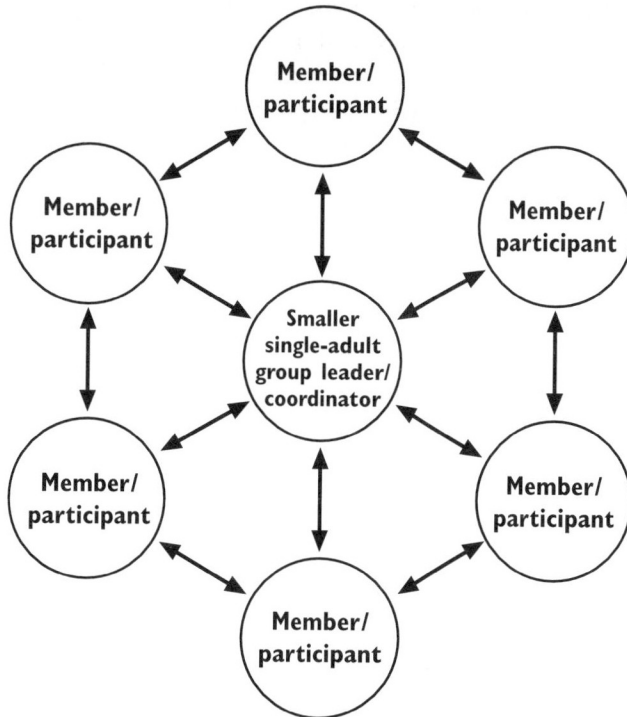

This diagram represents a very small group of single adults. Everyone maintains relationships with other members. Members/participants can be enlisted to assume the responsibilities for group functions.

Functions of a Single-Adult Group

Every single-adult group, regardless of its size and duration, has certain functions that must be conducted if the group is to be successful.

FUNCTIONS OF A SINGLE-ADULT GROUP
Coordination
Enlistment
Record keeping
Learning
Fellowship/caregiving

Here's an overview of the primary functions of a single-adult small group.

Coordination. Coordination is bringing together various parts of a group into a harmonious relationship so that it can learn, fellowship, and minister effectively. Some components of a group are members, study resources, equipment, schedules, events, relationships, planning, and leadership.

Enlistment. Enlistment is reaching and involving unenlisted persons. The key to enlistment is appealing to persons

on the basis of group fellowship, of what the group is studying, and of ways that study will speak to their needs.

Record keeping. Accurate records can be an important tool for evaluating and planning the group's work. They can also be a primary source of key information about group members. In most groups record keeping simply involves checking a roll. In some cases the secretary contacts group members when they are absent.

Learning. Learning is the most obvious of all group functions. At the same time, it can be the most misunderstood and the most abused. Learning in a single-adult group should be highly interactive. It may occur in a study group or in a variety of affinity groups, which are groups organized around common interests, such as hobbies, professions, and activities. Each member brings to the group a range of experience and knowledge to be shared. Group members are responsible for preparing and for feeding into the session the results of their preparation, their insights, and their prior learning experiences. Group members are not just presented material or taught answers by the leader. The leader's responsibility is to plan and lead the kinds of group experiences that enable members to work together to learn; to find answers; to formulate solutions; to develop Bible skills and other skills; to apply truths to life; and to develop, change, or reinforce attitudes.

Fellowship/caregiving. Fellowship is the dynamic often referred to as *koinonia*—that which is held in common in Christ. Fellowship results from the common experiences that bond a group together. Through fellowship openness, trust, mutual caring, and support are experienced. Fellowship is generally thought of as the social events the group does together, but these events are simply occasions that build genuine Christian fellowship and caring.

As a single-adult group grows in its membership and participation, the structure needs to change to ensure that group functions are conducted effectively. Some single-adult ministries have adopted a large-group/small-group structure. The large group has a leader/coordinator who guides the small groups' purpose and process as they relate to the overall single-adult and church ministries. Small-group leaders/coordinators provide and direct participants in coordination, enlistment, record keeping, learning, fellowship, and caregiving. Each small group represents some aspect of the single-adult ministry, helping it carry out its purpose. A small group could provide any number of services to its members, from divorce-recovery and single-parenting support to professional development and spiritual growth through seminars or Bible study. Each small group can have one or many functions and can be long- or short-term.

The most successful larger groups have discovered the importance of caring for members/participants. Small groups ensure that everyone can be touched in significant ways for ministry and fellowship.

Larger and More Complex

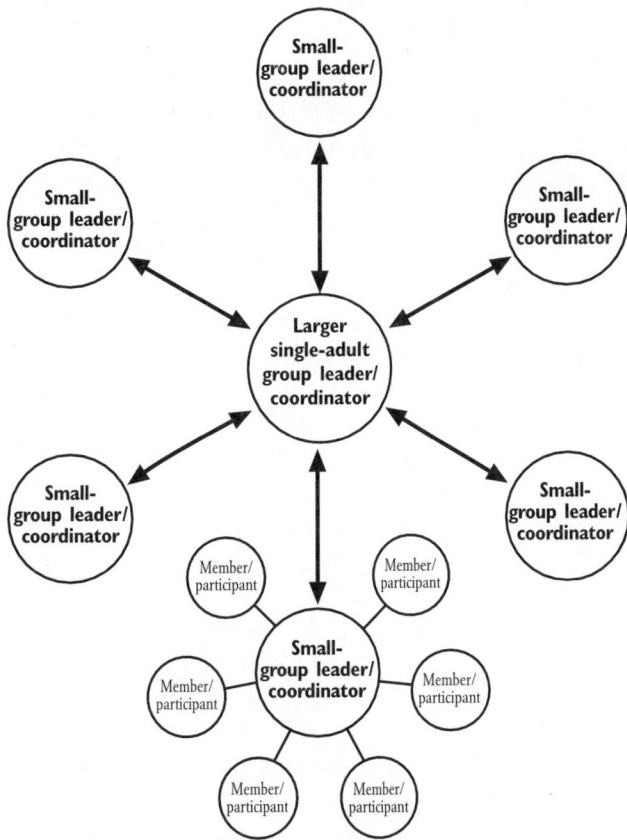

As the larger group increases in size, additional small groups might have to be created to meet the growing, diverse needs of the single adults in a church or community. In each new group the same patterns of organization that have been suggested to this point may be used.

Life stages or single-adult identities and ages play an extensive part in organizational structures. Many ministries to single adults are grouped by decades—20s, 30s, 40s, and so on—although you will not want to group by decades ending in zero. Consider a designation of 30-something, for example. Although age is a simple device for grouping, do not overlook other considerations. Persons might be grouped by ministry needs or by service, ministry, recreational, or professional interests. For example, some single-adult ministries are developing groups for women and men, single parents, 20-somethings and 30-somethings, hiking and outdoor activities, young professionals, divorce recovery, and other needs and interests.

A multiple-group structure calls for a different approach to organization. For instance, multiple groups or ministries require greater attention to coordination and planning than

a smaller organization. Coordination can be accomplished in a couple of ways. The leader can perform the task, or a representative leadership team can be formed from the members or participants. As long as a single-adult ministry has only a few ministry groups or teams, the single-adult leader can probably coordinate the ministries adequately. As ministry groups or teams proliferate, a leadership team is almost a necessity.

This diagram shows an organizational model that includes ministry groups or teams.

Larger and More Complex

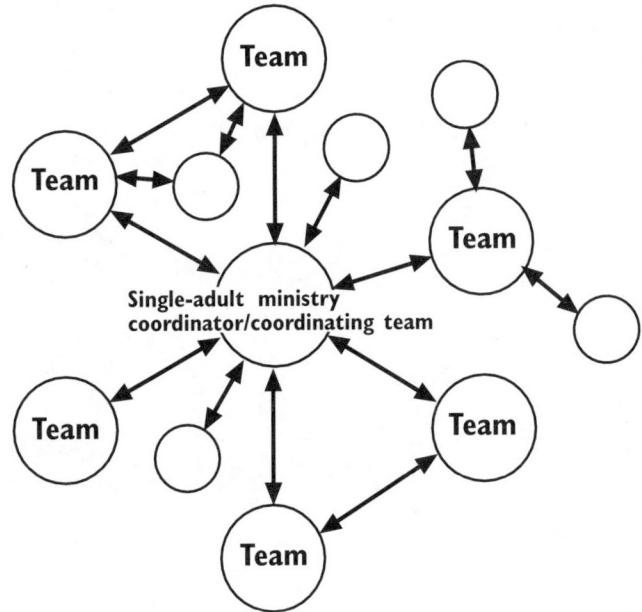

An organizational configuration like this accurately portrays the biblical model of empowerment. This configuration brings new ways of looking at the roles of leadership:
- The leader of the single-adult ministry becomes a coordinator, a player-coach, an equipper.
- As the single-adult ministry grows, a leadership team will probably be formed to handle planning and coordination.

The model suggests a degree of equality and authority among the teams:
- Teams are highly autonomous.
- Teams are formed around calling, ministry, and members' gifts.
- Some teams are connected with information and tasks, maybe even with common members.
- Some teams are entirely on their own.
- Some teams are large; some are small.

The diagram on the following page illustrates a segment of the previous diagram in more detail.

> ## factoid
> Teams provide entry points for single adults to receive and give ministry. At these entry points the church can touch the world in the name of Christ.
> Source: Larry Garner

Larger and More Complex

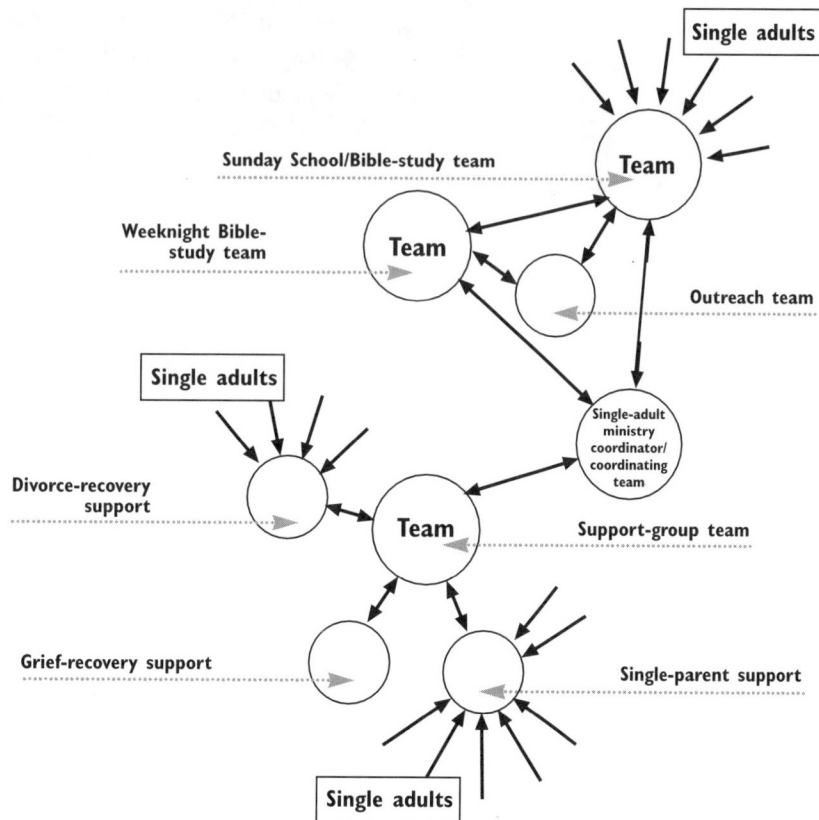

In this diagram two Bible-study teams have been formed—one for Sunday morning and another for a weeknight Bible-study group. Although these have a connection with each other, they are two separate teams. They might have members in common. They might, and probably will, reach different participants. Each team has a joint connection with the outreach team, which coordinates the single-adult ministry's efforts to reach those outside the group. As guests come to the various Bible-study groups, their names are channeled to the outreach team to be sure every guest receives appropriate follow-up.

The diagram also includes a support-group team and three support groups. These support groups vary, depending on the needs in a particular church or community.

Ministry teams are formed by the necessary members to conduct the specific ministry. Depending on the type and size of the ministry, teams vary in their composition. For example, for a number of years Anne has conducted a support ministry for single mothers. She is the only person needed to conduct this particular ministry. Steve, however, as the head of a ministry team that plans and coordinates disaster relief, has seven members on his team.

> ## factoid
> Organization should be flexible or fluid to allow for change, as needed, at any given time.
> Source: Larry Garner

Use the worksheet on page 92 to develop your single-adult ministry organization.

Issues of Control and Freedom in Organization

In single-adult ministry organization a key issue is control. If we try to exert control over all events, actions, and participants in a single-adult ministry, we might stifle what God wants to do. When God has freedom to work, we may need to relinquish our structures and charts. The disciples tried to exercise a degree of control when they told Jesus about someone who was ministering but was not connected to their group. Jesus said to leave the person alone: " 'Whoever is not against you is for you' " (Luke 9:50).

In the Book of Acts the Jerusalem church attempted to control what was happening as the early church was dispersed by persecution. Every time it heard that a new or different group had received the gospel, it sent envoys to investigate the situation. The Jerusalem conference must have been a riot with the control freaks showing their organizational charts and trying to straighten out the conferees.

As you organize your single-adult ministry, keep in mind these two concerns:

Freedom to respond to God's call to ministry. Single adults exercise their spiritual gifts in many different ministries. The vast majority of them find their ministries beyond the walls of the church. As single adults use their gifts, many avenues of ministry open to them, and most of those ministries aren't on anyone's charts. Single adults must have the freedom to exercise their gifts as God gives them opportunities.

Order to contain the chaos that could result from a lack of coordination and communication. At the end of a passage on public worship Paul admonished, "Everything should be done in a fitting and orderly way" (1 Cor. 14:40). While freedom must be provided to allow the spontaneity and dynamics of ministry, some elements of coordination and accountability are also needed. It is interesting that Paul always came back after his missionary journeys and gave an account of his ministry to the Jerusalem and Antioch churches. Accountability is a necessary part of stewardship.

A tension always exists between these two concerns. The tension is healthy and should be celebrated, not merely tolerated.

Organization should be flexible or fluid to allow for change, as needed, at any given time. Organization is a mixture of long-term, static structures and short-term, fluid structures. At any point a single-adult ministry has ongoing structures and short-term structures. If you avoid thinking of organization as constant structures, you can remain on the cutting edge of organizing to meet needs and can achieve your ministry purposes.

Resources

This section will help you develop a strategy for providing resources for your single-adult ministry. Developing a one-year strategy is recommended. However, most single-adult ministries that are led by volunteers maintain a plan from three to six months in advance. New single-adult ministries may have to develop a resource plan from week to week. Enlist a team to assist you in developing your plan. Consult with single-adult leaders from other churches and/or established ministries; denominational employees; church-staff members; a Christian book store or publishing house; and a Bible college, a seminary, or another educational institution. Also see "Resources for Single Adults and Their Leaders," beginning on page 138, and other resource lists.

Ask these questions as you develop your plan:
- For whom is the ministry intended?
- What are their needs?
- What are our related goals?
- What are our sources for materials?
- What is the cost, and how will it be funded?
- Who will provide leadership?
- How will we train leaders?
- What are our calendar opportunities and plans?

Review the ministry resource planning sampler on this page and complete the one in the toolbox for your ministry.

Budget

Successful single-adult ministries usually pay their own way and often more. Single adults commonly provide ⅓ of a church's annual ministry budget. Giving your single adults a line item in the church budget affirms your church's commitment to the single-adult ministry's purpose, potential, and leadership.

Consider these questions and answers to formulate your single-adult ministry's budget plan.

Does your single-adult ministry need a budget? The answer is yes if—
- it is a functioning ministry of your church;
- it is to be an important church outreach strategy;
- it will have significant Christian-educational value;
- single adults contribute money, time, and talent to

MINISTRY RESOURCE PLANNING SAMPLER

Who?	Divorced persons
Needs	Crisis help and support
Goals	Provide divorce recovery
Materials	*A Time for Healing: Coming to Terms with Your Divorce,* nine-week support-group resources. Order by calling 1-800-458-2772.
Cost	$12.95 per member book, funded through individual participant donations and supplemented by single-adult budget as needed.
Leaders	Enlist a group facilitator. If additional help is available, enlist a group host or a team to carry out actions for starting a group, as outlined in resources.
Training	Provide a training seminar with a divorce-recovery counselor interpreting material and discussing ways to handle various situations.
Time	Sunday morning from 10:30 a.m. until noon. Good time because Sunday School provides child care.
Calendar	Following Christmas and New Year holidays, often the most depressing time of year.

your church.

What is to be considered when doing budget planning for your single-adult ministry? Consider these factors:
- The number of single adults on church and Sunday School/Bible-study rolls—members and prospects. Determine the percentage of single adults enrolled and attending, compared to other church-ministry audiences.
- The single-adult demographics in your area and the challenges for ministry that you are able to address.
- The needs already provided through other church ministry budgets, for example, the church's general literature budget.
- The percentage of fair budget allotments to other

church ministries, compared to the single-adult ministry budget allotment.

- The maturity level of your current program, its vision, and projections for its future.
- The percentage of the general church budget given by single adults.

How should single-adult ministry budget money be spent? Consider the following guidelines.

- Always spend responsibly, considering the entire church's ministry goals. Single-adult ministry should be a team player.
- Generally, spend to subsidize special opportunities and needs, such as for community promotion to increase awareness of the single-adult ministry or for child-care provision during ministry activities.
- Spend, as a fair percentage of the church budget, for the single-adult ministry and its growth, compared to other church ministries.
- Do as much ministry programming as possible through cost recovery or program fees and, if commensurate with your church policy, a periodic fundraiser for a special mission trip or service opportunity.
- Always determine if a service or item could be donated by someone in the church or community.

The sample budget at right is compatible with a simple ministry organization led by a volunteer coordinating team.

---

[1]Malcolm S. Knowles, *The Modern Practice of Adult Education* (Chicago: Follett, 1980), 125.

SAMPLE SINGLE-ADULT MINISTRY ANNUAL BUDGET

Benevolence
(Provide through the church's benevolence fund.)

Literature
(Provide through the church's Christian-education budget.)

Community promotion **$500**
(Theme, art, and logo donated for business cards or ministry-information flier. Promotion through personal ads in the newspaper.)

Child care **$250**
(For key activities based on need, as well as donated child care.)

Conference and retreat subsidies **$500**
(To assist those who need fee paid, to pay for group transportation or a portion thereof, or to provide a discount incentive for early registration. Also consider donations and sponsorships for these opportunities.)

Total **$1,250**

Solution ③

Take Advantage of These Special Ministry Opportunities

Larry Garner

Single adults' diversity demands diverse strategies to meet their needs. Jesus used a variety of methods to meet similar ministry needs, as when He healed blindness. In Mark 8:22-26 Jesus spit on the man's eyes and touched him twice before sight was restored. In Luke 18:40-43 Jesus was asked to heal a blind man. "When he came near, Jesus asked him, 'What do you want me to do for you?' 'Lord, I want to see,' he replied. Jesus said to him, 'Receive your sight; your faith has healed you.' Immediately he received his sight and followed Jesus, praising God." In this instance Jesus pronounced the man healed. In John 9:1-7 Jesus made an ointment of clay, anointed the blind man's eyes, and told him to wash in the pool of Siloam.

We are not told in Scripture why Jesus healed the same condition in three different ways. We could speculate that each person's circumstances differed, the cultural conditions varied, or the individuals' specific needs demanded that they be treated in a slightly different manner. In each instance Jesus tailored His ministry response to the individual's exact needs. His ministry was need-specific.

The ministry actions commended in the parable in Matthew 25 are need-specific. The righteous are commended for meeting individuals' specific needs:

> "Come, you who are blessed by my Father; take your inheritance, the kingdom prepared for you since the creation of the world. For I was hungry and you gave me something to eat, I was thirsty and you gave me something to drink, I was a stranger and you invited me in, I needed clothes and you clothed me, I was sick and you looked after me, I was in prison and you came to visit me" (Matt. 25:34-36).

The hungry was fed, the thirsty was given drink, the stranger was welcomed, the naked was clothed, the sick received care, and the prisoner was visited. To follow biblical models of ministry, our strategies for ministry to and with single adults must be need-specific.

Part of the single-adult leader's responsibility is to identify gifted individuals and to equip them for the ministries they are to perform. Ministry teams can be formed to develop and conduct a variety of ministry strategies to meet the needs of specific identity groups in a church or community.

It might be best to think of single-adult ministry as a patchwork quilt rather than a uniform whole. A patchwork quilt is made up of many different patterns, colors, and types of material. New patterns and designs are formed as these are stitched together. Under the maker's direction, the various parts form a beautiful and useful new whole.

In a church's single-adult ministry the various pieces do not have to be of the same pattern, color, or fabric. In fact, the greater the variety, the better. All of these pieces can be formed into a ministry that is beautiful, useful, and whole—a ministry that addresses the specific needs of the identity groups forming the single-adult ministry population.

Following are some of the single-adult identities that might be addressed by a need-specific single-adult ministry. In the segments that follow, you will find characteristics of identity groups, some needs faced by each, and suggestions for meeting the specific needs of these groups.

Ministry with Divorced Persons[1]

Divorce is everywhere! The number of divorced people is rising. Currently, an estimated 1.3 million divorces occur each year, involving 2.6 million spouses, not to mention their children, stepchildren, parents, in-laws, friends, and colleagues. And these statistics are for just one year.

In the book *Marriage Savers* Michael J. McManus presents the breakup of the family as the central domestic problem of our time. He offers some strong evidence for his position.

- Six of 10 new marriages fail. Divorces have tripled since 1960. Before they are 18, ⅗ of children will see their parents divorce.
- Cohabitation has soared sixfold since 1970. The majority of marriages in America are preceded by cohabitation. Those who cohabit before marriage increase their odds of divorce by 50 percent.
- Fewer young people are getting married at all. In 1991 41 million adults had never married—twice the number in 1970 (21 million). The percentage of men ages 30 to 34 who have never married has tripled from 9 percent to 25 percent.
- Only 55 percent of adults are married today—the lowest figure ever.
- Who gets hurt the most? The innocent—the children.[2]

George Gallup, Jr., writes in the introduction to *Marriage Savers:*

> If a disease were to afflict the majority of a populace, spreading pain and dysfunction throughout all age groups, we would be frantically searching for reasons and solutions. Yet this particular scourge has become so endemic that it is virtually ignored.
>
> The scourge is *divorce,* an oddly neglected topic in a nation that has the worst record of broken marriages in the entire world. Divorce is a "root problem" in our country and is the cause of any number of other social ills.[3]

In its wake divorce leaves broken dreams and shattered lives. Divorced persons need hope and healing. The church can offer them both. One way a single-adult ministry can extend itself in ministry to the community is to offer or sponsor a divorce-recovery support group. Support groups are designed to be led by laypersons. These are not therapy groups but Christ-centered sharing groups—safe places—that help persons deal with the issues and struggles they encounter in crises. Sometimes expressing emotions is in itself an act of healing. Knowing that you are not the only one going through the devastation of divorce offers a degree of support and hope.

Harold Ivan Smith, who has done extensive work in the area of divorce recovery, offers excellent insight into the experience of divorce and divorce recovery. He has made the following observations about divorce recovery in churches.

> Many of the divorce-recovery models are based on the research of Elisabeth Kubler-Ross, a pioneer in the field of death and the grief process. [In her book *On Death and Dying* Kubler-Ross, a psychiatrist who specialized in death studies, shared stories of the agonies, expectations, and frustrations of dying patients and suggested that an orderly emotional stage system of dying exists.] Many writers and ministers, without closely reading Kubler-Ross, applied her theory of the grief process that the dying person undergoes to any grief or loss. They concluded that all divorced people must go though these five

factoid

Divorced persons need hope and healing. The church can offer them both.

Source: Larry Garner

stages: denial, anger, bargaining, depression, and acceptance. Some went a step further and suggested that people must experience these stages in the order listed. They concluded that if a person could not claim acceptance, he or she must not have successfully completed the previous stages.

Having completed my dissertation research in the area of spiritual formation and bereavement and having worked with many divorced and grieving people, I have concluded that this commonly accepted model is not the basis for the grief of the divorced and divorcing. I believe that Kubler-Ross offered a vehicle that has helped change the way people—particularly church members—think about divorce. Certainly, this model was initially helpful in summoning the compassion of the church to ministry with the divorced and divorcing. Far more critical is that we confront the agendas, or decisions, for healing and recovery.

Smith has provided another approach that goes well beyond the application of the five stages identified by Kubler-Ross. His work on divorce recovery, *A Time for Healing: Coming to Terms with Your Divorce,* is based on decision making rather than on feelings or stages. Smith feels that divorce recovery involves more than the five stages imply. Persons can go through the five stages in the "correct" order, but unless they make the decision to heal, they will not heal. A support group using *A Time for Healing* is designed to help divorced persons make and maintain the healthy decisions that lead to recovery.

Smith wrote:

Divorce is what I call a defining experience in a person's life. This becomes a part of who they are. A church has two basic options of ministering to these persons. One is program oriented—the emphasis is on getting over it. This type of ministry is mostly leader centered—providing the inspiration for participants by basically saying, "I made it through this and you can too." The second approach is ministry oriented. This approach points them to a future—to a redemptive future offering new opportunity. In this approach faith is the crucial element. Jesus Christ offers healing, forgiveness, restoring. The focus is on reconciling with the event: "The Lord can help me reconcile with this life experience."

The need for a divorce-recovery ministry is evident in almost any community. Need, however, doesn't mean that your church or single-adult ministry is the one to respond to that need. Unless a clear calling from God is evident to the church or the single-adult ministry, the ministry should not be undertaken. A single-adult ministry that plans to establish and maintain a divorce-recovery ministry must have a passion for it. If God has given you this passion, it is because He wants to use your ministry to make a difference.

Choosing a Facilitator for a Divorce-Recovery Support Group

Not every teacher or leader is ready to lead a divorce-recovery support group. This person must have compassion and a desire to minister to divorced individuals. Otherwise, he or she may be overwhelmed by the intensity of the losses, confusion, and anger that often accompany divorce. Because members deal with potentially intense and volatile emotions, the leader needs to be prepared to deal appropriately with these emotions. Patience and commitment are also required, because recovery is not always speedy, timely, or convenient.

A word of caution:

> Support-group facilitators might encounter situations that go beyond their level of counseling skills. They should know when to direct persons to more highly trained counselors.

In evaluating a potential facilitator, first consider basic qualities that are needed. A facilitator should—
- be a growing Christian, a person of prayer, and a person who has faith in what God can do;
- possess Christian values;
- be an active member of a local church;
- sense God's call to be involved in ministry;
- be spiritually gifted for the work;
- have a knowledge of Scripture;
- relate well to persons;
- have an absolute commitment to keep confidential information private;
- be willing to give time and energy to help group members;
- have a teachable spirit and a reachable heart;
- be emotionally stable;
- be comfortable with divorced and divorcing persons.

Emotional stability is essential for a facilitator. Sometimes a divorced person feels the need for a divorce-recovery group and volunteers to organize one and lead it. Unless that person has worked through the process of divorce recovery, it would probably be a mistake for that person to lead. Too many emotional pitfalls await.

The question is often raised, Should the facilitator be someone who has experienced divorce? Although identification with the group members is beneficial, it is not essential. Compassion for divorced persons, however, is necessary.

If an individual has not developed all of these characteristics, it does not mean the person cannot be an effective support-group facilitator. The person can continue to develop these qualities. God does His greatest work through imperfect, broken persons who are willing to serve and grow.

List potential facilitators of a divorce-recovery support group in your church.

Essential Steps in Launching a Divorce-Recovery Support Group
- Determine whether a support group is needed.
- Secure approval from your church's leadership.
- Enlist a leader.
- Determine the resources to use.
- Order materials.
- Set fees for materials and/or child care.
- Begin building group-leadership skills.
- Find a meeting place.
- Set a date and a time for launching the group.
- Decide on a schedule for the group.
- Decide on child care.
- Publicize the group.
- Interview prospective group members:
  - Discuss the goals for the group.
  - Explain that former spouses should be in separate groups.
  - Explain the group covenant.
  - Explain daily assignments.
  - Discuss a commitment.
  - Reassure the prospective group members.
- Prepare a group roster and name tags.
- Pray for each group member.
- Begin the group sessions.
- Help group members plan for follow-up.

Goals for a Divorce-Recovery Support Group
- To help group members identify and understand problems, issues, and feelings emerging from the divorce
- To help group members identify ways unresolved issues from the divorce affect them in the present
- To help group members understand that other persons have experienced similar problems and feelings
- To help group members admit responsibility for their contributions to the divorce or to the tension since the divorce
- To help group members experience an atmosphere of trust, honesty, and unconditional love

- To help group members identify and remove emotional, psychological, and spiritual barriers to fellowship with God
- To help group members experience a sense of hope and healing

A word of warning:

A divorce-recovery group is intended to move persons toward healing. Its purpose is not to nurture the pain of divorce but to nurture persons who have gone through divorce and to help them heal. Beware that the group doesn't become an enabling group.

Foundational Concepts for Support Groups
A divorce-recovery group works best when all members understand and commit to the following foundational concepts.
- All group members must sign the group covenant.
- We must face the divorce realistically.
- Feelings can be difficult to find.
- Feedback helps us discover our feelings.
- We must unpack our emotional baggage.
- We may feel worse before we feel better.
- We must establish or repair our boundaries.
- Former spouses should not be in the same group.
- Affirmation can change the way we think.
- Prayer can produce emotional healing.

Help All Ages with Divorce-Related Issues
Divorce is not an age-isolated event. It affects all family members. You can help whole families in your divorce-recovery ministry by offering support for each age division. A series of resources published by LifeWay Press can be integrated into a comprehensive divorce-recovery ministry: for adults, *A Time for Healing: Coming to Terms with Your Divorce;* for youth, *Healing the Wounds: Teenagers Learning to Cope with Divorce;* for children, *KidShare: What Do I Do Now?* (see "Resources for Single Adults and Their Leaders," p. 138). Your church can simultaneously offer ministry to adults, youth, and children. The leadership guide for each resource provides detailed plans for conducting the studies simultaneously.

A by-product of a divorce-recovery ministry is that families are reached for Christ and for church membership. Offering assistance for all ages shows that the church cares about ministering to the whole family. Divorce-recovery ministry is an effective way to make contact with persons in the community, often resulting in continuing ministry.

Many who have tried it feel that divorce recovery is a church's best access to unchurched persons.

What Your Church Can Do

Every church can do something in the area of divorce recovery. A smaller church might offer only one event or approach. A larger church or association or a network of churches might use several approaches to reach additional persons at different times and levels.

Consider these basic approaches:
- Provide individuals books on divorce recovery.
- Help divorced persons access counseling through a referrals list.
- Host a short-term, weekly seminar utilizing a speaker or a video-based study.
- Schedule a six- to nine-week divorce-recovery support group studying *A Time for Healing.*
- Sponsor a weekend divorce-recovery retreat.
- Sponsor a seminar during Sunday School/Bible study, integrating persons into follow-up groups and/or ongoing Bible-study groups at the close of the divorce-recovery group.
- Take a group to a local, state, or national divorce-recovery workshop.

If your church cannot offer a specialized ministry with divorced persons, consider one loss-recovery ministry for both divorced and widowed persons. Offer support-group studies of *Recovering from the Losses of Life* (see "Resources for Single Adults and Their Leaders," p. 138).

Ministry of Divorce Prevention[4]

In addition to ministering to the divorced, a church needs to emphasize divorce prevention. Many of those who will be married are presently in our single-adult ministries. Rather than waiting to repair and restore those damaged by the ravages of divorce, the church should take the initiative to prevent divorce.

Your church and single-adult ministry can work with single adults now to prevent divorce later.
- Equip single adults to screen the messages about morals, relationships, and marriage that constantly bombard them. One single-adult group recently conducted a retreat on single adults and sexuality. In one segment single adults viewed clips from recent, popular movies to heighten their sensitivity to their messages. One participant commented: "I never realized the overwhelming message approving illicit sexual relationships. I will never watch movies the same way."

> **factoid**
>
> A church needs to emphasize divorce prevention. Many of those who will be married are presently in our single-adult ministries.
> Source: Larry Garner

- Clearly present biblical teachings about relationships, singleness, sexuality, and marriage through Bible studies, counseling, and retreats. Create a culture that encourages single adults to live worthy of the calling they have received as Christians.
- Church members can provide role models that are strong, healthy examples of Christian marriage.
- Teach the reasons abstinence is the appropriate lifestyle for single adults, especially those who are Christians.
- Help single adults develop the relational skills necessary to make a relationship work. Many couples are swept into marriage by romantic love and never take time to develop the skills required to make a relationship work. They tend to seek romance, believing that a lasting relationship will be part of the package. In their book *Too Close, Too Soon* Jim Talley and Bobbie Reed state, "True intimacy takes time to develop as trust is built into each facet of a relationship by a series of shared experiences."[5]
- Administer a PREPARE questionnaire to couples who are dating. PREPARE (*Pre*marital *Pe*rsonal *a*nd *R*elationship *E*valuation) consists of 125 questions to ask the male and the female separately in 10 crucial areas. The inventory provides an excellent profile of a couple's potential for long-term compatibility. The results provide the couple a basis for developing or dissolving the relationship. (See "Resources for Single Adults and Their Leaders," p. 138.)
- Help single adults improve communication skills. Gallup polls found that at least ⅗ of all divorces are caused by poor communication. Take out "divorce insurance" for engaged couples by—
  - using the PREPARE premarital questionnaire;
  - offering small-group studies on male-female communication;
  - offer *Counsel for the Nearly and Newly Married* (see "Resources for Single Adults and Their Leaders," p. 138);
  - establishing relationships with mentor couples;
  - emphasizing scriptural teachings on marriage.
- Help single adults know how to sustain a loving, lasting relationship. Bettie Bilicki and Masa Goetz offer these suggestions:
  - Commit yourself to the relationship.
  - Keep the lines of communication open.
  - Develop and maintain your own identity.
  - Lighten up and have fun!
  - Invest time in the relationship.

—Develop a support system that's rooting for the relationship.
—Keep learning and growing.
—Remember and share love.
—Cherish and appreciate what you have worked hard to get.
—Anticipate the good times to come.
—Develop tolerance.
—Be friends.[6]

Ministry with Single-Parent Families[7]

Nearly half of the adult population is composed of single adults. A high percentage of those consists of single parents. More than 25 percent of all families are headed by a single parent. Although 85 percent of single parents are women, the number of custodial single fathers is rapidly increasing. The number of fathers rearing their children on their own climbed from 10 percent of single parents in 1980 to almost 15 percent in 1991. The trend toward single-parent families will not abate in the foreseeable future.

Today only about one of three families resembles the Ozzie-and-Harriet family of the 1950s. The divorce rate stubbornly refuses to decrease from its current level of one marriage in two. It is estimated that 50 percent of America's children will live in single-parent families at least a portion of their lives before age 18.

Single-parent families represent a growing mission field. Many are spiritually impoverished. Some are economically disadvantaged. Most desire to be freed from the bondage of past hurts. Others need to hear some good news and to see clearly that a loving God cares for them and their children. These families acutely sense their need and are open to ministry that offers hope and healing.

Single-parent families come into existence for a variety of reasons, such as divorce, a spouse's death, adoption, separation, and desertion. Another rapidly growing segment of single parents is unwed mothers. The number of unwed mothers has dramatically increased over the past 25 years, tripling since 1970.

> In an interview Senator Daniel Moynihan stated that in 1996 50 percent of the children born in New York City were born to unwed mothers. In the same week CNN broadcast a report titled "Babies Having Babies." The frequency with which children are born out of wedlock is reaching epidemic proportions. If this trend continues, the ramifications for society will be devastating.

Single parents face a variety of challenges. Emotional struggles often arise from the events that created the single-parent situation. Parents, children, and persons to whom they relate may wrestle with anger, rejection, confusion, guilt, fear, hopelessness, and despair. With so many different emotions at play, single-parent-family situations are often volatile.

Children's Stressors

A complex set of stressors may influence children in a single-parent family. In addition to the normal stress of growing up, they may experience resentment at losing a parent; low self-esteem from being treated as different or unacceptable in the neighborhood or church; loss of another adult for support; weariness from the custodial parent's resentment and frustration; feelings of being torn between two families after a divorce; and a sense of guilt and responsibility for causing the divorce or death of a parent.

As a result of these stressors, children from single-parent homes have far more than their share of problems coping with school, developing self-esteem, and finding healthy relationships. Sometimes the children behave improperly and even commit crimes as a result of emotional stress.

Parents' Stressors

Whether custodial or noncustodial, single parents experience similar emotional upheavals following failed relationships. Like their children, single parents may have difficulty appropriately expressing their confusion, rejection, anger, bitterness, loneliness, and guilt. Like their children, they may improperly act out rather than find appropriate ways of expressing themselves.

Financial strain. Adding to the considerable emotional stress is the financial strain that often accompanies the circumstances bringing about single parenthood. A Census Bureau study indicated that of women with children under the age of 21 with no father present in the household, 42 percent were not awarded child support. Of those awarded support, only 50 percent received the full amount. One-quarter received partial payments, and another quarter received none of the awarded amount.

The income of a single-parent family with the mother retaining custody decreases an average of 23 percent. Single dads may also face financial difficulties, either as one-income custodial parents or as noncustodial parents paying child support while establishing their own households. Single-parent families represent one of the fastest-growing segments of the U.S. population living below the recognized poverty level.[8]

Improving work skills. Closely associated with financial concerns is the need to improve work skills. These concerns cover a broad range of issues. Although it is becoming a less frequent occurrence, some single parents, primarily mothers, have never worked outside the home and feel that they have no marketable skills; they require basic skill development or specialized education. Those who have experience in the job market may need to enhance their skill levels to increase their earning potential. The lack of financial resources and readily available and affordable child care can hinder a single parent's efforts to take advantage of educational opportunities.

Unhealthy self-esteem. Sometimes unhealthy self-esteem results when single-parent situations are created. Feelings of rejection accompany many divorces. With a significantly lower income in a society that often values individuals by their earnings, a person's self-worth sometimes suffers. In the breakup of some marriages demeaning, hurtful comments are sometimes hurled at each other, damaging self-esteem.

Relationship skills. Many single parents, having experienced the pain of a failed relationship, are motivated to improve their ability to relate to others and to determine another's ability to relate to them. They need relationships with others who might be struggling as well as with those who are healthier. These relationships, formed in Sunday School/Bible-study groups, small-group studies, and support groups, facilitate the healing process and provide the foundation for building enduring relationships in the future.

Since many single parents remarry, the church has an opportunity through teaching and modeling loving relationships to help break dysfunctional family patterns that may have existed for several generations. Children from single-parent families also have the opportunity to learn more appropriate ways of relating to their peers and, eventually, to their spouses and children. Ministry in this area affords the church a discipleship opportunity that can have a positive, lasting impact on future families.

Single fathers. Patrick Batchelder of Single Fathers Ministry has identified specific issues single fathers face. He says: "Many think dating is the number one need of single fathers. In the conferences I've done, men list this much farther down the scale." Batchelder lists as the number one issue the fathers' willingness to put aside their own needs and to make the sacrifices single parenting requires for the welfare of the children. In addition, he lists these issues as important for single fathers:

• Feelings of abandonment, especially if the wife initiated the act of divorce or desertion.
• Societal perceptions: single fathers often suffer from negative stereotyping.
• Isolation, sometimes described as a crushing loneliness.
• The lack of programming for single fathers, especially in churches. Because the majority of single parents are mothers, churches that offer anything for single parents usually target mothers.[9]

Intensified needs. Although many concerns of single-parent families are the same as those of dual-parent families, the needs are often heightened because single parents face the challenge of parenting alone. One parent shared her sense of weariness: "Sometimes I just want someone to make a decision. You get tired of making all of the decisions yourself." The continual weight of earning a living, running a household, and parenting has created an identity group in our churches and communities that is receptive to ministry efforts on its behalf.

Leadership for Single-Parent Ministry

Those who work with single parents must empathize with their needs. Often, empathy and a sense of calling grow from having been single parents or having grown up in single-parent families. Leaders may have adult children who have been divorced or who are unwed mothers. This is not to say that persons who have not experienced such losses cannot be effective leaders. However, single parents have a more positive perception of a director or teacher who has had similar experiences.

Leaders of single-parent Sunday School/Bible-study groups should most often be pastor-teachers like those identified in Ephesians 4:11. The pastor, or shepherd, is sensitive to the needs of the flock. This person spends time with participants, listens to them, empathizes with them, protects them, and always seeks the one who is lost. Look for leaders who have the gifts of shepherding and mercy to work in single-parent ministry.

Reaching Out to Single-Parent Families in Your Community

To reach unchurched single parents, your ministry must seek to understand and develop programs to respond to their interests, needs, and concerns. Create and publicize workshops to answer questions and meet needs. Use members of your congregation or other Christian leaders with expertise in particular areas of concern. Some topics might be:

• Cooking on a budget
• Parenting skills
• Money management
• Healthy self-esteem

---

f a c t o i d

Although many concerns of single-parent families are the same as those of dual-parent families, the needs are often heightened because single parents face the challenge of parenting alone.

Source: Larry Garner

- Photography
- Car care
- Decorating on a shoestring
- Computer basics
- Weight loss
- Divorce recovery

Events should either include children or offer free or inexpensive child care at least for preschoolers. Allow sufficient lead time for adequate planning and publicity. Keep in mind tight budgets in all cost considerations and offer scholarships and fund-raisers for higher-ticket events.

Be careful to avoid church jargon when preparing promotional material designed to reach the unsaved and unchurched.

What Your Church Can Do

Here are a few ideas for starting your church's single-parent ministry.

- Understand the general dynamics of most single-parent families: more stress, less money, possible resentment, and worries about children.
- Carefully choose labels and descriptors to refer to single-parent households, avoiding terms like *broken homes.*
- Provide free child care for every event held at the church.
- Offer scholarships to needy single parents so that they can attend programs and events.
- Regularly sponsor a single-parents night out.
- Offer a parenting seminar for single parents.
- Start an after-school program for all children.
- Purchase books for the church media library that deal with single-parent issues.
- Provide counseling and/or make referrals to qualified psychological therapists.
- Mobilize helpers when single parents need help with housework and yard work.
- Don't expect single parents to attend every church-committee meeting.
- Create a sense of openness so that single parents will call when necessary to discuss their needs and problems.
- Establish an adopt-a-grandchild program in the church. Grandparents share with child care and participate in special times like the children's birthdays and holidays.
- Include positive illustrations of single-parent families in sermons.
- Be aware of community programs that offer services for single-parent families.
- Encourage a positive relationship with the other parent unless it is clearly destructive.
- Invite single parents and their children to suggest specific ways the single-adult ministry can help.[10]

Realize that many who come through the doors of a single-parent ministry are in pain and can hardly take care of themselves and their children, much less reach out to others. However, once their situations are stabilized, single parents need to be given opportunities to invest themselves in the lives of others. They have been given spiritual gifts that need to be used in ministry. In serving others, they often find a sense of freedom.

Ministry with Blended Families

One result of a rising divorce rate is an increased number of blended families. A blended family is a family composed of any configuration other than a husband and wife and the children of those two persons. By definition a blended family must include at least one stepparent, stepsibling, and/or half-sibling.[11]

Blended families in the United States are becoming more and more normative. According to the U.S. Census Bureau:

- As of 1986 35 million adults and 7 million children were living in stepfamilies. By 1991 9,807,000 children were living in blended families.[12] This nearly 10 million children represents 14.9 percent of the total population of children in the United States.
- Currently, each month about 50,000 people become members of stepfamilies.
- One of four children will live in a stepfamily before age 18.
- One-third of all American children do not live with both natural parents.
- About 1,350,000 children became members of stepfamilies in 1990—55 percent because of remarriage after a divorce, 15 percent because of remarriage after a spouse's death, and 30 percent because a never-married mother wedded.
- Nearly 26 percent of all marriages are second or third marriages.
- Eighty percent of all divorced Americans remarry, and 60 percent of these have children from former marriages.[13]

In a resource about single adults why discuss married and/or remarried persons? Because of high divorce and remarriage rates, many persons in single-adult groups are members of blended families. If 80 percent of all divorced

factoid

By 1991 9,807,000 children were living in blended families. This nearly 10 million children represents 14.9 percent of the total population of children in the United States. Source: U.S. Census Bureau

Americans remarry and 60 percent of these have children from former marriages, the issue of blended families needs to be addressed within the context of single-adult ministry. These figures do not even include the marriages of widowed persons with children.

Blended families are often thought to be a fairly recent development. Actually, they have always been part of all cultures. The Bible contains several examples of blended families. In the Old Testament some examples are Abraham, David, and Solomon, all of whom were beset by problems. One New Testament example is the family composed of Mary, Joseph, and Jesus.

factoid
Sixty percent of second marriages end in divorce.
Source: Larry Garner

The trend toward blended families is reflected in the secular world. The entertainment industry has depicted blended families in a variety of productions, although many models are unrealistic, like the movie *The Sound of Music* and the television show "The Brady Bunch," or extreme, like the movie *The Stepfather.*

Churches, however, have been reluctant to address the issue, partially because of the standard the church holds for the family. Because the ideal is one man, one woman, and their children for life, openly dealing with the reality of the blended family might appear to be a compromise.

The complexity and difficulty of the issues confronting blended families might be additional reasons churches neglect these families. Blended families might face some of the most complex relational problems in any family arrangement. But not all blended families are riddled with problems. Some blended families are strong and healthy for the same reasons any family is strong: faith, love, commitment, and forgiveness.

Blended Families Are Complicated

Regardless of the circumstances, all stepparents experience situations a traditional nuclear family never faces. Any family demands work to make it succeed. A blended family demands even more work because of the complexity of relationships. From the beginning a blended family must squarely face the realities of the new situation.

Since singleness by divorce is far more prevalent than singleness by death, the issues of a blended family must factor into the equation the presence of former spouses. The relationships in a blended family are also complicated by relationships with the grandparents of all who have connections with blended-family members. The ages of the children can also complicate the relationships in a blended family. For example, the presence of teenagers who are well on their way to independence can disrupt a smooth transition.

If both parents in a blended family were previously married, children might have come from both marriages. The

situation can be further complicated if the parents then have a child together. Resentment toward one or both parents can create difficult situations. Sometimes the difficulty can come from persons who are not in the present family structure.

At a recent conference on blended families one participant shared her story. She had gone through a divorce after a tumultuous eight years of marriage. The divorce and the continuing relationship with her former spouse was as difficult as the marriage had been. After a couple of years she met and married a man whose wife had died the previous year in a car accident, leaving the husband with two small children.

The most difficult issue for this woman was dealing not with her spouse but with her husband's dead spouse. The former wife was a constant presence that haunted the relationship between the present wife and her husband. Because the first wife had died at an early age, she was viewed as a saint who had never done anything wrong. The present wife always felt as if she were being compared to the former wife—a person against whom she could not compete.

In families the parents must answer the question of what constitutes proper discipline. In a blended family the stepparent's role in discipline complicates the picture. This issue is one of the largest contributing factors in the breakup of blended families—something that occurs all too often in second marriages. Sixty percent of second marriages end in divorce.

Other issues, like relating appropriately to former spouses or setting reasonable limits for stepchildren, must also be addressed.

In *Blended Families: Yours, Mine, Ours* William Cutler and Richard Peace list realities that must be faced by members of a blended family. They assert that—

- the children consider at least one adult in the house an outsider;
- initially at least, the parent-child bond may be stronger than the bond between spouses;
- financial commitments must be made to former spouses and perhaps to children who live away from home;
- some members of the stepfamily may feel out of place where they are supposed to feel at home;
- holidays, instead of being times of joy, become logistical nightmares, as various children are shuttled to various parents at various times.[14]

What Your Church Can Do

Because single adults in our churches and communities are likely to become members of blended families, churches can help prepare them for the realities they will encounter. Jerry Wilkinson, involved in blended-family ministry for several years, offers these insights for a church's ministry to blended families.

- A church must adopt a policy or theology on divorce and remarriage. This is not a ministry to begin without considerable thought. For example, one issue is the roles persons in blended families can fill in the church. Clear understanding and communication at the outset can help you avoid difficult, hurtful experiences.
- Develop a close alliance across ministry areas of your church to address the needs of all members of blended families. Workers with children or youth might become aware of problems before workers with the parents do. Others can then be informed and involved in counseling and ministry to help all family members.
- A church can offer workshops on blended-family issues like establishing new family traditions, discipline, and communication.
- Support groups can be developed as needed for blended families who are having difficulty adjusting. Use the LIFE Support course *New Faces in the Frame: A Guide to Marriage and Parenting in the Blended Family* (see "Resources for Single Adults and Their Leaders," p. 138).
- Offer a course or a seminar on blended-family parenting for the single adults in your church or community. If you have single adults who are in serious dating relationships that might result in blended-family situations, also target these persons in your enlistment.
- Consider whether your church needs to adjust its approach to premarital counseling. Persons who are entering a blended-family situation have different needs than a couple going into a first marriage. For instance:
  - Persons entering a blended-family relationship often have emotional baggage that needs to be unpacked before they enter another marriage.
  - The issue of disciplining children needs to be decided before the marriage. Issues related to child rearing are the most critical ones facing a blended family.
  - Couples must agree on a plan for managing their finances. In developing a plan, couples need to explore value systems and strategies for managing money.
  - Expectations should be clarified. Rather than expecting the person to be all the former spouse was not, couples must look at the relationship realistically.

Wilkinson recommends approaching a ministry to blended families primarily through material and programming offered through Sunday School/Bible study. He suggests that before couples can deal with child-rearing issues, they must first strengthen their own relationship. Marriage building is aided by short-term courses of study offered during the Sunday School/Bible-study period. These studies are alternated with the regular Bible-study curriculum. He warns against a steady diet of blended-family emphases for couples. A sense of abnormality can develop if partners maintain a single-issue or problem-related focus.

Men's and women's discussion and support groups are also offered on a short-term basis on weekdays or weeknights as needed. Couples in blended families are encouraged to participate in marriage-enrichment opportunities offered to the larger church body, as well as in national events like Marriage Encounter or Fall Festival of Marriage.

Leadership of a Ministry to Blended Families

Leaders of study groups for blended-family couples might best be drawn from persons who have been in blended families for a period of time and have worked through situations faced by blended families. The leaders' experience will be highly valued by participants. Be sure the leaders meet the criteria outlined on pages 76–77.

Ministry with 20-Somethings

Loud, freedom-loving, individualistic, in-your-face, denigrated, and practical—all describe the 20-somethings—the first wave of Busters, the children of Boomers. Born between 1965 and 1976, Busters number 68 million—not a small population segment but smaller than their parents' generation. Twenty-somethings (ages 18 to 31) represent 41 million Americans.

Who Are 20-Somethings?

Busters are more like their grandparents than they or their grandparents would ever believe. This generation differs distinctly in one important way: it has been called the first atheistic generation in America. Busters do not have the basic religious background or orientation their parents and grandparents had. They lack basic biblical knowledge. And even if they had that knowledge, they still do not believe that the Bible is the authoritative source of truth. Therefore, more effort and time are required to reach them. Yet this generation has the potential to revolutionize the church.

Many 20-somethings, as children of divorce, grew up in single-parent and blended-family homes. Consequently, 20-somethings wait longer to marry and have a higher commitment to parenting and spending time with their children.

> **factoid**
> Twenty-somethings (ages 18 to 31) represent 41 million Americans.
> Source: U.S. Census Bureau

Growing up with working mothers, 20-somethings were latchkey kids. This lifestyle engendered a spirit of independence and freedom—characteristics that still mark 20-somethings. Members of this generation are radically individualistic and want to determine what is best for themselves.

Family doesn't mean the same as in past generations. The television comedy "Friends" is indicative of this generation. "Family" is found with friends, at work, in gangs, and with sports teams. These parafamily groups give 20-somethings a place of acceptance and a sense of belonging.

Twenty-somethings stay at home longer. The average age for launching adult children is 28. The economy, to a degree, is responsible for this delay. Often, 20-somethings make attempts to be on their own, but these periods are short-lived. They frequently return to their parents' home or must have their incomes supplemented to remain on their own.

Twenty-somethings reject the workaholic syndrome they have seen in their parents. Freedom and time are more important to them than money. Although they reject the drive to work long hours, they like the lifestyle to which they have become accustomed. They consider it better to remain at home and enjoy the comforts and amenities of home than to enter an economic struggle. This trend, in effect, extends their adolescence.

This generation is the first truly technological generation. Twenty-somethings have been reared with television, computers, CDs, and video games. Often, they have many different sensory experiences at once. High tech has conditioned them to short attention spans.

Without an objective source of authority, the 20-something individual is his or her sole basis of authority. With no moral fixed point, this generation is riddled with problems. Early sexual activity and alcoholism are extremely high in this population segment.

A degree of hopelessness drives some 20-somethings to a live-for-the-moment philosophy. They have inherited from their parents a degree of despair about the world, primarily because of ecological, economic, and social problems.

Many 20-somethings feel a spiritual void. The absence of moral and authoritative standards can lead them on a spiritual quest, making them open to religion. They are especially willing to listen to a message that promises a sense of tranquillity and well-being.

What Your Church Can Do

Your ministry to 20-somethings may look very different

from your ministry to previous generations. Knowing what is important to them is essential for reaching this unique group. Begin by considering these needs.

- *Spirituality.* An interest in spirituality generates an openness to the gospel, with which they may or may not be familiar. A direct link must be made between spiritual principles set forth in Scripture and a credible Christian lifestyle.
- *Candor.* They want Christian leaders to be up-front and to give it to them straight.
- *Confrontational evangelism.* They understand the place of relationship and lifestyle evangelism, but they are also up-front and personal.
- *Functional living.* They want messages that help them in practical ways in their daily problems and challenges.
- *Character formation.* The church must present content and material to help persons grow in Christ, including corporate programs and individual disciplines.
- *Relationship.* Provide opportunities to learn, pray, serve, and fellowship together.
- *Fellowship.* Provide experiences for food, fun, and informal interaction.

Understanding these needs can help a church design strategies to reach 20-somethings. Because they are largely unchurched, they need to be convinced that the institutional church can have a place in their lives. Here are a few suggestions to help you reach 20-somethings.

- Informality, casual dress, and relationships appeal to 20-somethings. Churches that have begun offering user-friendly, seeker services have success reaching 20-somethings. Although some churches have dramatically altered their services to attract Busters, this population's diversity reveals that it responds to a variety of styles. Any church that adopts a Buster-friendly attitude will find Busters responsive.
- Some contemporary single-adult groups utilize a large-group format with music and a presentation on Sunday mornings or even during the week. This model features short, lively segments. Bible studies focus on practical problem solving of life issues. Worship services vary in approach, using music; visual presentations; and short, clear messages to focus on the practical application of biblical truth and spiritual principles.
- The small-group learning experience can work well with 20-somethings. Ministry teams—small, practical, purpose-driven groups—are attractive to them.
- Learning is ultra- or multisensory. Twenty-somethings

factoid

Because 20-somethings are largely unchurched, they need to be convinced that the institutional church can have a place in their lives.
Source: Larry Garner

enjoy having many different sensory experiences at the same time. Visual, auditory stimuli should be varied and loud. Paradoxically, 20-somethings want high-tech, up-to-date delivery systems but a simple, basic Christian message.

- Twenty-somethings respond better to positive than to negative motivation. Guilt does little to move this generation, whereas realizing potential, using gifts in ministry, and making a contribution in ministry make quite an impact.
- Offer a variety of times and types of meetings that involve 20-somethings. Personal participation, planning, and performing in worship services appeal to 20-somethings. Create teams and give them authority and responsibility for conducting events.
- Because 20-somethings have been conditioned by television and video games for short attention spans, churches and study groups must be fast-paced and technologically on the edge. Use short dramas, short sermons, and video-driven images.
- The church must be attuned to 20-somethings' musical wavelength. They like music, and they like it loud.
- Twenty-somethings' in-your-face style demands that we be direct with the message. Help them answer some of their questions. Deal with real-life issues in studies and sermons.
- Their practical nature requires down-to-earth stories about real people. Their lack of biblical knowledge requires a somewhat different approach to using the Scripture. First capture their attention with contemporary, real-life stories. Then use the Bible to make a spiritual application.
- Highly structured activities are not necessary for 20-somethings. Casual gatherings with friends, food, sports, and physical activity appeal to them. Cost, however, is a factor since they have limited discretionary funds.
- Develop a clearly defined vision for your church. Twenty-somethings respond positively to churches that demonstrate commitment to achieving their stated mission. The more local that vision, the better. International missions is not as important as responding to local issues and needs. Perhaps the tangible, sensory elements of seeing and becoming involved in a project attract them.
- Young adults have high energy levels. They give that energy to their work, friendships, and recreation. They are also willing to expend it in ministry. Initially, a short-term ministry is the best way to engage 20-

somethings. After they have committed to a short-term project, they might lengthen their time and energy commitments.

- Use small-group and large-group strategies to reach and disciple 20-somethings. A small group of between 8 and 12 allows interaction and accountability in discipleship. Some 20-something groups in larger cities sponsor large metro rallies. The approach is not either/or but both/and. Even churches that have the large gathering need to offer small-group discipleship that incorporates accountability. Small discipleship, Bible-study, and mission/ministry groups can develop the sense of family that appeals to 20-somethings.
- A needs-driven, responsive ministry attracts 20-somethings. Although many of them might not need crisis services or ministries, they appreciate a church that is willing to meet practical needs.

David Edwards, a popular 20-something speaker at metro Bible studies, offers the following suggestions for communicating with 20-somethings.

> **factoid**
> For 20-somethings credibility is everything. They want to know that the messenger is living the message.
> Source: David Edwards

- Be authentic—with your faith and your language. For 20-somethings credibility is everything. They want to know that the messenger is living the message. Since they do not have extensive backgrounds with church, they do not know the language of Zion. Avoid Christian clichés and jargon. Communicate in everyday language.
- Relate to them with your life; connect with them by revealing your struggles and feelings. Transparency allows them to see you as a fellow traveler in faith. Deal with them on a level of equality.
- Use what they know; be contemporary. Use music, movies, television, and sports. Get to know them and seek to understand them.

Edwards offers these suggestions for teachers:

- Use humor and object lessons.
- Use concise Bible texts. Busters do not have extensive biblical knowledge. Focusing on one passage is better than using multiple passages in a variety of books of the Bible.
- Shape a truth into a principle for living. Give them something concrete on which to build their lives.

Ministry with Widowed Persons

Don, Faralyn, and Vera have something in common: they all lost their spouses to death. That's practically the only thing they have in common.

- Don is a young father with two children. His wife died after a short bout with cancer.
- Faralyn is a healthy, vibrant woman in her mid-50s.

She and her husband retired early from their teaching professions to pursue interests and activities they both enjoyed. Less than one year after they retired, Jack died of an aneurysm in the brain.

- Vera, in her 70s, stayed by her husband's side as he battled a slow form of cancer before he finally succumbed to death. They had been married for more than 50 years.

Although these individuals share the common experience of a spouse's death, their needs and their perceptions of their experiences are quite different. Their particular experiences and developmental stages in life determine the kind of ministry they need and are willing to receive. If you asked them if they are single, only two of them would say yes. Although the Census Bureau classifies her as single, Vera still considers herself married; she and Gene are merely separated for a brief period.

All three have experienced the grief process.

- Part of Don's grief process involved moving to another city and church.
- After a two-year period of grieving for Jack, Faralyn was invited by an acquaintance to join a single-adult group at her church. She found a group of persons near her age with whom she could have companionship and support.
- Vera had been a member of her church for most of her life. Her Sunday School class had been part of her life for the past 20 years. Many in the class who had already lost their husbands were especially helpful to Vera in the recovery process after Gene's death.

The Grief Process

Our understanding of the grief process has been greatly influenced by the research of Elisabeth Kubler-Ross. Her ground-breaking research with dying patients identified five distinct stages of their grief process: denial, anger, bargaining, depression, and acceptance. Many ministers, writers, and counselors have applied these five stages to every experience of loss. Although they might be applied in general to dying persons, the five stages do not apply to every experience of loss. In survivors' grief experience, for example, bargaining is probably not a part of the equation.

I believe the following stages more accurately describe the grief-recovery process that survivors experience. Not every person goes through all of these stages. Furthermore, the stages do not always occur in a predictable sequence, and some of the stages may overlap. Each person's grief experience is unique.

1. *Shock* is an early stage of grief. It serves as an emotional anesthetic and can be beneficial. Because the loss seems overwhelming, a person may go around in a kind of a trance. In the face of a loss, especially a sudden loss such as the sudden, unanticipated death of a loved one or another type of loss that occurred without warning, the emotional pain may have been too much to deal with. A voice inside the person says: "This is more than you can cope with! I'm shutting you down."[15] Shock may last for a few minutes, hours, or days.

2. *A flood of grief* often follows the initial stage of shock. The grieving person needs to express his or her emotions at this time. This stage can be a healing catharsis for grief's wounds. We need to learn to express emotion in a healthy way. Bottling it up indefinitely usually makes matters worse. We may choose to express grief privately but should not be afraid to express it.

3. *Loneliness* is still another stage in the grief process. After the relatives and neighbors leave, we may feel even more acutely the loss of our loved one.

4. Often, *guilt* is associated with grief. We may feel guilty for failure to aid the person who has died or for some hurt we might have caused. We may blame ourselves for some action or neglect, real or imagined. This guilt can only add to the burden of our grief.

5. The bereaved person may harbor feelings of *resentment* or even *hostility*. He or she might blame the patient's physician for operating or not operating. The person might even go through a stage in which he or she blames God for the death of the loved one. Resentment and hostility must run their course until the person can think and act logically.

6. Eventually *hope* returns, and we take up the threads of life again. The bereaved person can again affirm reality. It is unrealistic to expect someone with strong faith not to experience grief. Christians are not exempt from any phase of our humanity. Even Jesus felt grief and disappointment. When Paul wrote to the Thessalonians about their dead loved ones, he urged them not "to grieve like the rest of men, who have no hope" (1 Thess. 4:13). He did not tell them not to sorrow; they would have the sorrow that was natural to the loss of any loved one. But their sorrow was not without hope. In Christ we have hope through the resurrection. Even in a time of death, we have hope. While grief might darken the sky at death, we know that the sunshine of hope will again break through.

Granger E. Westberg presented a similar list in his book *Good Grief*:

1. We are in a state of shock.
2. We express emotion.

> **factoid**
>
> There are six stages in the grief process: shock, a flood of grief, loneliness, guilt, resentment, and hope.
> Source: Larry Garner

3. We feel depressed and very lonely.
4. We may experience physical symptoms of distress.
5. We may become panicky.
6. We feel a sense of guilt about the loss.
7. We are filled with anger and resentment.
8. We resist returning.
9. Gradually, hope comes through.
10. We struggle to affirm reality.[16]

What Your Church Can Do

A single-adult ministry probably cannot minister to all who experience grief, not because they don't need the ministry but because they will not accept the ministry. Of the three persons mentioned earlier in this section, probably Don and Faralyn would be open to ministry from a church's single-adult ministry. Vera doesn't consider herself to be single. That is not to say that ministry cannot be done on her behalf but that it may need to be inconspicuous. The ministry efforts might be sponsored by the single-adult ministry but performed by a variety of persons, including Sunday School/Bible-study classes, friends, or staff members.

Remember that not all grieving persons are widowed. Many single adults experience grief when they lose a family member, a friend, a job, or a significant relationship. Use this material and the information in issue 7, solution 3 to minister to all single adults who are grieving.

How can your church minister to grieving persons? Ron Mumbower, a minister to families, offers several suggestions.

Establish a crisis-ministry response team. Many churches respond to crises through the deacon ministry or the Sunday School/Bible-study organization. Consider developing and training a crisis-ministry response team in your single-adult ministry. Persons with the spiritual gifts of encouragement, mercy, and healing would be especially good prospects for this ministry team.

Offer a grief-recovery support group. Use the LIFE Support course *Recovering from the Losses of Life* (see "Resources for Single Adults and Their Leaders," p. 138) in support groups for widowed persons. If your church membership is large enough, the group might be an ongoing ministry. Persons can enter the group at any stage of the grief experience. Because factors such as age, emotional makeup, and length and quality of the relationship affect the grief-recovery process, individuals recover at their own pace. Those who are farther along can minister to others who are just entering the grief-recovery process.

If your church cannot offer a specialized ministry with the widowed, consider one loss-recovery ministry for both widowed and divorced persons. Offer support-group studies of *Recovering from the Losses of Life.* Another option is to offer the support-group study for all church members, since everyone experiences grief.

Conduct a recognition luncheon or dinner. One church conducts a luncheon for persons who have lost spouses during the past year. They remember their loved ones, celebrate their lives and contributions, and express loving care to survivors. Sometimes connections are made that result in supportive friendships.

Encourage Sunday School/Bible-study groups to extend care and ministry to the grieving. Because Sunday School/Bible-study groups are age-graded, they can do much to minister to their members who lose loved ones. Ministry is part of a Sunday School/Bible-study group's responsibilities and opportunities. Some groups of older adults assume a support ministry almost as a matter of course, especially when many of the members have lost spouses or children. These members have experienced grief and have learned coping and caring skills. Those who have emerged healthy and hopeful from grief can be great resources for others.

Younger groups that have less experience with grief might need guidance in extending ministry to those of their age group who experience deaths of loved ones.

Maintain contact, especially through the first year. For the first year everything is a new experience for a grieving person. Every holiday, birthday, anniversary, and special occasion brings painful memories, which constantly renew grief. Most studies hold that essential grief-recovery work takes from 1½ to 2 years.

Especially during the first year of the grief process, contact can be maintained by writing notes on significant occasions or by contacting survivors during holidays. Some churches have a ministry team that places memorial flowers in the sanctuary for Sundays, then reworks them into arrangements that are taken to survivors.

Offer a discipleship course to explore questions raised by death. Those who have experienced loss through death often turn to the church when confronted with the finality of death. Facing the eternal questions that our mortality raises, they have deep, honest questions. In a discipleship group they can seek deep, honest answers. One church asked a surgeon to lead a study that focused on concerns about the death process, such as what to do when a loved one is on life support, when death occurs, what happens after death, and living wills.

> ## factoid
> Because factors such as age, emotional makeup, and length and quality of the relationship affect the grief-recovery process, individuals recover at their own pace.
> Source: Larry Garner

Stand with the survivors in silence. Some questions have no answers. In those cases survivors simply need someone to care and to grieve with them. When they turn to the church, they want to know if we have a word from God for them. One of the oldest written works of literature, the Book of Job, confronts questions and responses to loss. Job raised many questions about his experiences of pain and loss. Pleading his innocence, he wanted to confront God with his questions. At the end of the book God came to Job in the whirlwind, but He never told Job why he had suffered. In the end Job's response was a faith response that recognized the Lord's sovereignty and majesty. For some issues and situations related to death, we have no words, no answers. We simply stand with the survivors in their pain until it begins to subside.

Allow the survivors to grieve. Don't short-circuit the grief process. Grief is a natural emotional response and process that, in many ways, marks us as human. All cultures share the common bonds of grief. Each person who has experienced loss needs to do grief work. Grief work is a gift from God that allows us to move from pain and distress toward hope and healing.

Individuals who have lost a loved one, especially a spouse, have been subjected to one of the most intense stresses anyone can experience. One study revealed that the death of a spouse rated as the highest life stressor of the 43 examined.[17] The pain can be so intense that many adults learn to shut down certain feelings.

Survivors may be out of touch with their feelings, or they may not have grieved over their loss in a healthy way. They may assume that because they no longer cry, they are finished with their grief work. The absence of tears does not necessarily mean that grief work is over. If tears are shut down or have never been allowed, the person may still have much work to do. A get-over-it attitude exists in our culture today: "It's been a year since your mother died; aren't you over it yet?"

Well-meaning friends may say to a bereaved person: "Just trust God, and you'll be OK. Read the Bible more. Pray more. Have faith." Trusting God, reading the Bible, praying, and having faith are important things to do in a time of loss. However, often such statements prove frustrating for a bereaved person because they make the person feel ashamed. Many bereaved persons are troubled by the notion that if they had tried more diligently or had had more faith, they could have prevented the loss.

Others know that although they have tried trusting, reading God's Word, and praying, something is still not right inside them. They have not yet processed their grief to the point that they can move toward hope. Such individuals need biblically based insights into their pain so that they can come to terms with the impact of their loss. Their loss may have caused them to erect barriers between themselves and God. By gaining insights into the reasons behind these barriers, they can be freed to receive God's love, grace, and strength.[18]

Ministry with Senior Single Adults

One difficulty in addressing the needs of senior single adults is identifying who is a senior. In a culture in which youth is prized and age is regarded negatively, most people are unwilling to admit to the aging process. Even the designation *senior* is rejected. Many euphemisms are used, including *mature, older, young at heart,* and *grays.*

Several single-adult groups have elected to use the AARP entry point of 50 to designate senior adulthood. This is fairly reasonable, since 50 marks the beginning of what many consider to be the latter third or half of life. In organizational structures like Sunday School/Bible study, some churches have found it best to avoid decadal breaks like 30, 40, and 50, because many people have difficulty with decadal birthdays. It is usually easier to organize if breaks are made a couple of years before or after decadal points.

> ## factoid
> Baby Boomers are entering the senior years at the rate of one every seven seconds.
> Source: U.S. Census Bureau

Some people who are single adults in their senior years do not consider themselves to be single. Many widowed persons, though technically single, still think of themselves as married and merely waiting to rejoin their spouses. They maintain associations with their Sunday School/Bible-study groups and circle of friends, which were cultivated during married years. Those who consider themselves senior single adults are usually persons who never married or who divorced at an early age and never remarried.

A Time of Transition

Ministry to senior single adults is beginning to change, precipitated by the entrance of Baby Boomers into the ranks of senior adulthood. In 1996 the first wave of Baby Boomers began turning 50. This generation is entering the senior years at the rate of one every seven seconds. They are the most affluent, educated, entertained, and egocentric generation of U.S. citizens. This generation will likely revolutionize the world of senior adults, as they have changed every preceding period of development through which they have passed.

In the past many single-adult ministries focused primarily on trips and social events as key ingredients for ministry to senior single adults. Boomer seniors will no longer be content with a trip to the mall and lunch. They will demand a greater degree of self-determination. A church with an effective ministry to senior single adults will focus on ministry opportunities *with* them, not just *to* them. This new wave will respond to opportunities for social involvement and for improving physical, intellectual, and spiritual well-being.

Boomers are adding steam to senior adults' momentum as the fastest-growing population segment in America. In the past reaching the age of one hundred was rare. Increasingly, medical advances are extending life. People are living longer, healthier, more active lives. This significant change makes it more important for a church to minister with senior single adults and not just to them.

Do not expect Boomer single seniors who are content with their singleness and are active in strong single-adult ministries to join a docile seniors program. Instead, create a new programming paradigm with them.

The Needs of Senior Single Adults

Robert Havighurst offers a seven-stage explanation of human development that covers life from birth to the grave. In every stage a person must complete a variety of tasks. Following are the tasks Havighurst assigned to middle and late adulthood.

```
┌─────────────────────────────────────────────┐
│ MIDDLE ADULTHOOD                              │
│ • Achieving adult civic and social responsibility │
│ • Assisting teenage children to become responsible and │
│   happy adults                                │
│ • Developing adult leisuretime activities     │
│ • Relating to one's spouse as a person        │
│ • Accepting and adjusting to the physiological changes of │
│   middle age                                  │
│ • Reaching and maintaining satisfactory performance in │
│   one's career                                │
│ • Adjusting to aging parents                  │
└─────────────────────────────────────────────┘
```

```
┌─────────────────────────────────────────────┐
│ LATE ADULTHOOD                                │
│ • Adjusting to decreasing physical strength and health │
│ • Adjusting to retirement and reduced income  │
│ • Adjusting to the death of spouse            │
│ • Establishing an explicit affiliation with members of one's │
│   age group                                   │
│ • Establishing satisfactory physical living arrangements │
│ • Adapting to social roles in a flexible way[19] │
└─────────────────────────────────────────────┘
```

Note the number of developmental tasks that apply to senior adults. With only a few exceptions, all tasks must be achieved by single adults. Additional tasks can be listed for single adults. For instance, single adults must come to terms with their singleness. A single adult might have to develop a compatible circle of friends with whom to share life. Instead of adjusting to the death of a spouse, a single adult might experience and accept the deaths of close friends.

Senior single adults deal with the question of singleness differently than younger or middle-aged single adults. They come to a point of acceptance of and contentment with their identity or state of life. Nevertheless, they may still have concerns about a variety of issues, such as health, adequate financial provision, long-term housing, companionship or social needs, and security. Although married senior adults also face these issues, for senior single adults the issues are intensified.

What Your Church Can Do

A church's ministry with senior single adults should help them—

- maintain physical health;
- determine living and care arrangements;
- cultivate healthy attitudes and interests;
- enjoy social relationships;
- learn and grow spiritually.

Consider some of the following suggestions for developing a ministry with senior single adults.

Provide opportunities to enhance the physical well-being of senior single adults. Special activities that can help meet physical, as well as social, needs of senior adults are recreation, sports, drama, art, crafts, music, and hobbies. A favorite activity of senior single adults is travel. Enhance a trip for senior single adults by incorporating a ministry opportunity. Remember that senior single adults may not have the same income as senior couples, making their participation in expensive trips impossible.

One of the greatest fears senior single adults have is not having someone to care for them in old age and, consequently, losing their independence. Churches can provide an environment of care to ease this fear. Some senior single adults may need only certain types of physical assistance to remain independent. Consider a ministry that includes shopping assistance, transportation assistance, or home-repair services. One church organized a ministry team of deacons to care for single adults in later adulthood.

Provide counseling for financial concerns. Many senior single adults fear not being able to provide for themselves adequately in their later years. This fear is further compounded by the fact that persons over 65 compose slightly more than 10 percent of our population but make up approximately 15 percent of the poor.

Single adults must plan carefully to ensure an adequate

income to see them through their later years. One way a church can minister is to help them develop a sound financial plan. Since people are living longer and since pensions and Social Security are not always guaranteed, the individual must assume more responsibility for financial well-being.

Financially, single adults are often at a disadvantage when compared to married couples. Couples are often two-earner households with the benefit of two pension plans or a greater amount of discretionary income. Even a spouse's death doesn't necessarily mean financial hardship for couples who have provided adequate life insurance or benefits for the surviving spouse.

Provide opportunities for social contact. Life is lived in relationship with others. Relationships nurtured through activities with others contribute to a sense of belonging and purpose that enables us to give and receive. The need for interaction with others continues for a lifetime. Local churches are uniquely suited to provide many of these social needs in a balanced program.

Senior single adults who have been together for a number of years form a "family" network. They watch out for one another. In time of sickness or trouble they often turn to their friends for support and care. A church can assist senior single adults in developing care networks.

Provide opportunities for ministry and spiritual development. Prayer groups, retreats, and conferences are only a few ways to enhance continued spiritual growth. Places of service in a church and community are unlimited. Retired persons, who have more free time than ever before, should give priority consideration to opportunities for ministry through their churches. An excellent resource giving ideas and instructions for ministry is *Meeting Needs, Sharing Christ* (see "Resources for Single Adults and Their Leaders," p. 138).

factoid

Persons over 65 compose slightly more than 10 percent of our population but make up approximately 15 percent of the poor. Source: U.S. Census Bureau

[1]Much of the material in this section has been drawn from Harold Ivan Smith, *A Time for Healing: Coming to Terms with Your Divorce, Facilitator Guide* (Nashville: Life-Way, 1995).

[2]Michael J. McManus, *Marriage Savers: Helping Your Friends and Family Stay Married* (Grand Rapids: Zondervan, 1993), 27.

[3]Ibid., 9.

[4]Much of the material in this section has been drawn from Michael J. McManus, *Marriage Savers: Helping Your Friends and Family Stay Married* (Grand Rapids: Zondervan, 1993).

[5]Jim Talley and Bobbie Reed, *Too Close, Too Soon* (Nashville: Thomas Nelson, 1982), 25.

[6]Bettie Bilicki and Masa Goetz, *Getting Back Together* (Holbrook, Mass.: Bob Adams, 1990), 127–36.

[7]Much of the material in this section has been drawn Jerry and Lana Wilkinson, *Developing Ministries with Single-Parent Families* (Nashville: Convention, 1993), 9.

[8]Stephen Waldman, "Deadbeat Dads," *Newsweek*, 4 May 1992, 46, in Wilkinson, *Developing Ministries with Single-Parent Families*, 11.

[9]Patrick Batchelder, interview with Larry Garner, 15 January 1996.

[10]Don Davidson, *How to Build an Exciting Singles Ministry* (Nashville: Thomas Nelson, 1993), 202–3.

[11]Stacy Furukawa, *The Diverse Living Arrangements of Children: Summer 1991*, U.S. Bureau of the Census Current Population Reports, Series P70, No. 38 (Washington, D.C.: U.S. Government Printing Office, 1994), 4.

[12]Ibid., 6.

[13]William Cutler and Richard Peace, *Blended Families: Yours, Mine, Ours* (Littleton, Colo: Serendipity House, 1990), 8.

[14]Ibid., 18.

[15]Kay W. Moore, *Recovering from the Losses of Life, Facilitator's Guide* (Nashville: Life-Way, 1995), 18.

[16]Granger E. Westberg, *Good Grief* (Philadelphia: Fortress, 1962), 7–8.

[17]Thomas H. Holmes and Minoru Masuda, "Life Change and Illness Susceptibility," in *Stressful Life Events: Their Nature and Effects,* ed. Barbara Snell Dohrenwend and Bruce P. Dohrenwend (New York: John Wiley & Sons, 1974), 52.

[18]Adapted from Moore, *Recovering from the Losses of Life,* 18.

[19]Robert Havighurst, in Lucien E. Coleman, Jr., *Understanding Today's Adults* (Nashville: Convention, 1982), 52.

Solution ④
use the single-adult
ministry toolbox

Tools for Organizing

Identifying Your Audience
Ask each class, department, and special group in your church to provide this information. Prepare a composite form to depict the potential audience for single-adult ministry in your church and community.

Who is your primary single-adult ministry target group?
_____

How many persons constitute the potential ministry group?
    Church: _____
    Community: _____

What are the identities of single adults in your church or community?
    Never married: ____ percent
    Divorced: ____ percent
    Widowed: ____ percent
    Single parents: ____ percent
    Other: ____ percent

What is the socioeconomic status of the single adults in your target audience?
    Church: _____
    Community: _____

What is the educational level of the single adults in your target audience?
    Church: _____
    Community: _____

What vocations are represented in your single-adult audience?
    Church:
    • Professional: ____ percent
    • White collar: ____ percent
    • Blue collar: ____ percent

Community:
• Professional: ____ percent
• White collar: ____ percent
• Blue collar: ____ percent

What is the spiritual level of the single adults in your target group?
    Church:
    • Committed believers: ____ percent
    • Nominal believers: ____ percent
    • Nonbelievers: ____ percent

    Community:
    • Committed believers: ____ percent
    • Nominal believers: ____ percent
    • Nonbelievers: ____ percent

What are the generational groupings of most of your single adults?

Church:	Community:
20s: ____ percent	20s: ____ percent
30s: ____ percent	30s: ____ percent
40s: ____ percent	40s: ____ percent
50s: ____ percent	50s: ____ percent
60+: ____ percent	60+: ____ percent

What affinity groups (special-interest clubs, hobbies, and so on) are represented?
Church: _____
_____

Community: _____
_____

Developing Your Single-Adult Ministry Organization

The symbols in the diagrams on pages 69–72 represent various components of a single-adult ministry's organization. After thorough study of this information, draw your ministry's current and potential organizational leadership structure. When possible, record the names of leaders and roles unique to your structure. For a larger ministry you may want to draw configurations for both larger and smaller ministries since the larger includes small groups. A smaller ministry may want to project a larger structure as a growth strategy.

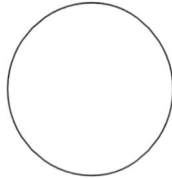

Members/participants; smaller or larger groups; leadership/coordination groups, roles, or tasks

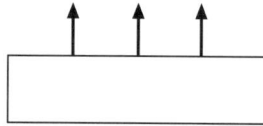

Single adults and their entry points to the single-adult ministry and church

Relationship between components

Ministry Resource Planning Tool

Use this grid each time you need to provide resources for your single-adult ministry. You can plan a resource strategy by asking these questions:

• For whom is the ministry intended?
• What are their needs?
• What are our related goals?
• What are our sources for materials?
• What is the cost, and how will it be funded?
• Who will provide leadership?
• How will we train leaders?
• What are our calendar opportunities and plans?

Who?	
Needs	
Goals	
Materials	
Cost	
Leaders	
Training	
Time	
Calendar	

Issue ⑥
expanding and growing a
single-adult ministry

Churches with effective ministries to single adults capitalize on two key concepts:

1. *Warm, caring relationships.* A distressed society, filled with countless hurts and loneliness, is ready to accept true friendship. This is the point at which the opportunity for ministry begins. A single-adult ministry that is built on the foundation of Christ's love offers a place to meet persons who are growing in their faith and who desire to encourage others in their walk with the Lord.

2. *A strong emphasis on Bible-study with application to life.* Single adults will grow stronger in the Lord only if they feed on the truths of God's Word. Single adults respond to Bible study in all forms, from ongoing groups to small-group studies that meet at other times. They eagerly accept responsibilities as Bible-study leaders and, in most cases, provide the most faithful base of dedicated leaders participating in ongoing leadership training.

A church that does not have an aggressive plan to reach single adults has decided to go out of business. A church that wants to reach the vast single-adult audience will offer single adults the best: the truths of God's Word. Start building your ministry on this foundation today. *–Bill Taylor*

Solution ①

Understand the Dynamics of Single-Adult Sunday School/Bible-Study Ministry
Steve Cretin

A Sunday School/Bible-study ministry consists of six unique tasks that directly relate to the Great Commission: " 'Go and make disciples of all nations, baptizing them in the name of the Father and of the Son and of the Holy Spirit, and teaching them to obey everything I have commanded you. And surely I am with you always, to the very end of the age' " (Matt. 28:19-20). These tasks are:

1. *Reaching people.* Reaching includes discovering people who are not in Sunday School/Bible study and determining their spiritual conditions in an effort to lead them to salvation and spiritual growth.

2. *Teaching people the Bible.* Teaching the Word is the cornerstone of Sunday School/Bible study that provides knowledge as well as understanding and application. Teaching should not only produce spiritual growth but also thrust learners into active service.

3. *Caring for people.* Caring for people builds relationships and a sense of family in the Sunday School/Bible-study ministry. Caring meets needs through Christ.

4. *Witnessing to people.* Obeying Christ's mandate to reach the lost, witnessing involves praying for unbelievers and sharing Christ with them.

5. *Fellowshipping with people.* Fellowship allows relationships to deepen through wholesome social activities.

6. *Leading people to worship.* Worship is the outcome of Bible study. As God continues to reveal Himself through His Word, worship continues and grows.

A single-adult ministry can build a solid Sunday

> **factoid**
> Teaching should not only produce spiritual growth but also thrust learners into active service.
> Source: Steve Cretin

School/Bible-study organization by incorporating these tasks:

1. *Reaching* single adults is becoming a more defined task as that population continues to grow and identify itself as unique among adults. The latest figures show that approximately 40 percent of the adult population are single adults. This number has steadily grown over the past several decades. In metroplex cities the single-adult population now outnumbers the married-adult population.

2. *Teaching* single adults takes on a new dynamic as different social, age, and experience groupings come into play. There are divorced single adults, single-adult parents, never-married single adults, young single adults, median single adults, and senior single adults. Within these categories are professional single adults, single adults who are students, and single adults who are starting careers. Such diversity challenges a single-adult ministry as Sunday School/Bible study is designed to meet specific needs.

3. *Caring* takes on a deeper meaning for single adults than for other adult groupings. Single adults are looking for a sense of family. A strong caring-and-fellowship ministry can fulfill a single adult's need for family and community. Single adults, especially in larger cities, are away from their family support groups and depend much more on one another to meet their needs for fulfillment, encouragement, and belonging. Caring offers support, a sense of family, and an opportunity to express genuine Christian love.

4. *Witnessing* to single adults takes on a unique dimension. Often, single adults are in the midst of change in their lives because of work, relationships, or other factors that make them open to the claims of the Scripture and to the impact Christ can have on their lives. In these transitional times single adults' search for purpose and meaning leads to tremendous opportunities to share the claims of Christ. Like no other group, single adults are open to evangelism, and the church needs to take every opportunity to reach them for Christ.

5. *Fellowship*, like caring, takes on a deeper meaning with single adults because of their need for family. Except for single parents, most single adults do not have the family obligations that married adults have. In general, single adults place a high priority on meaningful fellowship that is deep in relationship and commitment. Fellowship among single adults is an open door to reaching, caring, and witnessing. Fellowship is key in building a strong single-adult Sunday School/Bible study and enhances every aspect of it.

6. Leading single adults to *worship* is the ultimate goal of single-adult ministry. Worship is the natural result when single adults discover who they are and who God is. It is an outpouring of faith in response to the claims of Christ. Although worship is an individual response and can be nurtured individually through personal Bible study and prayer, it takes on new energy when done corporately in the single-adult environment or in the larger church setting.

Knowing single adults increases the challenge of significant Bible study for them. Because of this group's diversity in age, skills, occupation, previous marital status, children, and other factors, finding the right leadership team to minister with single adults is important. In most cases the best leaders for single adults are single adults, because they know single adults' mind-set, needs, hurts, successes, failures, temptations, trials, and heartaches. Often, single adults are a tremendous, untapped resource that a church can mobilize to minister to the single-adult population in the community. Single adults best minister to single adults!

Sometimes the church sees single adults as difficult to reach and teach. Single-adult Sunday School/Bible study, administered properly, can be a vast source of outreach and ministry in a community. It can also lead to fulfilling, rewarding opportunities for single adults to use their gifts and abilities to reach others for Christ.

Ministering to single adults through Sunday School/Bible study is unique, dynamic, and rewarding. A church that does not accept this challenge chooses to ignore almost half of the adult population. Single-adult Sunday School/Bible study is perfectly designed to fulfill a vital ministry with single adults.

factoid
A strong caring-and-fellowship ministry can fulfill a single adult's need for family and community.
Source: Steve Cretin

Solution ②

Build a Growing Sunday School/Bible-Study Ministry
Steve Cretin

Single-adult ministry comes in all shapes and sizes, from a small group of single adults in a rural setting to megachurch, metroplex single-adult organizations. The following six guidelines can help you meet the Bible-study needs of your single adults, no matter what size ministry you have. These strategies can tie together all facets of your single-adult ministry, as well as ensure that your single-adult Sunday School/Bible study is an enriching experience.

Pray

Pray as if all depends on God. It does! Unfortunately, most Christians neglect prayer, and this is no less true of most single-adult ministries. Prayer is the key. Only God knows what His ultimate mission is for single adults in a particular setting. Because prayer taps into the source of wisdom and power, it must be the first step before planning begins. Intense, sincere, searching, committed prayer is the beginning of a successful single-adult Sunday School/Bible-study ministry.

Plan

Plan as if all depends on you. Thank God it doesn't! Planning is paramount in successful mission and ministry. Because planning is hard work, it must be shared. One can touch 100, but 100 can touch 10,000. Planning requires a shared ministry with single adults.

Prioritize

Single adults live by their priorities. Sometimes elaborate plans are made for single adults that do not meet their needs. A good idea is good only if it meets a need. Listen to single adults. They will tell you what they need in ministry. Listening to single adults will develop priorities for your ministry that only single adults can set.

Promote

Tell them, tell them that you told them, and tell them again! Communication is a must in successful single-adult Sunday Schools/Bible studies. Announcements, fliers, newsletters, phone calls, and other methods increase communication and advertise ministry. The best advertisement for single-adult Sunday School/Bible study, however, is a satisfied participant. As needs are met, promotion occurs by word of mouth.

Persist

There is no such thing as instant Sunday School/Bible study. Persistence and consistency build stability and promote growth. "Keep on keeping on" does more for ministry than most other principles do. Single adults are looking for stability, for something solid to connect with, and for something in which to invest their lives long-term.

Produce

Because Sunday School/Bible study seeks to reach single adults for Christ, giving attention to the bottom line is not unspiritual but appropriate. People count. Growth is measured not only in numbers but also in depth. As single-adult ministry produces and grows disciples, it also builds a leadership base that expands and grows single-adult Sunday School/Bible study.

Single-adult Sunday School/Bible study can be an effective tool for reaching the majority of single adults in any community. Try these proven methods to enhance your ministry or to establish new work with single adults.

> **factoid**
>
> A good idea is good only if it meets a need. Listen to single adults. They will tell you what they need in ministry.
>
> Source: Steve Cretin

Solution ③

Reach Single Adults Through Small Groups: The WillowCreek Model

Jon Bodin

Imagine a place where relationships go beyond surface issues. Imagine a place where you can be vulnerable and disclose your true self. Imagine a place where you feel really cared about. Single adults are looking for a safe place like that.

There is such a place. It is called a small group, and it is found in the church. God created every person with the need to relate intimately both to Him and to others. I believe that a small group in the church is one of God's ordained ways to meet this need.

My church used to be a place that had small groups. We are now a church that *is* small groups. The reason for this change is simple: a small group is the optimal place for life change to occur. It is the place where God's love is manifested and persons minister to one another. Members then go into a world that is desperately seeking these types of relationships.

It has been thrilling to be involved in leading the single-adult small-group ministry in my church for the past 14 years. Currently, single adults form approximately 225 small groups with 1,500 participants, representing approximately 20 percent of the total small groups in the church.

Our small-group structure is patterned on the metachurch concept, described by Carl F. George in *Prepare Your Church for the Future* and *The Coming Church Revolution*. The metachurch model employs small groups to win persons to Christ as it cares for and disciples them, at the same time developing leaders who then form new groups. A typical small group comprises between 6 and 14 persons and is led by a qualified leader and an apprentice leader, or potential leader in training. The apprentice-leader role is critical because eventually, that person will become the leader of a new group, enabling the ministry to grow. Typically, groups consist of persons of the same gender and meet in homes at least twice a month.

Each group has four basic functions:
• Learn
• Love
• Serve
• Reach

Each group has the freedom to custom-design its group to focus on the function it has chosen to emphasize. For example, a group may want to emphasize learning the doctrines of the faith. Another group may want to reach out to persons who are spiritually seeking. The curriculum selected would be determined by the group's primary focus. See page 73 for help with selecting resources. Also see "Resources for Single Adults and Their Leaders," page 138.

Groups grow in size by filling the open chair. Each group has an open chair that symbolizes the next person God wants to bring into the group. Each group determines the frequency with which new persons are invited in. We have discovered that if a group remains closed, the group life will eventually stagnate.

Usually, in from 12 to 18 months the group becomes relatively large. With the apprentice leader now prepared to lead, the group gives birth to a new group, giving more persons the opportunity to experience group life.

For small-group leaders to be effective, it is essential that they regularly receive Vision-Huddle-Skill (VHS) Training. Usually, the staff is responsible for orchestrating a monthly VHS gathering. Another support system for leaders is the ministry of a volunteer "coach," who provides personalized care, training, and leadership for between three and six small-group leaders. This coaching role allows the ministry to grow beyond the pastor's influence. Although our single-adult ministry is small-group-driven, it is supported by strategic mid- and large-size gatherings.

Churches that are Sunday School/Bible-study-driven can gain a new perspective on the ministry of Sunday School/Bible study by thinking of the program as the church's original small-group process. Of course, small groups often need more time to meet, and they meet for purposes other than Bible study and at a variety of times and locations.

One saying around our church is "Nobody does life alone." A world is starving for the intimacy that only God through His Spirit and His people can provide. Undergirded with small groups, our single-adult ministries can be places where God meets that need.

> **factoid**
> A small group is the optimal place for life change to occur.
> Source: Jon Bodin

Solution ④

Apply the Great Commission Factor
Ron Proctor

I remember landing on foreign soil and thinking, *I am in a strange land!* I had received information about cultural differences and instructions for approaching the people of this country. Soon I realized that I did not speak the language and that I had a different value system from the people of this land. But my objective was very clear: I was there to present the gospel effectively, quickly, and passionately.

To be more effective today in reaching non-Christian single adults, we must approach them with the same principles we would use to reach non-Christians on foreign soil. Learning single adults' language and understanding their culture are necessities for effectively sharing the gospel with them. Our objective must be clear: we must present the gospel effectively, quickly, and passionately.

Because most single adults are not believers, they provide exciting opportunities to share the gospel. Single adults are receptive to the message of good news in a world of frustration and confusion.

Who is responsible for reaching lost single adults today? Every Christian! Unfortunately, many Christians question their responsibility to share the gospel, making statements like "That is not my gift" or "I do not have that kind of personality." However, the Bible emphatically tells us that every Christian is responsible for sharing the gospel. For example, Proverbs 11:30 states, "He who wins souls is wise." If we fail to warn others of the eternal danger of hell, their blood will be on our hands (see Ezek. 33:6).

The church is responsible for aggressively taking the gospel to the lost. The Great Commission commands us to make disciples, and the first step is to lead the lost to personal relationships with Jesus Christ (see Matt. 28:19-20). Jesus said that believers would be His witnesses to the world when the Holy Spirit comes upon us (see Acts 1:8). We are exhorted to warn every person by proclaiming Christ (see Col. 1:28). We have received the ministry of leading others into right relationships with God through the ministry of reconciliation (see 2 Cor. 5:17-20). Therefore, the Bible is very clear when it says that every Christian has the responsibility of presenting the gospel of Christ to others.

Since single adults need the gospel and are open to hearing the gospel, why aren't we sharing the gospel? If single adults do not hear the true gospel of Jesus Christ, they will fall prey to the false gospels of cults, New Age philosophies, humanism, materialism, and secularism.

> **factoid**
> Because most single adults are not believers, they provide exciting opportunities to share the gospel.
> Source: Ron Proctor

Single adults usually respond positively if you follow these guidelines as you approach them with the gospel:
- Be authentic.
- Do not be judgmental toward any unacceptable lifestyles you encounter.
- Single adults, like married adults, have been influenced by a narcissistic value system that leads many to live compartmentally in their religious, personal, business, and family lives. Challenge single adults to know the reality of Christ in all aspects of their lives.

In addition to these general guidelines, you will want to use the following specific strategies based on single adults' receptivity to the gospel and the church.

Receptive Prospects

How can you reach receptive single-adult prospects—believers and unbelievers who express interest in attending your single-adult and/or church activities? Capitalize on the interest the prospect shows or on a referral to your ministry and church. We can best accomplish the goal of sharing Christ by using three different but complementary methods to reach, win, teach, and send:
- The least threatening method for participants is writing letters and cards to these prospects.
- The second method, which is more personal and creates greater participation by church members, is calling a prospect on the phone.
- The third method of involvement is the most personal contact and requires the most dedication. It is a personal visit or appointment in a home or at another location. The personal visit/appointment is an intimate and informative time with the prospect, ideal for sharing not only the gospel but also information about Bible-study opportunities and fellowship activities. The most important goal of this visit/appointment is to communicate genuineness and identification.

These three methods encourage church members and receptive prospects to become involved in the single-adult ministry and the church.

Even though nothing replaces a personal visit or appointment, you may find it difficult to make appointments with single adults. Do not underestimate the effectiveness of a personal letter or a phone call. If you reach an answering machine, leave a brief, caring message with your name and number.

Another idea for connecting with receptive prospects is

a prospect event such as a cookout or a meal. Invite church members to be hosts, sharing fellowship, information, and the gospel with participants. Also consider providing an opportunity for prospects to meet as a group with your pastor in his home, at church, or at a location in the community.

Whatever methods you utilize, include a personal, clear presentation of the gospel. Seek to build relationships with prospects and give opportunities for them to respond by praying to receive Christ.

Closed Prospects

In contrast to the methods used to reach receptive prospects, who have shown some degree of interest in your ministry or church, you need to employ different strategies to reach non-Christian single adults who have no awareness of or interest in attending ministry activities.

The first step is to get these single adults' attention, to interest them in becoming seekers. After making contact with single adults who respond, build relationships one by one, perhaps outside an immediate connection with your church. Consider these ideas.

- A community event or concert and creative, needs-focused advertising, such as the personals in a newspaper, may open the door to single adults.
- One church sponsors a ministry called Outdoor Outreach. Single adults invite friends and acquaintances on a bimonthly day hike, camp-out, or recreational outing. These events have no church agenda besides developing friendships. As friendships are built, they often lead to opportunities for sharing faith.
- Another church mailed the Jesus film to selected ZIP codes with high concentrations of single adults. A letter included an offer to discover more about Christ through a follow-up appointment.
- One single-adult group felt that churches' single-adult ministries reached mostly church-oriented and receptive single adults, disregarding the large number of disinterested single-adults. Consequently, the group began a single-adult church that looks like a coffee-house, does not meet in a church building, and seeks to meet single adults' felt needs. This ministry is promoted by news ads on entertainment pages and billboards. In the first six months of operation, more than three hundred single-adult prospects attended, most of whom indicated that they came because the church promised to meet their felt needs. Surveys were taken of participants, and the information gathered was used to design future message headlines and advertising.

factoid
The best person to lead a single adult to Christ is another single adult.
Source: Ron Proctor

Great Commission Principles

Whether directed to receptive or closed prospects, Great Commission outreach keeps these principles in mind.

- Scripture instructs us to pray to the Lord of the harvest (see Matt. 9:38). Prepare to win single adults' lost souls through prayer. Involve participants in your single-adult ministry and church in intercessory prayer for your efforts.
- Make the acquaintance of and build friendships with non-Christian single adults. If all of your acquaintances and friends are Christians, you have no opportunities to lead non-Christians to Christ.
- Train yourself and others to share your personal testimonies effectively. Then memorize a simple gospel presentation, clear and concise, explaining how to receive Christ as Savior.
- Offer single adults opportunities to respond by trusting and accepting Christ in prayer.
- Get around to it. The goal of all activities in your single-adult ministry and in your church is to claim lost souls. Activities and programs designed to meet single adults' needs holistically must also offer participants the opportunity to receive Christ.
- Carry out the rest of the Great Commission by helping new believers recognize the importance of membership in a local church and of growth in their faith, equipping them in turn to share their faith with others. This step completes the holistic goal of reaching, winning, teaching, and sending.
- Above all, remember that the best person to lead a single adult to Christ is another single adult. Equipping your single adults to do so will bear fruit. In reality, each single adult is a single-adult leader or minister. The official leader or minister is simply an equipper.

Because every Christian is responsible for sharing the good news of Jesus Christ, let us present the gospel effectively, quickly, and passionately.

Solution ⑤

Market Your Single-Adult Ministry
Bill Pentak

"Jesus went throughout Galilee, teaching in their synagogues, preaching the good news of the kingdom, and healing every disease and sickness among the people. News about him spread all over Syria. ... Large crowds from Galilee, the Decapolis, Jerusalem, Judea and the region across the Jordan followed him" (Matt. 4:23-25). Jesus always drew a crowd. Immersed as He was in a world of poverty, disillusionment, and moral decay, Jesus' person and message could not be overlooked or ignored. Jesus had an uncanny ability to arrest the attention of those around Him. He always knew how to use a pressing issue or situation to draw attention to Himself. In the temple Jesus said, " 'Destroy this temple, and I will raise it again in three days' " (John 2:19). At the tomb of Lazarus He said, " 'I am the resurrection and the life' " (John 11:25). After feeding the five thousand, Jesus declared: " 'I am the bread of life. He who comes to me will never go hungry' " (John 6:35). To the woman at the well Jesus said, " 'Whoever drinks the water I give him will never thirst' " (John 4:14). The Gospels are replete with examples of Jesus' using an issue or a need to connect with persons.

Each day in the United States 75 million single adults awake to a world riddled with rising crime, growing dissatisfaction, increasing instability, and eroding moral boundaries. The fields are as ready for harvest now as they were in Jesus' day. Unlike Jesus, however, His church often appears powerless to influence its world. Sadly, the good news of the Kingdom is not spreading in a society that is insensitive to the gospel message. It is a tragic reality that "churches and single-adult ministries are casually neglected by the very people they are so desperately trying to reach."[1] Usually, if the church is noticed today, it's for all of the wrong reasons.

The questions every concerned ministry leader must ask are: How can we penetrate an increasingly secular culture and arrest single adults' attention with the good news of the Kingdom? How can we connect with today's lost single adults? The answer is found in a communication tool and a discovery process called marketing.

Many church members and leaders reject the idea of using marketing principles to reach people, arguing that such practices are too worldly, manipulative, and intrusive. Images often come to mind of pushy salespersons or of inferior products hawked by inflated and empty promises. The idea of "selling" the church or its ministries is uncomfortable for many.

Although many people use marketing principles only for selfish, materialistic gain, the truth is that marketing is nothing more than a "communication tool whose use depends solely upon the hand that wields it."[2] Marketing, like a hammer, can be used to tear down or build up.[3] We should not hesitate to use marketing to spread the gospel simply because some people use it to profit materially.

Unfortunately, while we argue about the appropriateness of marketing in the church, our adversary is using it to sell an empty bill of goods to single adults by the millions. "It is high time, I think, for us to take this tool into our hands and use it to reach singles with a message that they are 'complete in Christ' and that places exist where they can be accepted for who they are."[4] Marketing can be a mighty weapon in our proclamation arsenal. When used well, it yields powerful results.

When I became the minister with single adults at a church in Houston, I entered a ministry that had declined during the period without a single-adult minister. After spending a year resolving issues and rebuilding foundations, our single-adult leadership team felt that it was time to unveil our new and improved single-adult ministry. Our challenge was to capture the attention of Houston's single adults with the news of our revitalized ministry.

Our team decided to launch our ministry with a Sunday School rally featuring a contemporary Christian band, a brunch served on china, and a message from the new minister with single adults. The leadership team also decided to set a high-attendance goal of 200 for our grand opening. At that time our Bible-study attendance averaged from the high 70s to the low 90s. We planned a media blitz utilizing several different advertising mechanisms. As a result, communication about our event reached more than 1.5 million people in the Houston metropolitan area. On Sunday morning 351 single adults attended our grand opening. Rather than meeting our attendance goal, we almost doubled it! We were equally impressed by the fact that the most effective technique we used—the one that reached the most single adults—cost under one hundred dollars!

Before examining the marketing techniques we used to reach single adults for our event, we need to understand the fundamental marketing principles that made them so powerfully effective.

> **f a c t o i d**
>
> Marketing can be a mighty weapon in our proclamation arsenal. When used well, it yields powerful results.
> Source: Bill Pentak

Marketing 101: What You Need to Know Before Promoting Your Single-Adult Ministry

Before marketing your single-adult ministry, you need to understand what marketing is and is not. Norman Shawchuck states that marketing is not "selling, advertising, or promotion."[5] Marketing, at some point, may involve these, but it is much more. Neither should marketing be construed as a panacea for all ills that might plague a ministry. Shawchuck defines *church marketing* as "a process for making concrete decisions about what the congregation is going to do, and not do, to achieve its mission."[6] It involves understanding who your audience or mission field is, discovering its needs, and then meeting its needs. Marketing, therefore, is an exchange that involves meeting needs.

Unfortunately, many church members and leaders do not understand this concept. Erroneously equating marketing with advertising, they assume that effective marketing is taking out an ad in the local newspaper. To use marketing to reach people for Christ, you must understand the distinction between marketing and advertising. Advertising that is not based on sound marketing principles and strategies represents poor stewardship of God's resources. Marketing tells you what to communicate and to whom so that you will receive the desired response. Advertising is merely one method of that communication.

Too many churches and their single-adult ministries advertise without marketing. A local newspaper, for example, contained ads from churches of various denominations inviting readers to attend. The ads resonated with religious symbolism and language, such as *holy eucharist, sacrament of reconciliation, liturgy schedule,* and *missionettes.* It is doubtful that unbelievers would understand what these ads attempted to communicate; yet the ads were intended for these persons! Church slogans were promoted and events advertised that would not appeal to the average unchurched person. For example, an invitation to attend an evangelistic service would not draw those for whom the service was intended. The message conveyed by these ads was clear: "Come to church on our terms, not on yours." Sadly, these ads were not worth the paper on which they were printed.

Jesus was the most effective communicator who ever lived. What made Him so effective? He approached persons on the basis of their needs and desires. He always initially appealed to them on the basis of their self-interest. The account of the woman at the well is a classic example. Jesus began the conversation by talking to the woman about water that would never run out. The idea of never having to come to the well in the heat of the day appealed to her and captured her interest. From there Jesus addressed the cause of her spiritual thirst. Jesus began where the woman was and then moved her where He wanted her to be.

Because Jesus was God's Son, He had the divine ability to discern the needs of this woman's heart instantly. Looking into her eyes, He could see that she needed living Water and that she was trying to satisfy her thirst in unhealthy ways. Unfortunately, we can't look at someone on the outside and know what they're dealing with on the inside. Therefore, we have to engage in the first and most important step of marketing: research our audience. We have to do our homework about the persons we are trying to reach.

Know your ministry environment. The first step in church marketing is to collect information about your ministry environment. This means researching the place where you minister and the people with whom God has called you to minister. God does not call us to minister in a vacuum but in a context—to a specific person at a specific time in a specific place. Our first task, as ministry leaders, is to understand this context fully.

Find answers to these questions: Who are we? What do we have to offer? This information provides the age, education level, and income of the average member of your single-adult ministry or church. You might want to know the average length of time members have attended; the percentage of those with children; and how many live within 3, 5, and 10 or more miles of the church. Determine your church's greatest strengths, weaknesses, and overriding passion. Some congregations, for instance, have a passion for worship or evangelism, while others have a passion for missions or discipleship. Your goal is to build profiles of the persons who have been drawn to your church and your single-adult ministry. I constantly ask our members, What attracted you to our single-adult ministry and to our church? If you identify who has been drawn to your ministry and why, you know to whom your ministry has the broadest appeal. Then you can identify your ministry's unique place in the body of Christ.

Know your mission field. You also need to understand your mission field: your community and the persons who live there. Try to answer these questions: Who are they? What are they looking for? Discover the population of your city or county and its breakdown according to household type: the percentage of single-family units, average household income, housing transience, age, and average education level. Discover the current trends and lifestyles within your ministry's reach. Most importantly, learn persons' needs, hurts, and interests.

You can find this demographic information by contact-

factoid

Marketing is understanding who your audience or mission field is, discovering its needs, and then meeting its needs.
Source: Bill Pentak

ing your state's census office, which provides a wealth of information free of charge. On-line services such as CompuServe, Dialogue, and Dow Jones also have forums that charge fees to download the latest demographic information for your area. The local library is another good resource, as well as numerous publications like *American Demographics* and *Emerging Trends*. Perhaps the best resource to help you get started is the Research Department of the North American Mission Board of the Southern Baptist Convention (see "Resources for Single Adults and Their Leaders," p. 138). Its staff can help you develop a profile of single adults in your area.

Your goal in obtaining information about your mission field is to find a connection point between your congregation or single-adult ministry and your community. If you can align who you are and what you have to offer as a ministry with the needs of the persons you are trying to reach, you will see a combustion of ministry and growth.

Only after you have researched your target audience are you ready to begin the communication process. With the vast array of advertising tools and methods available today, choosing the right ones can be a daunting task. In my ministry experience the two techniques that have made maximal impact and have been the most cost-efficient are direct mail and a carefully written news release. These tools produced a record harvest at our church on high-attendance Sunday.

Direct Mail: The Next-Best Thing to Being There

Two thousand adults were asked to to choose from a list of 21 items the one daily activity they enjoyed most. Sixty-three percent of the respondents selected "Getting the mail." Most people look forward to getting the mail. Statistics also reveal, contrary to many claims, that people respond to junk mail! Thousands of mail-order companies would not spend billions of dollars each year on direct mail if they were not getting rich returns on their investments.

Although space does not permit an exhaustive analysis of the benefits of direct mail, two are especially pertinent for single-adult ministry leaders. The first is that direct mail can penetrate closed doors. Two of the greatest obstacles single-adult ministry leaders face in visiting single adults are finding a time when single adults are home and getting past apartment communities' security gates. Direct mail penetrates security gates, and it is waiting in the mailbox when the single adult arrives home.

The second great advantage of direct mail is that it can be read at the reader's convenience. A call or a visit, especially an unannounced one, can intimidate an unchurched prospect. That same prospect, however, can sit back and relax while reading your direct mail. The nonthreatening nature of direct mail makes it very effective. "It communicates a message at a time when the receiver's defensive barriers are down."[7]

Using direct mail is nothing new to the church community. Churches and their single-adult ministries send newsletters and mailings to their members every week. However, most of these direct-mail pieces are worthless because they fail to communicate effectively to the target audience. I urge pastors to ensure that as much effort is put into their church's weekly newsletter as is put into their weekly sermon. Far more people read their church's newsletter than will ever hear their pastors' sermons.

Use the following guidelines to prepare effective direct-mail letters, newsletters, or fliers.

Write from the reader's perspective. Unfortunately, this is where most churches' public relations break down. Too often, church communication is written from the writer's point of view instead of the reader's. Remember that the goal is to connect and communicate. We cannot communicate with people until we first connect with them. We can do so by approaching them from their perspective. The persons we are trying to reach are already interested in their own points of view. Appealing to their viewpoints, then, is a guaranteed method of arresting their attention.

Focus on benefits, not features.[8] Features deal with the what of your event. Benefits deal with the why. Most single-adult ministry advertisements do no more than tell the reader what the event is, where it will be, what time it will start, and how much it will cost. This approach is grossly ineffective because today's single adults are skeptical, critical, and questioning of what they see and hear. We must move the focus of our communication from the what to the why. We must tell single adults why they should come to our ministry or event. We need to communicate how they will feel as a result of attending.

Rick Warren, the pastor of Saddleback Valley Community Church in Mission Viejo, California, and an expert at church marketing, says that every church public-relations piece needs to offer a solution, an advantage, or a benefit. One slogan frequently appearing in his church advertisements is "Life was meant to be enjoyed, not endured. Enjoy life to the fullest at Saddleback Valley Community Church." Second Baptist Church in Houston claims, "You just feel good inside." One theme we continually use is "Find en-

f a c t o i d

Two of the greatest obstacles single-adult ministry leaders face in visiting single adults are finding a time when single adults are home and getting past apartment communities' security gates.
Source: Bill Pentak

the single-adult ministry solution

couragement for today and hope for tomorrow." These slogans illustrate that an invitation to enjoy life, feel good, and find hope is more likely to draw single adults to your ministry than an explanation of what your next event will be. They connect with people at their point of need. Telling people why they should attend your ministry activities is the modern equivalent of telling them where they can find living Water that satisfies their thirst forever.

Don't use church language.[9] Our goal of communicating means speaking in the vernacular of the persons we are trying to reach. It means speaking to them in terms they can understand. This principle precludes using much of the religious jargon with which we may be comfortable. For example, instead of saying: "You need to get saved. Let me tell you about the Roman Road," try: "You need a life change that only God can bring. Let's look at how God wants to help you."

Capitalize on current events. Nothing captures people's attention more readily than addressing current issues or events that draw attention to fundamental life needs. A number of years ago Eric Clapton won a Grammy for "Tears in Heaven," a song that concerned the untimely death of Clapton's son. If I had been preaching the following Sunday, I would have scrapped my message and placed an ad or a news release in the newspaper promoting my upcoming message, "Will There Be Any Tears in Heaven?" It would have drawn a crowd.

At the time of this writing, jurors have acquitted O. J. Simpson of double homicide. His trial attracted a lot of attention and raised many questions. A ministry leader could tactfully use the issues suggested by this trial to draw people to Christ. A sermon or a Bible study titled "God's Verdict: Innocent or Guilty?" would attract a large crowd. Learn to capitalize on current events by relating them to universal spiritual needs.

Always proofread your communication. A church once decided to hold a churchwide sing-along during the Sunday-evening service. They called it a singspiration. Unfortunately, when the event was advertised on the front of the Sunday bulletin, the letter *g* was inadvertently dropped, making it a sinspiration! Always proofread your material. And remember that spell checkers on computers do not do all the work of proofreading.

Use a logo for identification. Almost every corporation uses a logo for name identification and recognition. Your single-adult ministry needs to have a logo that appears on every piece of printed material you produce. Follow these guidelines in designing your logo.

- Make sure the logo accurately conveys your ministry's identity and purpose.
- Make sure the logo reproduces well in one color. Logos used in newspaper ads or in fliers duplicated on a photocopier are usually printed in black ink, so ask your artist to design a two-color logo that will also look good in one color.
- Make sure the logo is professionally drawn. Because this logo represents your ministry, hire an experienced professional. The result will be well worth the cost.
- Make sure the logo reduces well. Because your logo may sometimes be printed small, such as on business cards and stationery, ask your artist not to design a logo that has fine lines or too much detail.

Be flexible to stretch your promotion budget. When creating an ad or securing an artist to design an ad, specify a size that will allow multiple uses. When creating a newspaper ad, for example, you could ask the artist to assign dimensions that could be enlarged to fit on an 8½-by-11 sheet of paper, giving you not only an ad but also a flier or one side of a direct-mail piece. The artwork could be enlarged again to fit on an 11-by-17 sheet of paper, giving you a poster. Another budget saver is to use a variety of tints of the same color. This way you create the perception of more than one color but pay for only a one-color job. In addition, many commercial print shops print a color of the day at a discount if you can be flexible in your color selection.

Above all, remember that it takes less than three seconds for the average reader to decide whether he or she will read your mail. Make sure that the design is clean, balanced, and appealing to the eye. Use a headline that grabs the reader's attention by addressing a need. When it is done well, direct mail is a powerful advertising tool.

News You Can Use: How to Get Free Publicity from a News Release

"By far and away, ... the singularly most important [and cost-effective] promotional tool I have found [is] the news release. With it I have received free advertising from newspapers, periodicals, and radio [and television] stations which otherwise would have cost literally thousands of dollars."[10] News releases are relatively easy to write. With some practice you too can receive thousands of dollars of free publicity through news releases.

A news release is a one-page, double-spaced, typewritten news brief that covers the who, what, when, where, and why of your event. (See the sample news release at the end of this solution.) It should be as factually and concisely written as

f a c t o i d

Telling people why they should attend your ministry activities is the modern equivalent of telling them where they can find living Water that satisfies their thirst forever.

Source: Bill Pentak

possible. "For immediate release" should appear at the top right or left margin of the news release, with the date of issue underneath. The opposite margin should read, "For more information contact … ," followed by your name and phone numbers. Center the headline immediately below the release date and contact information. Make sure the headline succinctly captures the essence of your event or project.

The first paragraph of the news release should contain the most important information so that it could stand alone if necessary. Subsequent paragraphs contain details or quotations explaining why you are conducting the event or project. The last sentence should refer readers to your single-adult ministry for further details. The annotation "End" should be centered on the line immediately following your last sentence.

Finally, the news release should be sent to every media organization in your locale between 10 days and two weeks before the date you wish it to be printed. A media mailing list can be purchased for a reasonable price from a local mailing house or can be generated by scanning the local phone book. Include in your media database every television station, radio station, and newspaper in your area. When your single-adult ministry or church engages in a major, newsworthy activity, send a news release to your local media outlets.

Newspapers and radio and television stations have a lot of space or airtime to fill. When editors have placed all of the stories their reporters have written and have positioned all of the ads the local businesses have purchased, they may publish your single-adult ministry news release. Sometimes they also print a black-and-white photograph if you provide one.

How did 1.5 million people in the Houston area hear about our single-adult rally? We sent a one-page news release to more than one hundred media organizations in the Houston area. With the releases sent to the larger newspapers we included a black-and-white photo of our singing group.

The day before our grand opening the *Houston Chronicle,* with a readership of more than one million, ran the photograph with a byline about our rally. The photograph and release were also printed in the *Pasadena Citizen,* with mentions in the *Clear Lake Times* and numerous neighborhood publications. Houston's Christian radio stations aired free promotional spots, as well. To purchase the equivalent ad space in the *Houston Chronicle* alone would have cost eight hundred dollars. Our actual cost was a little effort and the price of a postage stamp.

When sending a news release, remember these important guidelines.

> **factoid**
>
> The most important and cost-effective promotional tool is the news release.
> Source: Bill Pentak

- Don't overuse them. Save your releases for events that have the best capacity to reach people. If you send releases for all of your events, newspaper editors will eventually disregard them.
- Include the name of the editor on the mailing label. No one likes to receive mail addressed to Occupant. Make it personal.
- Realize that you are competing for attention with every organization that has a social calendar. Plan your big events and send your news releases during slow times in your area. If possible, don't hold your biggest event of the year at the same time another big event is held.
- Don't take it personally if the newspaper doesn't use your release. The editor determines what is newsworthy for your area.
- Never call reporters to ask if they received your news release. They won't know at the moment, and they are too busy to look.
- Don't doubt your ability to write effective news releases. You can if you try. If you can prepare an article for your church newsletter, you can prepare a news release for a newspaper. You have hundreds of dollars of free publicity to gain and nothing to lose.

Marketing, without a doubt, is a powerful tool for reaching single adults of all ages and persuasions. Contrary to popular opinion, it doesn't always require a great deal of money. It does require a thorough understanding of the persons you are trying to reach and of the ministry you wish to offer them. When the marketing tool is used properly, we will have much the same response that Jesus did: news about our ministries will spread, and large crowds will follow Jesus.

[1]Bill Pentak, "Viewpoint: Practical Guidelines for Advertising Your Singles Ministry," *Single Adult Ministries Journal,* July–August 1990, 3.
[2]Ibid.
[3]Norman Shawchuck, *Marketing for Congregations: Choosing to Serve People More Effectively* (Nashville: Abingdon, 1992), 43.
[4]Pentak, "Viewpoint," 3.
[5]Shawchuck, *Marketing for Congregations,* 22.
[6]Ibid., 45.
[7]Rick Warren, "How to Advertise Your Ministry," message delivered at Saddleback Valley Community Church Growth Conference, Mission Viejo, Calif., 1989.
[8]George Barna, *Church Marketing: Breaking Ground for the Harvest* (Ventura, Calif.: Regal, 1992), 202, 212.
[9]Warren, "How to Advertise Your Ministry."
[10]Pentak, "Viewpoint," 5.

NEWSRELEASE

For immediate release
23 March 1995

The Tallowood Singles
555 Tallowood Drive
Houston, TX 77024

For more information contact:
Bill Pentak
Minister with Single Adults
(713) 468-8241, extension 133
(713) 493-6156

Single Adults to Sponsor Divorce-Recovery Workshop

Houston, Texas—23 March 1995—"New Beginnings," an eight-week divorce-recovery workshop sponsored by The Tallowood Singles, will be offered Tuesday evenings at 7:00 p.m., starting April 4. The workshop, led by prominent local psychologists Kathy Galvin and Lavonnia Duck, is for the divorced and separated and will be held at Tallowood Baptist Church. The cost of $30 a person includes workbook materials, snack food, and beverages. Child care is available by advance reservation only.

Topics covered during the workshop will include "Identity and Self-esteem," "Getting Your Ex in Focus," "Assuming Responsibility," "The Process of Forgiveness," "Relationship Building," "Single Parenting," and "Let Go and Live."

The workshop will also host an eight-week support group for the children of divorced and separated parents. Meeting concurrently with "New Beginnings," the children's workshop will be led by Dr. JoAnn VanWey.

"We're trying to help rebuild lives that have been traumatized by the emotional pain of divorce and separation," stated Bill Pentak, minister with single adults at Tallowood Baptist. "We're hoping to meet real needs and heal real hurts during this workshop," Pentak said.

For more information and a free brochure, contact The Tallowood Singles at 468-8241.

End

SAMPLE NEWSPAPER AD COPY

A cutline like the following would accompany an appropriate publicity photo.

Gabriel to sing for single adults

A single-adult rally at 11:15 a.m. Sunday at Sagemont Singles Center, 11514 Hughes Road at Southbelt, will feature the gospel band Gabriel.

A free lunch will be provided.

Solution ⑥
use the single-adult
ministry toolbox

Tools for Expanding and Growing

Who's Who in Single-Adult Sunday School/Bible-Study Ministry

Copy these job descriptions and distribute to leaders you enlist.

Teacher
Studies and prepares to teach each week. Attends teacher-preparation opportunities. Enlists substitute teachers when needed.

Secretary
Keeps records for the group by maintaining lists of members and prospects and by assisting care, outreach-evangelism, and prayer leaders with contact information.

Fellowship Leader
Leads in planning and conducting social and missions activities to encourage fellowship among members and prospects.

Care Leader
Cares for and encourages four or five other members, recognizing their needs and meeting them through the resources of the Christian community. Celebrates special events in their lives, such as birthdays, graduations, and job promotions.

Outreach-Evangelism Leader
Leads in ensuring that all visitors and prospects receive follow-up contacts and have opportunities to know Christ and to become involved in His church.

Prayer Leader
Leads efforts to involve participants in prayer for one another and for God's activity in the group, church, and community.

Greeter
Meets visitors in a friendly manner, introducing them to others and helping them find meeting areas and choose study groups.

Ideas for Single-Adult Sunday School/Bible-Study Groupings

As you read the following ideas, place an *X* beside each idea you currently use. Place check marks beside others to consider for future use.

❑ Use a large-group master-teacher approach. Single adults often enjoy the anonymity of a large group.

❑ Use small groups or a combination of large group and small groups. Divide single adults into small groups for discussion after a large-group time. Many single adults feel threatened when they enter a room and see small groups, realizing that they may have to talk and relate immediately to others. This approach allows them time to adapt to the group.

❑ Use the standard Sunday School/Bible-study model with choices of ongoing studies of dated curriculum. Departments and groups can be either age-grouped or peer-grouped.

❑ Use multiple interest-driven curriculum resources that focus on single adults' life needs.

❑ Use quarterly or monthly special programs with music, speakers, drama, and so on to increase interest in ongoing attendance. Generally, new single adults are added as a result.

❑ Combine an alternative Sunday School/Bible study with a contemporary worship model. Meet in alternative locations, such as a restaurant, a hotel meeting room, or a home and at a time other than Sunday morning.

❑ Target niche or affinity groups for starting new units based on peer needs. Examples are single parents, 20-somethings, and young professionals.

❑ Schedule divorce recovery on Sunday morning and promote it in the community. Make it short-term—from 4 to 6 weeks. If desired, follow up with a 12-week, 12-step Bible study. Those who want to continue should be given opportunities for continued participation. Approximately ¼ of the individuals who respond to this format are absorbed as new members into the ongoing Sunday School/Bible study.

❑ If your group needs more members, try meeting together in a high-energy opening with Christian music, videos, food, greeters, and promotional time. Then dismiss to individual units. This approach can help you move to a new tier in attendance if small groups discourage visitors from returning.

❑ Use a combination of multiple ideas to maintain energy in your Sunday School/Bible study throughout the year. For example, change the format of your Sunday School/Bible study, utilizing some of the previous suggestions.

A Team Approach to Single-Adult Sunday School/Bible-Study Organization

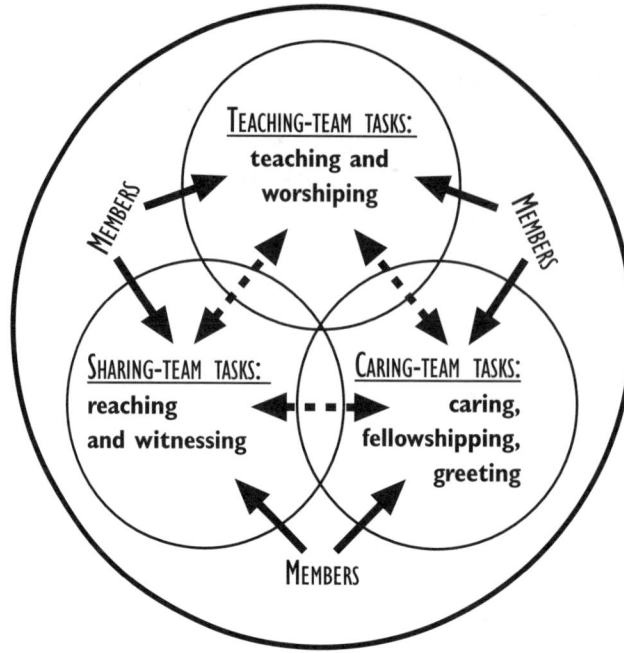

Basic Organizational Approach

How are you organized? Write on a separate sheet of paper the names and positions of leaders in your group. If you have leaders other than those suggested here (such as a president), consider how the responsibilities of these leaders match the tasks. Then write changes you think could be made to improve the effectiveness of your leadership.

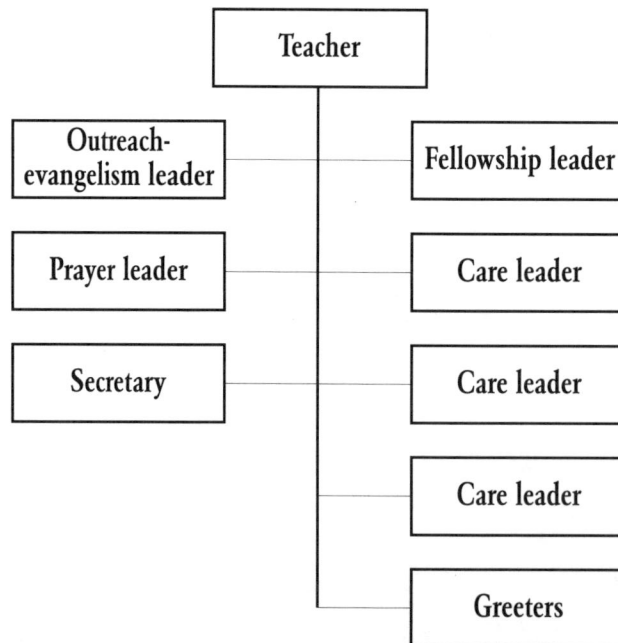

A new group would begin with the teacher, an outreach-evangelism leader, and two care leaders if possible but would enlist additional workers as the group grows.

Richard E. Dodge, comp., *Toward 2000: Leading Adults in Sunday School* (Nashville: Convention, 1995), 26–27.

Issue ⑦
facing the challenge of critical issues
in single-adult ministry

The Single-Adult Ministry Great Commission reminds us to have no fear. Fear keeps many churches from ministering with single adults. Information in this issue will help you move past your fears and risk ministry with single persons who have special needs. Remember that you have not only greater understanding of single-adult ministry but also the reality of Christ's presence. —*Tim Cleary*

Solution ①

Lead Your Church to Face the Challenge
Jerry Wilkinson

A church that begins ministering with single adults must confront several major issues. In many churches the most pressing challenge may be to overcome negative stereotypes commonly held by some church-staff members and by uninformed laypersons. Many see single adults as uncommitted, uninvolved persons who always take and never give. Some may believe that all single adults are promiscuous. Others may believe that single adults have enormous needs that drain ministers of time and energy and overload the church's counseling ministry.

It is important that church leaders help their congregations understand that these kinds of images are no more true of all single adults than are stereotypes of any other demographic group. In reality, single adults want to be involved, to give, and to be fellow ministers. In my church more than ⅓ of the adults who attend each Sunday are single. They invest themselves in almost every area of ministry. They faithfully serve as Sunday School/Bible-study directors, teachers, and care leaders. They are greeters, ushers, and shuttle drivers. Single adults participate in our worship ministry as vocalists, instrumentalists, drama-team members, and technical-support persons. They serve on key committees and on our church staff.

As a church grows, the staff's counseling load also increases. If you grow a single-adult ministry, your counseling load will increase. Some unmarried adults, like married ones, will need the attention of their pastor or of another minister as they try to cope with their emotional and spiritual pain. However, effective, preplanned strategies can help minimize the pastor's direct involvement (see "Utilize Counseling

Techniques and Resources," beginning on the next page.

Some church leaders may believe that aggressively pursuing ministry with single adults signals an abandonment of a historical and vital marriage-and-family ministry. However, more and more churches are recognizing the need to minister to diverse groups of people. They are learning to broaden the umbrella under which they minister. These churches may help more young people feel comfortable with senior adults and may help one ethnic group feel more at home with another ethnic group. Preachers and teachers help single adults feel accepted and included by regularly using illustrations that reflect the lives of unmarried single adults, divorced men and women, single-parent families, and widowed persons.

Others feel that opening the church to single adults indicates that the church condones divorce. The truth is that no church should condone any sin. However, we are called to be redemptive and restorative to those who have sinned and are hurting. Ministry with divorced individuals may include individual counseling, divorce-recovery workshops, or support groups. In light of concerns about family ministry and divorce, churches that minister with single adults should carefully examine and articulate their positions on divorce and remarriage. Single adults are drawn to churches that extend grace in these areas and are alienated by churches that don't.

While some single adults choose to remain unmarried, most want to marry. Therefore, churches that minister with single adults should recognize single adults' need to build healthy relationships across gender lines, and they should expect dating relationships to develop. Programming should provide help in building successful friendships, in developing appropriate dating relationships, and in preparing for marriage. These areas can be addressed through sermons, Bible-study lessons, and topical workshops. Single adults who are encouraged to participate in small groups have opportunities to practice what they learn in an environment that also provides accountability. For resource ideas, see "Resources for Single Adults and Their Leaders," beginning on page 138.

Closely related to dating and marriage readiness is the need to help single adults manage their sexual desires appropriately. Leaders in single-adult ministries must be prepared to teach biblical standards of sexual purity regularly. Single adults should understand the physical, emotional, and spiritual implications of immoral sexual behavior.

In addition to providing regular, open, and frank teaching on and discussion of sexual behavior, consider asking single-adult leaders to contract with church leaders to remain sexually pure. Teach those in leadership positions to watch for sexual predators who may join the group for the sole purpose of finding sexual partners. These persons should be confronted quickly and the ministry's rules of participation defined. Leaders should also be prepared to confront any members who become involved in immoral sexual behavior.

Ministry to single-parent families is emerging in many churches. As the name implies, this is a family ministry. Churches that minister with single parents must also be prepared to minister with their children. Workers in children's and youth ministries should be aware of the special concerns common in single-parent families. Programming for children and parents may be affected by issues such as custody and visitation, child care, and limited financial resources.

Finally, churches should settle the issue of limiting single men or women who wish to serve in the church. The more successful single-adult ministries are led by single adults, both men and women. As mentioned earlier, many single adults are eager to participate in all areas of ministry. They bring a wealth of gifts, abilities, and energy to help the body of Christ advance the Kingdom. Remove barriers to service for single adults in your congregation.

> **factoid**
>
> Single adults are drawn to churches that extend grace and are alienated by churches that don't.
>
> Source: Jerry Wilkinson

Solution ②

Utilize Counseling Techniques and Resources
Jerry Wilkinson

As emotional and spiritual problems and challenges arise in the lives of the single adults in your ministry, you will want to assist with appropriate counseling and discipleship. This task need not be overwhelming if you have a well-understood strategic plan and if you plan to use a multifaceted approach to meeting needs.

You can easily develop a counseling plan for your single-adult ministry by assessing your available resources and by arranging them in tiers or levels of assistance. The list below shows resource referrals arranged in a strategic order. The levels, with 1 meaning least complex and 4 meaning most complex, indicate where individuals may be referred for help.

LEVEL	RESOURCE PERSON	ADDITIONAL REFERRAL TO
1	Trained volunteer, peer listener	Other lay leader, teacher, deacon, elder
2	Lay leader, teacher	Pastor, staff minister, related support group, discipleship/accountability group
3	Pastor, staff minister	Related lay or professionally led support group, professional Christian counselor, discipleship/accountability group
4	Professional Christian counselor	Other appropriate mental-health professional

The first line of assistance will likely come from properly equipped volunteer leaders in your group. The second level may include your other lay leaders and teachers. Your pastor or another staff minister may represent the third line of assistance. If your pastor/staff minister carries a small counseling load or counsels persons for only a few sessions, then a local Christian counselor can serve as the fourth level of assistance and can recommend other Christian mental-health professionals as needed. Individuals at every assistance level should recognize their limitations and must know when and to whom they should refer counselees for the next assistance level.

Volunteer listeners can provide valuable help when single adults need a listening ear more than professional therapy. These listeners, whether Sunday School/Bible-study leaders, other group leaders, or other laypersons, need to be trained for their listening role. A pastor or a local counselor can help your team with this project. Volunteer listeners may wish to complete the course *WiseCounsel: Skills for Lay Counseling* (see "Resources for Single Adults and Their Leaders," p. 138). Also see the information on peer listeners in issue 3, solution 4.

Listeners should quickly acquire active listening skills. These skills include—
- learning to be present for the speaker;
- maintaining appropriate eye contact;
- encouraging the speaker to label feelings;
- clarifying thoughts;
- reflecting the speaker's feelings and thoughts.

Volunteer listeners should be taught to resist giving advice. Rather, they need to focus on hearing what the speaker is saying. As the intensity of emotions decreases, listeners also need to help individuals focus on accepting the reality and truth of their circumstances. Scripture teaches us that freedom comes with truth (see John 8:32).

Listeners need to establish boundaries with those to whom they seek to minister. For example, they should communicate the limits of their availability—when they are available, how long they can listen, and what type of encouragement the individual may expect.

Teach volunteer listeners to pray with those to whom they minister. We know that "the prayer of a righteous man is powerful and effective" (Jas. 5:16). Prayer increases the persons' faith and hope in God and assures them of the listeners' genuine concern.

Your listening team can also benefit from understanding issues commonly encountered on the single-adult journey. For example, listeners may want to be familiar with the stages of grief experienced by those who have endured broken relationships, desertions, separations, divorces, or the deaths of mates. Understanding the process of forgiveness and its relationship to anger and bitterness is another key topic that deserves attention.

Listeners should also be alert to critical issues of depression, threatened suicide, and other potentially harmful behaviors. If symptoms of depression are prolonged, the person should be referred to a pastor or a counselor. Most states require that threatened suicides be reported immediately. Be sure that your volunteers, as well as your church-staff members, know how to report a threatened suicide.

Persons providing help through listening or counseling may find useful a list of community resources and agencies. Your resource list might include a contact's name, as well as addresses and phone numbers of community food banks, transitional-housing services, crisis-intervention groups, public mental-health agencies, public health services, travelers-aid groups, crisis-pregnancy centers, and shelters for victims of family violence. Also include local Christian groups like the Salvation Army.

A well-stocked library can also help your listeners and counselors. Include books by Christian authors and publishers that address topics like divorce, single parenting, friendship building, dating relationships, and single-adult sexuality. Also include books that encourage spiritual growth.

Spiritual growth, as well as healing from painful experiences and dysfunctional relationships, is facilitated in the Christian community. For this reason, small discipleship groups can help your single adults deal with some of the issues for which they routinely seek counsel. A trip to the local Christian book store will reveal a wealth of material that can be used in small, midweek Bible-study/fellowship groups. Also see "Resources for Single Adults and Their Leaders," beginning on page 138. To be most helpful, these kinds of groups should provide opportunities for worship, study, discussion, sharing concerns, and prayer for group members.

Church-sponsored support groups, led by trained laypersons, can also be very helpful to many single adults. These types of groups help relieve the pastor's counseling load and expand the church's ministry. The LIFE Support Series is anchored by a support-group leader's training program and includes resources designed to help those who struggle with self-esteem, hurtful family relationships, eating disorders, chemical dependency, physical or sexual abuse, and divorce recovery (see "Resources for Single Adults and Their Leaders," p. 138).

factoid
Volunteer listeners can provide valuable help when single adults need a listening ear more than professional therapy.
Source: Jerry Wilkinson

Regularly scheduled workshops on current topics of concern or critical issues can also help your single adults. Enlist knowledgeable individuals from your congregation or community as leaders. Publicize well. Half-day or whole-day events work best in many locations. Keep the cost low.

Provide child care on site.

Counseling and discipling are gratifying elements of single-adult ministry. The key to effective ministry in these areas is to develop a strategic plan that distributes the workload and utilizes multiple resources.

Solution ③

Tackle These Critical Issues
Jerry Wilkinson

Personal Growth

Singleness: A Biblically Valid Lifestyle

We live in a society that has historically promoted marriage as the only normal lifestyle. However, our culture is progressively becoming more aware of the validity of singleness as a normal, socially acceptable lifestyle. Even so, most single adults want to be married. It is important that the church teach the following points.

- Singleness is a biblically valid lifestyle. Jesus was a single adult. The apostle Paul, also single, encouraged those who could remain single to do so (see 1 Cor. 7).
- Singleness should not be viewed as a transitional phase or stage. Life should not be postponed while waiting for a marriage partner.
- Marriage does not produce happiness. Individuals must learn to be happy with themselves before they can be happy in marriage.

Self-esteem/Identity in Christ

To esteem means *to value, respect, or appreciate.* In modern Western culture, individuals often learn that self-esteem is derived from comparing themselves to others. Similarly, many believe that their value is based on appearance, achievement, and status.

- Teach single adults that genuine self-esteem is not based on comparison or the world's false standards. Rather, genuine self-esteem is based on their identity in Christ. In Him we are loved, accepted, and valued.
- Use the LIFE Support course *Search for Significance* for individual, personal, or group study (see "Resources for Single Adults and Their Leaders," p. 138).

Shame, Guilt, and Rejection

Some single adults live with feelings of regret, shame, guilt,

and/or rejection. These painful feelings have their roots in many causes, but the solution is found in Christ's forgiveness and unconditional love.

- Teach single adults that God loves, forgives, values, and accepts them.
- Demonstrate love, forgiveness, and acceptance. Single adults also feel valued when you entrust ministry to them.
- Use the LIFE Support courses *Search for Significance* and *Making Peace with Your Past* (see "Resources for Single Adults and Their Leaders," p. 138).

Addictive Behaviors

Some single adults may struggle with addictive behaviors centered on food, alcohol, drugs, or sex. It is important that churches help them find freedom from their addictions.

- Recognize that recovery is more than a matter of prayer and willpower.
- Recovery is a process usually requiring accountability in the Christian community. Church-sponsored 12-step groups can help those who struggle with most forms of addictive behavior.
- Use the LIFE Support courses *Conquering Eating Disorders, Conquering Chemical Dependency,* and *Faithful and True: Sexual Integrity in a Fallen World* (see "Resources for Single Adults and Their Leaders," p. 138).

Sexual Abuse

Experts estimate that as many as 25 percent of American women have been sexually abused. Unresolved issues resulting from abuse often interfere with a woman's ability to function in relationships with family, friends, and coworkers. Many single victims of abuse unknowingly invite unhealthy relationships with the opposite sex. Victims of sexual abuse should be referred to a professional counselor or to a support group. Church-sponsored groups using the LIFE Support course *Shelter from the Storm: Hope for Victims of Sexual Abuse* can help (see "Resources for Single Adults and Their Leaders," p. 138).

> **factoid**
>
> Our culture is progressively becoming more aware of the validity of singleness as a normal, socially acceptable lifestyle.
> Source: Jerry Wilkinson

Dysfunctional-Family Issues

None of us come from perfect families. Everyone has had to overcome pain experienced in hurtful family relationships. Persons who come from severely dysfunctional families may still experience immense emotional pain. On the other hand, other individuals may not be conscious of their emotional pain but may recognize their inability to relate to others in healthy ways. Refer single adults who struggle with painful family experiences to a pastor, minister, or counselor for assistance. Some may benefit from church-sponsored support groups that study LIFE Support courses like *Breaking the Cycle of Hurtful Family Experiences* or *Making Peace with Your Past* (see "Resources for Single Adults and Their Leaders," p. 138).

Managing Stress

Most adults live with some level of stress. When stress escalates or reaches high levels, it can endanger physical and mental health. Although stress cannot be totally eliminated, it can be managed.

> **factoid**
> Although stress cannot be totally eliminated, it can be managed.
> Source: Jerry Wilkinson

- The negative effects of stress can be minimized through regular exercise, a healthful diet, and adequate rest.
- Teach single adults to balance their work with time for prayer, spiritual growth, healthy interaction with others, and recreation.
- Teach single adults to give time to pursuits they value most and to identify and eliminate unnecessary activities and tasks.
- Stress can be minimized by simplifying life. Single adults should be counseled to remove unnecessary stressors from their routines.

Career Planning and Employment Networking

Establishing themselves in a career is a primary developmental task for most young single adults. Older single adults who have recently been divorced may also need to find permanent employment and to develop feasible career paths. Local churches can provide practical help in this area.

- Most community colleges and universities offer testing and career-planning services, many at no charge. Private consulting agencies also offer such services. You may prefer to refer single adults to such groups.
- Consider hosting a workshop at your church. Often, skilled Christian individuals from public and private agencies lead workshops for a small church group at little or no charge.
- Help single adults who are searching for jobs develop strong résumés. Guidelines can be found in your local book store's career-and-business section. Your church may help type and duplicate résumés for members who are searching for jobs.
- Develop a network among the local businesspersons in your congregation. Circulate résumés through the network. No-obligation referrals can frequently be very helpful. Start a prayer-and-encouragement group for persons who are unemployed. Let them share their frustrations, hopes, and successes as they search for employment.

Budgeting and Financial Management

Some single adults experience great stress because of inadequate financial resources, which may be caused by many factors. For some, insufficient skills (either social or employment) and/or inadequate education may make it difficult for them to find work. Others may be limited to minimum-wage jobs for similar reasons. On the other end of the continuum, some single adults are employed in professional positions that provide a comfortable living. Help single adults be good stewards or trustees of whatever God provides.

- Teach those with limited incomes to prepare and follow a budget, as well as to become more effective shoppers. A home economist can provide help with money-saving cooking and shopping ideas.
- When consumer debt is a problem, refer single adults to consumer-credit counseling agencies. These agencies often help individuals work with creditors to restructure or reduce monthly payments.
- Overspending or unnecessary spending is sometimes caused by unresolved emotional issues. For example, some individuals buy presents to cheer themselves when they feel down or depressed. Help single adults identify these patterns and learn appropriate ways to manage their emotions.
- Single adults who have good incomes usually welcome help with wisely managing and investing their money. Often, Christian accountants and financial planners are willing to present workshops that stress the biblical principles of money management.
- Books and training materials written by Larry Burkett or Ron Blue are good resources on stewardship and budgeting (see "Resources for Single Adults and Their Leaders," p. 138). These materials can be used by individuals or groups.

Relationships
Building Friendships

Many young single adults grew up as latchkey kids, learning to take care of themselves and to function independently of

others. In addition, many endured the pain of their parents' divorces. Persons they thought they could trust proved themselves untrustworthy in significant ways. As a result, younger single adults often have little confidence or trust in others. These factors, coupled with a growing distrust of formerly respected institutions, make it difficult for this generation to trust. They want to develop trusting, caring relationships, but they find it difficult. They sometimes lack essential trust, have limited understanding of the need to be interdependent, and have few credible role models.

Older single adults may also have difficulty developing friendships. Many who have experienced painful divorces are reluctant to establish close relationships because they fear being hurt again. Their confidence in their ability to relate successfully to others may also be low. You can help your single adults learn to develop trusting, caring, and lasting friendships.

- Create low-risk opportunities for single adults to interact with others. For example, replace lecture-style Sunday School/Bible-study lessons with ones that combine brief presentations of biblical principles and thought-provoking discussions.
- Create programming that encourages groups to get together for fellowship, recreation, and relaxation.
- As group members become comfortable with one another, encourage them to participate in small discipleship and study groups. As they learn to apply Scripture to their daily lives, share their concerns with one another, and pray for one another, they will naturally begin to deepen their friendships.
- Regularly teach principles for building healthy friendships. *The Friendship Factor* and *Becoming a Friend and Lover* are excellent resources (see "Resources for Single Adults and Their Leaders," p. 138).
- Those who continually become involved in unhealthy relationships should be referred for professional counseling or should be encouraged to join an appropriate support group. LIFE Support courses such as *Untangling Relationships* may help (see "Resources for Single Adults and Their Leaders," p. 138).
- If individuals who lack social or relational skills disrupt your group, privately and lovingly confront them. Clearly describe the offensive behavior and clearly communicate necessary boundaries. Contract with them for acceptable behavior.

Dating Relationships

Dating relationships develop in almost any thriving single-adult group. Most single adults want to develop good friend-ships and possibly to find marriage partners. Take steps to ensure that dating relationships are both emotionally healthy and biblically appropriate.

- Regularly teach your single adults how to date. They need to know how to get to know one another while keeping their emotions and sexual urges in check. Teach them to pace the development of emotional intimacy. Use *Too Close, Too Soon* (see "Resources for Single Adults and Their Leaders," p. 138). Because new single adults continually enter a growing single-adult group, address this topic often.
- Regularly teach single adults what Scripture says about all forms of sexual behavior. It says much more than no. Single adults need to know the emotional, physical, and spiritual dangers of sexual intercourse outside marriage. Communicate often that they are expected to remain sexually pure. See the section "Sex, Sexuality, and Intimacy," beginning on the next page, for more information.
- Ask single adults in leadership to covenant with you to keep their dating relationships discreet and to remain sexually pure. They should avoid becoming the objects of conversation or envy (see Eph. 5:8).
- Help single adults who have been sexually active to deal with regret. Teach them to seek forgiveness from God and from former sexual partners (when possible) and to forgive themselves. Use *Free to Love Again: Coming to Terms with Sexual Regret* (see "Resources for Single Adults and Their Leaders," p. 138).
- Know your church's position on divorce and remarriage. When a relationship develops between two individuals whose marriage your church could not sanction, address the issue with the dating couple as early as possible in their relationship.

Marriage Readiness

It is very important that single adults considering marriage are properly counseled. In many instances premarital counseling is a formality that a couple endures because of church policy rather than a genuine discipling process that prepares the couple for a life together. In addition, counseling often occurs after the engagement has been announced. This makes it very embarrassing for a couple to postpone a wedding date or to decide not to marry. Encourage your single adults to begin a counseling or discipling process as soon as they begin considering marriage. This should be done before engagements are announced or wedding dates set.

- Hold a workshop for all single adults—even those who are not currently involved with anyone—that deals with important marriage-readiness issues.

factoid
Younger single adults often have little confidence or trust in others.
Source: Jerry Wilkinson

- Offer a Sunday School/Bible-study group for nearly married couples.
- Establish a marriage-preparation procedure in your church that specifies a length of time for counseling, as well as the number of counseling sessions—12 sessions over three months, for example. Be certain this premarital counseling or discipling includes biblical concepts of marriage; identifying the husband's and wife's scriptural roles and responsibilities; training in communication; understanding and valuing each other's personality; and assessing and coping with differing values in areas such as money, entertainment, vacations, holiday and family observances, and parenting strategies. Use *Counsel for the Nearly and Newly Married* (see "Resources for Single Adults and Their Leaders," p. 138).
- When children from previous marriages are involved, be sure that counseling includes discussions of realistic expectations of family life, philosophies of discipline, children's expectations, and strategies for coping with former spouses. Use the LIFE Support course *New Faces in the Frame: A Guide to Marriage and Parenting in the Blended Family* (see "Resources for Single Adults and Their Leaders," p. 138).

f a c t o i d

It is very important for single-adult ministries to present regularly what Scripture teaches about sexual behavior.
Source: Jerry Wilkinson

Sex, Sexuality, and Intimacy

The Need to Address Sexual Issues

In the past, sexual behavior was not discussed in society. Today human sexuality is openly used to sell products and to arouse interest in magazines, books, movies, and television programs. What purports to be sex education is being taught in public schools. In today's culture heterosexual sex outside marriage is considered the norm, but gay and lesbian relationships are becoming more accepted as alternative lifestyles. The world openly and aggressively promotes a sexual system that stands in direct opposition to the teachings of Scripture.

It is very important for single-adult ministries to present regularly what Scripture teaches about sexual behavior. Biblical standards must be held high. Your single adults need to know what God and His church expect. It is no longer enough to tell single adults just to say no. Help single adults develop healthy, biblically based attitudes toward sexuality and sexual behavior.

- Openly and frankly, without embarrassment, address from the pulpit issues of sexual behavior.
- Teach single adults appropriate expressions of masculine and feminine characteristics. Keep in mind that traits like tenderness and assertiveness are not exclu-

sive to one gender.
- Regularly teach single adults effective ways to cope with their sexual drives. For example, individuals with close friendships in which many of their needs for emotional intimacy are met find it easier to control their sexual behavior. Similarly, those with close friends and/or family often find it easier to give and receive appropriate physical expressions of affection. They are also less tempted to become involved in inappropriate relationships.
- It is important that your frank discussions and teachings include information about the physical, emotional, and spiritual dangers of immoral sexual behavior (see Rom. 1:26-27; 1 Cor. 6:18).

Purity, Abstinence, and Celibacy

Help your single adults understand the biblical principles of holiness, purity, abstinence, and celibacy.

- Christians are to be holy and pure. To be holy means, in part, to be set aside for service to God. To be pure means to remain uncontaminated by the world. All believers are God's servants. Our service is more effective and more pleasing if we remain uncontaminated by sin—sexual or otherwise (see Lev. 20:26; Eph. 1:4; Heb. 7:26; 1 Pet. 1:15-16).
- Abstinence is the method single adults use to remain sexually pure. They abstain from, or refuse to participate in, sexual immorality (see Acts 15:20,29; 21:25; Rom. 13:13; 1 Thess. 4:3).
- *Celibacy* and *abstinence* are often used interchangeably. However, important shades of difference exist. An individual who chooses to remain celibate, or to practice abstinence for a lifetime, does so in order to devote full attention to serving God. While many persons abstain from sexual intercourse until marriage, celibate individuals abstain for a lifetime (Matt. 19:10-12; 1 Cor. 7:1-2,7-9; Rev. 14:1-5).

Cohabitation

Many couples choose to cohabit, or live together, before marriage. Most who make this decision do so because they lack trust in the concept of marriage. Having seen "good" marriages fail, they reason that something is wrong with the institution of marriage. Older single adults often choose cohabitation because they have experienced painful divorces and fear making commitments to another lifelong relationship. A recent trend also shows that older adults sometimes cohabit for economic reasons.

- Build nonjudgmental relationships with these couples, accept them as they are, and pray for an opportunity to present biblical and sociological evidence on the dangers of cohabitation. Emphasize that God's laws are for our benefit.

- Decide in advance whether you want to minister with these couples through your single-adult or married-adult ministry. Your married-adult ministry probably offers the best opportunity to influence couples who live together.
- Stress to your single-adult leaders the difference between the need to minister to non-Christian or carnal-Christian couples who are cohabiting and the need to restrict Christian leaders who may want to live together.

Homosexuality[1]

As your church and single-adult ministry grow, gay single adults will probably want to attend your Bible studies and activities. When working with homosexuals in your ministry, help your leaders deal with the issue by teaching them to separate the sin from the sinner, just as God hates the sin but loves the sinner. In *Issues in Focus,* compiled by Margaret Rosenberger, the following teaching and ministry facts and suggestions are offered.

- Homosexuality is a result of the fall rather than a part of God's good creation. It is contrary to God's original order and plan for the sexes.
- Desire for the same gender, while not consciously chosen by a homosexual, is an unhealthy distortion or corruption of the sexual desire God planted in humankind.
- Homosexual desire, a form of temptation, becomes sin when it is nurtured and acted on (see Jas. 1:13-15).
- Even when the desire is not acted on, it can be guilt-provoking and damaging. Healing of past hurts and emotional damage can often be facilitated by a professional Christian counselor who uses a combination of counseling and prayer therapy.
- Homosexuals come to Christ in the same manner as heterosexuals—by repenting of their sins and by accepting Jesus Christ as Savior and Lord. As new believers, they need a Christian community in which they can experience love and can be nurtured and discipled.
- Encourage single adults with same-gender desires, as well as heterosexual single adults, to remain sexually pure.
- Refer those leaving a gay lifestyle to Christian support groups like Exodus International.

AIDS[2]

Acquired Immune-Deficiency Syndrome (AIDS) is a fatal disease that attacks the immune system, leaving the body defenseless to illnesses it can normally resist, such as pneumonia or meningitis. Sexually active single adults are at risk of contracting AIDS and other sexually transmitted diseases. However, your church may confront the AIDS issue in other arenas as well. For example, some married couples in your church or a child in the nursery may have AIDS.

- AIDS is not a homosexual disease, although 65 percent of the known cases in the United States are homosexual men. Twenty-five percent of the cases are intravenous drug users. The remaining cases acquire the virus through heterosexual sex, blood transfusions, an infected mother, or an undetermined cause.[3]
- Romans 1:26-27 is often used to argue that AIDS is God's righteous judgment on homosexual sin. This is a dangerous, emotionally charged assumption. For example, the passage mentions both male and female homosexuals. Few lesbians have AIDS. Does God practice sexual discrimination by withholding judgment from homosexual women? And what about persons with AIDS who are not homosexuals? In addition, homosexual behavior is not a recent phenomenon. It seems to be as old as recorded history. However, the first AIDS cases were not confirmed in the United States until 1981.
- Single-adult leaders, as well as other leaders, should be taught the facts about AIDS. They need to learn to minister with compassion to persons with AIDS. Jesus provided us a model when He ministered to a man with leprosy (see Mark 1:40-42). Looking beyond the man's decaying skin, Jesus saw a soul in desperate need of a compassionate touch from another human being.
- Obtain information about AIDS from your local Red Cross or from an AIDS support group or agency. Share the information with your single adults.
- Privacy laws restrict your communicating your knowledge that someone has AIDS—even when you believe that another person needs to know. Be very careful about telling others what you know. Often, it is advisable to contact your local public-health service and to let it take responsibility for communicating needed information to others.

> **factoid**
>
> AIDS is not a homosexual disease.
> Source: Kathleen McAuliffe

Sexual Predators

Jude 1:4 addresses the problem of persons who join a single-adult ministry for the purpose of finding sexual partners. These sexual predators seem to know instinctively who is vulnerable. With experience you can quickly identify and appropriately confront these individuals.

- At an orientation session for new group members, outline the expectations for sexual purity. Make clear that leaders will confront persons seeking sexual partners.
- Teach your members and leaders to identify those who encourage immorality. They should know how to confront those who seek to lead others astray.
- When a predator is identified, two members of your leadership team should take the individual to lunch or coffee and should explain their concerns as well as their expectations. Often, the individual will correct his or her behavior and will become a fruitful member of the group. If the sole intent was to find a sexual partner, he or she will likely move on.
- If inappropriate behavior continues, the individual should be confronted by ministers or deacons. If the confronted individual remains unrepentant, ask him or her either to attend a men's or women's group or to leave the church (see Matt. 18:15-17).

Never-Married Parents

Build nonjudgmental relationships with unwed parents. Remember, not all unwed parents are guilty of sexual immorality. Many single adults choose to adopt children. Others may be victims of rape or incest. Those who repent of immoral conduct should be forgiven and welcomed into the group. Ongoing sexual immorality should be confronted. Be certain that the children of never-married single adults are treated with grace and compassion by those who minister to the children in your church.

Loss Recovery

Many single adults struggle with issues stemming from loss. Their losses may have resulted from broken engagements, desertion, separation, divorce, or the death of a mate or another significant person. Each type of loss brings a different kind of painful experience. However, all losses share a similar grief process.

Grief

Most authorities recognize several stages of the grief process, including denial, shock, panic, an outpouring of emotions, emotional repression, anger, depression, acceptance, and hope. Not everyone moves through each stage. The length of time spent in a stage depends on circumstances, personality style, coping skills, and maturity of faith. Most people cycle through some of the stages several times. Recovery from grief may take up to three or four years. The minimal time required for healthily processing grief is about one year.

- Help single adults who are experiencing grief understand that it is a normal and natural process. This is good news for many whose their painful emotions may cause them to believe that they might be emotionally disturbed. Assure them that they are not losing their minds.
- Offer studies of the LIFE Support course *Recovering from the Losses of Life* (see "Resources for Single Adults and Their Leaders," p. 138).
- Remind those who are grieving that the process will probably take longer to complete than their friends and relatives think is necessary. Encourage them to find two or three friends or a counselor with whom they can discuss their feelings. Tell them not to discuss matters with anyone else.
- Although cycling through grief stages is natural, individuals should beware of stagnating in any particular stage. For example, depression following a loss is normal. However, grief-related depression may become clinical depression. If deep depression lasts for more than a few weeks, refer the individual to a counselor.
- Encourage single adults to grieve and heal before becoming involved in a serious dating relationship. Otherwise, they are likely to carry unresolved issues into the new relationship.

Broken Engagements

Breaking long-term dating relationships or engagements leads to genuine grief. Do not discount or minimize the feelings of persons who suffer these losses. Treat these individuals with the same compassion with which you treat others who experience loss.

- Encourage these persons to give themselves permission to grieve and heal, allowing plenty of time for this process before becoming involved in other romantic relationships.
- The healing process is facilitated by sharing thoughts and feelings in a safe environment. Encourage participation in small-group activities.
- Enlist one or two same-gender volunteer listeners to provide ongoing support.

Desertion and Separation

Persons who have been deserted and those who are separated also experience feelings of loss. However, some may be reluctant to give themselves permission to grieve because they hope to be reunited with the absent spouse.

- Encourage these persons to deal with reality. Help them process strong, painful feelings. For many, dealing with anger will be a challenge. Forgiveness is the biblical antidote to anger and bitterness.

factoid
The grief process takes longer to complete than friends and relatives think is necessary.
Source: Jerry Wilkinson

- Women who have been deserted or are separated from their husbands may need practical help with finances; child care; or basics like shelter, food, and clothing.
- Although these persons are still married, most feel more comfortable in a single-adult group than in a married-adult group. If they fellowship with single adults, carefully communicate guidelines about developing emotionally intimate relationships with opposite-gender group members. You may choose to ask these individuals to participate in an appropriate women's or men's group.
- Enlist one or two same-gender volunteer listeners to provide ongoing support.
- Be certain always to encourage marriage reconciliation. Discourage hasty decisions about divorce. However, be prepared to acknowledge that reconciliation may not be possible or realistic in certain situations.

Divorce

Divorced single adults also experience the painful emotions associated with grief. Their feelings may be further complicated by concern for their children and by feelings of failure, guilt, shame, rejection, and loneliness.

- Single adults who have been through divorce, like others who have endured significant loss, need help in dealing with painful emotions. They need to know that God loves them. Also make sure they are certain of the church's love for them. Show them how to be reconciled with God. Teach them to trust others. In addition, provide help in understanding the process of forgiveness and its relationship to their healing.
- Divorced single adults usually benefit from a loss- or divorce-recovery program. Use the LIFE Support course *A Time for Healing: Coming to Terms with Your Divorce* (see "Resources for Single Adults and Their Leaders," p. 138).
- Do not let ongoing Sunday School/Bible study become support groups for persons in pain. Instead, encourage them to process most of their issues with a same-gender volunteer listener, the pastor, or a professional counselor. You might refer them to a divorce-recovery support group in your church or community.
- Be sure divorced single adults understand that the recovery-and-healing process takes a long time—usually one year or more. Discourage involvement in serious dating relationships until old issues are resolved.
- Offer divorce recovery for children and youth, using

Healing the Wounds: Teenagers Learning to Cope with Divorce and *KidShare: What Do I Do Now?* (see "Resources for Single Adults and Their Leaders," p. 138).

The Death of a Spouse

Most churches minister effectively to individuals who have lost mates through death, especially during the days and weeks immediately following the death. However, their long-term ministry is usually not as effective.

- The grieving process following death is very similar to that which occurs after divorce, with most widowed persons cycling through the same stages of grief. Help them understand that grieving is natural. Remind them that the process takes time.
- Enlist volunteer listeners for widowed persons.
- Many widowed persons choose to remain in married-adult Sunday School/Bible-study groups. Some may be more comfortable attending men's or women's groups. Others may wish to join appropriate single-adult groups.
- Many who are widowed find that they desire and need to develop a new set of friends who are single. Organize activities that encourage this process.

Single-Parent Families

U.S. census figures reveal that approximately 25 percent of households with children are headed by single parents. Approximately 85 percent of custodial single parents are women. However, the number of custodial fathers is rapidly increasing.

> **factoid**
> Sometimes the fear of not being loved or the fear that a child will want to live with the other parent keeps single parents from effectively disciplining their children.
> Source: Jerry Wilkinson

Parenting Skills

Parenting alone presents unique challenges. Circumstantial factors like insufficient resources, time constraints, child-care problems, home-and-car maintenance, and housekeeping chores can seem overwhelming when there is no one with whom responsibilities can be shared. Often, single parents, thinking that their children have suffered enough, feel guilty about establishing firm behavioral boundaries. Sometimes the fear of not being loved or the fear that a child will want to live with the other parent keeps single parents from effectively disciplining their children.

- Some single-parent families may need professional help to sort through all of their issues. Refer them to Christian counselors who have expertise in dealing with children.
- Organize a study or support group for single parents. Consider using *Helping Single Parents with Troubled Kids*

(see "Resources for Single Adults and Their Leaders," p. 138).

Role Models for Children

Many single mothers are concerned about the lack of positive male influences for their young sons. Churches can help fill the gap created by an absent or uninvolved father.

- Develop two-man teams who are willing to spend regular time with young boys. On appointed days the team can meet with two assigned boys for all-day fun. Carefully screen the men and send them out in pairs to minimize the risk of child abuse.
- Often, the leaders of boys' Sunday School/Bible study, Royal Ambassadors, TeamKid, and Scouts are willing to spend extra time with young boys and can serve as good role models.
- Help single mothers make connections with a Big Brothers program.

Home-and-Car Repair

Many single mothers have difficulty with home repairs and car maintenance. Churches can provide practical help.

- Hold single-mom car clinics twice a year. Recruit qualified persons from your congregation to check transmission, power-steering, and brake fluids and to change oil, sparkplugs, air filters, fuel filters, wiper blades, and so on. Perform a safety inspection and refer more complicated work to a trusted mechanic. Churches may also want to help cover repair expenses.
- Organize teams of persons who are skilled in making home repairs. Often, the single parent can provide the cost of the materials if the church furnishes the labor.

Child Care

Most single parents live on very tight budgets. Child care for two or more children can represent a significant percentage of a working single parent's take-home pay.

- Organize child-care co-ops among single parents. A parent donates an hour of child care for every hour the service is used.
- Make certain that affordable child care is available when single parents have opportunities to participate in counseling, support groups, Bible studies, and other activities.
- Recruit couples to provide child care when single parents have opportunities to attend weekend retreats or conferences.

factoid

Child care for two or more children can represent a significant percentage of a working single parent's take-home pay.
Source: Jerry Wilkinson

- Organize senior adults who can serve as surrogate grandparents to help provide transportation to soccer games, piano lessons, and other activities.

Dating Relationships

Single parents need adult companionship and may start dating. It is important that single parents avoid letting relationships develop too early between their children and the persons they are dating. They should also avoid doing things that resemble family activities, such as taking children on picnics or other outings with their dates. Avoiding such "family" situations keeps children from becoming emotionally attached to someone who may be part of their lives only temporarily. Children who have already suffered through one loss should not be allowed to experience another unnecessarily.

Children's Programming

Separation, divorce, and custody issues affect church programming. When churches plan to minister with single adults, they should also plan to minister to the children from single-parent families.

- Program awards based on perfect attendance are rarely attainable by children who spend every other weekend with the opposite parent.
- Plan teaching units that stand alone rather than ones that depend on preceding lessons.
- Mother's Day and Father's Day may present problems. For example, making Father's Day cards as a crafts project may be emotionally disturbing or confusing for children who have no relationships with their fathers. Similarly, other children may feel uncomfortable choosing whether to give their cards to their fathers, who may be absent, or to their stepfathers.
- If your church holds annual father-son or mother-daughter activities, have a deacon or a Sunday School/Bible-study teacher accompany a child from a single-parent home.

[1]This section is adapted from Don Williams, "Homosexuality," in *Issues in Focus*, comp. Margaret Rosenberger (Ventura, Calif.: Regal, 1989), 37–38.
[2]This section is adapted from Americans for a Sound AIDS Policy, "AIDS: What We Should Know About It," in Rosenberger, *Issues in Focus*, 39–52.
[3]Kathleen McAuliffe, "AIDS: At the Dawn of Fear," *U.S. News & World Report*, 12 January 1987, 66, as summarized in Rosenberger, *Issues in Focus*, 40–41.

Solution ④
use the single-adult
ministry toolbox

Tools for Facing Critical Issues

SAMPLE COUNSELING STRATEGY

ASSISTANCE LEVEL 1	EQUIPPING NEEDED	Resources
• Care-group leader • Volunteer listeners	• Active listening skills • Boundaries defined • Referral procedures • Knowledge of church and community resources	• Pastor or local Christian counselor to provide training in active listening skills and to make referrals • Directory of church and community resources
ASSISTANCE LEVEL 2	**EQUIPPING NEEDED**	**Resources**
• Sunday School/Bible study directors • Bible teachers • Deacons, elders • Ministry leaders	• Active listening skills • Boundaries defined • Referral procedures • Knowledge of church and community resources • Basic lay-counseling skills	• Pastor or local Christian counselor to provide training in active listening skills and to make referrals • Directory of church and community resources • LIFE Support Series and *WiseCounsel: Skills for Lay Counseling*
ASSISTANCE LEVEL 3	**EQUIPPING NEEDED**	**Resources**
• Pastor • Minister of education • Staff counselor	• Active listening skills • Referral procedures • Knowledge of church and community resources • Advanced counseling skills	• Directory of church and community resources • Appropriate education
ASSISTANCE LEVEL 4	**EQUIPPING NEEDED**	**Resources**
• Professional Christian counselor • Christian psychologist or psychiatrist	• Appropriate education and licensing	• Professional

PLAN YOUR COUNSELING STRATEGY

ASSISTANCE LEVEL 1	EQUIPPING NEEDED	Resources
ASSISTANCE LEVEL 2	EQUIPPING NEEDED	Resources
ASSISTANCE LEVEL 3	EQUIPPING NEEDED	Resources
ASSISTANCE LEVEL 4	EQUIPPING NEEDED	Resources

Issue ⑧

discovering fresh ideas for
ministry with single adults

Sometimes a single-adult ministry makes a leader feel like Benjamin Franklin flying a kite in a storm, trying somehow to harness the power of nature. You don't know what you need until a lightning bolt electrifies the process. Ideas are the lightning bolts that can electrify your single-adult ministry. Issue 8 will introduce you to some new ideas and will teach you how to develop your own ideas for ministry.
—Tim Cleary

Solution ①

Find Ideas That Work
Tim Cleary

Ideas come and go on the winds of paradigm shifts in our ministry audience and its unique culture. A single-adult ministry cannot become dependent on the need to create an endless succession of big ideas to keep single adults attending and happy.

The following strategic ministry-development process will help you incorporate big ideas into the context of your ongoing ministry strategy.

1. Determine the context or framework for your single-adult ministry. Issue 2 in this manual gives the benefits of choosing empowerment as your primary ministry model.
2. Develop a process to discover and implement new ideas. The persons filling roles in your organization—such as volunteer coordinator, single-adult minister,

ministry or leadership team, Sunday School/Bible-study departments and groups, and other small groups—will put hands, feet, and action to ideas. Issues 3, 5, and 6 in this manual can assist you with processes for relating to these individuals and groups.

3. Choose ideas based on your mission statement. If an idea accomplishes one of your ministry's purposes, go for it! Context and process function in a ministry the same way a skeletal frame and key organs support and give substance to a human body. Ideas are the electromagnetic charges that keep us activated and functioning!

In the remainder of this issue's agenda we will go on a hunt for ideas. Keep in mind this introductory material as you consider and maximize the ideas you find. Happy hunting!

Solution ②

Use This Catalog of Ideas
Chris Elkins

Fresh ideas for ministry with single adults are organized here around the various functions and goals of a single-adult Sunday School/Bible-study ministry. Many ideas presented can be used in other contexts in your ministry organization.

Innovative Inreach
Dinner for five. Persons who eat together get to know one an-

other. Ask your Sunday School/Bible-study group members to sign up for a monthly dinner for five. Randomly group five persons who have signed up, recruit a leader among them, and ask that person to organize the dinner. Or organize groups around announced topics for dinner conversation. It may be a potluck, home-cooked, or catered meal, but each participant should share equally in the event. Ask that each group have a camera and take pictures to display on the bulletin board the following Sunday.

Nearly-weds seminar. Many single adults come to church to find a mate. When that happens, give them a good start. Keep engaged couples involved in your single-adult ministry by offering a Sunday-morning marriage-preparation course for between 8 and 12 weeks. Consider using a printed instrument to help couples understand each other better. One of the best is the PREPARE Inventory, which gives couples insight in 13 areas, including conflict resolution, finances, religious orientation, children and parenting, communication, and recreation (see "Resources for Single Adults and Their Leaders," p. 138). Personality inventories can also be used. Study material for a nearly-weds seminar may be found in *Counsel for the Nearly and Newly Married* (see "Resources for Single Adults and Their Leaders," p. 138). Topics include commitment, family of origin, self-image, communication, conflict resolution, and decision making.

Divorce-recovery/grief-recovery seminar. Many persons come to a single-adult ministry as a result of a crisis. Often, a Sunday School/Bible-study group is not equipped to help newly divorced or widowed persons. Offering a Sunday-morning seminar allows grieving, hurting single adults to receive specific help for their needs. Of course, child care should be available. Many churches offer this group on an ongoing basis so that a person can enter it at any point and then leave it when ready. Recovery groups also make the transition to single-adult Sunday School/Bible study somewhat easier.

Use these age-graded divorce-recovery resources: *A Time for Healing* for adults, *Healing the Wounds* for teenagers, and *KidShare* for children. *Recovering from the Losses of Life* helps persons working through the grief process. (See "Resources for Single Adults and Their Leaders," p. 138.) Video divorce-recovery resources are available if you do not have a Christian psychologist or counselor in your area to teach the sessions.

Care groups. A growing ministry must find ways to stay in touch with every member. Care groups can help you do this if—

• your Sunday School/Bible-study rolls are up-to-date;
• someone is responsible for maintaining rolls: adding new members, removing inactive members or dropouts, creating new groups, and training and recruiting leaders;
• each group is limited to eight persons.

These groups should not be seen as social groups or discussion groups. In fact, a group does not even need to realize that it is a group. The purpose is for the group leader to keep in touch with between six and eight persons to ensure that they are involved, ministered to, and offered opportunities to grow and develop. Personal contact should be made at least monthly. You may want to develop a phone tree within a care group to encourage interaction.

Newsletter. A newsletter helps a group define itself by seeing itself in print and photos. Avoid the common mistakes of being overly wordy and short on art, photos, and white space. Most desktop-publishing packages can help you format an attractive, easy-to-read newsletter. Use as many photos as you can of single adults doing missions work, ministering to others, having fun, praying, and studying. Be sure to send your newsletter to prospects. If a monthly publication is too much work, publish it quarterly. If mailing costs are prohibitive, distribute the newsletter at your weekly group meetings.

Outstanding Outreach

Talk it over. As often as quarterly, host a meal at which single-adult prospects can meet the pastor/staff. Plan this meal away from the church building, at little or no cost to prospects. Have the pastor speak briefly about the benefits of joining your church. Bring church-membership cards to show prospects what they will fill out if they join. Have your group officers serve as hosts of the event. Send out formal invitations with an RSVP about two weeks in advance. Outreach leaders should contact all who have not responded about five days before the event.

Message-machine ministry. Ask church leaders and single-adult ministry leaders to include a word about the ministry as part of their message to incoming callers, such as "Be sure to ask me about my church's single-adult ministry when we talk." You can also promote a special event this way. If your church has a telephone line designated for the single-adult ministry, use a machine to give announcements to callers 24 hours a day. Publish that number in the personals column and on the entertainment page of your newspaper.

Contact cards. Print cards the size of business cards with the pertinent information about your ministry, including directions to your church. Include group-meeting times, ongoing weekday events, and a telephone number to call for more information. Encourage members to give the cards to friends and other day-to-day contacts.

Cookiethon. Have the group meet on a Saturday morning and bake cookies to take to prospects. Divide the group to deliver the cookies. Include a brochure or other information about your ministry. Have bags available to hang on doorknobs if the person is not at home. Almost everyone likes homemade cookies, and the personal touch of making them and delivering them is refreshing to a prospect.

factoid

Offering a Sunday-morning seminar allows grieving, hurting single adults to receive specific help for their needs.

Source: Chris Elkins

Phone blitz. If your church does not have several telephone lines, get permission to use a business's phones one evening to make local calls to prospects. Conduct brief training and provide pizza and beverages for the callers. Have a goal of reaching all prospects. Leave messages on the answering machines of those you do not reach personally. Use the calls to update information, conduct a survey, extend an invitation to a special event, or just say hello.

Discounts or freebies. If your single-adult ministry hosts a monthly after-church luncheon, offer it free or at a discount to nonmembers if they return the invitation you send.

Perhaps through a local Christian book store offer a significant discount on a book and send a coupon to your prospects. To follow up, ask the book store to register anyone who uses the coupon.

Give gift bags to first-time visitors that include ministry information and freebies that department stores, book stores, or other local businesses might give you in exchange for the exposure.

"Happy hour." To discover new prospects, host a "happy hour" at a central location. Provide upbeat taped or live music, food, and beverages. Enlist volunteer servers who are excited about this opportunity to attract persons to your ministry. Aggressively promote this event through print, word of mouth, public-service announcements on radio and television, and your church's business leaders' company newsletters and bulletin boards.

Fun run. Sponsor a fun run and use the proceeds to help a local charity. Offer well-designed T-shirts at registration. Include as many single-adult nonmembers as possible. Recruit help from a professional race organization to supervise the event properly.

Jobs fair. Often, local banks and other community-minded businesses agree to cosponsor a jobs fair. Offer seminars on networking, interview skills, writing résumés, and finding the right job-search organization. Sell booth space to employment agencies and large employers in your area. Prominently display information about your ministry to single adults.

Apartment ministry. Find a member who is willing to be an outreach leader in his or her apartment complex. He or she should reserve the club room and coordinate the publicity for an event like a games night, hot-topic seminar, or film/video series. Because tenant turnover is about 100 percent every 18 months, don't let bad experiences in the past keep you from trying again.

Joint efforts. Smaller churches can work together to offer a monthly fellowship or another event. Your pastor may be more comfortable with an event that is not dominated by one church and is held either at rotating church sites or at a neutral site, such as an apartment club room, a hotel meeting room, or a community center.

Lunch club. Lunch is a great way to minister to single-adult professionals. Offer a weekly or monthly event at a restaurant or in the cafeteria of a business. Enlist a speaker to address a topic like dating and relating, conflict resolution, consumer buying skills, and job-advancement skills. More specialized lunch clubs could focus on divorce recovery, single parenting, or marriage preparation.

Great-catch cards. Insert cards in your church's worship bulletin that ask church members to write the names of single adults they would like to be invited. Have them drop the cards in the offering plates. Include a question on the card that asks whether you may use the contributor's name when you contact the single adult.

Super Socials and Fantastic Fellowships

How many different ideas can you think of for a party? Some of the best ideas are the ones your group generates. Don't underestimate the value of a brainstorming session. The following social and fellowship ideas have worked in a variety of churches.

- Host a monthly/bimonthly Sunday brunch, either potluck or catered. Keep it simple and consistent. You may want to ask a different group to host it each month and to be responsible for a theme, games, or entertainment.
- Host a monthly birthday party for everyone in your group having a birthday that month. Ask each person to bring a baby picture.
- Celebrate holidays and special occasions together, such as New Year, Thanksgiving, Independence Day, and the Super Bowl. The plans do not have to be elaborate.
- Theme parties are fun. Use decades, cultures, or old or current television shows as themes.
- Have an all-saints party in the fall and ask persons to dress as their favorite saints—Mount Saint Helens, Saint Louis, or Saint Nick, for example.
- Attend concerts together.
- Attend sporting events together.
- Sponsor a build-a-_____ party, featuring pizza, ice-cream sundaes, submarine sandwiches, and so on.
- Take trips together—camping, sight-seeing, tubing, or shopping.
- Have a scavenger hunt.
- Have a monthly new-members dinner.
- Have a volleyball game or tournament. Offer different teams for a variety of skill levels.

factoid
Some of the best ideas are the ones your group generates.
Source: Chris Elkins

- Go to dinner and the theater together.
- Have a progressive dinner from church to church, to church-staff members' homes, or to single-adult Sunday School/Bible-study teachers' homes.
- Have a New Year's Eve party at which participants write themselves letters about what they would like to have accomplished spiritually, professionally, and physically by the next New Year. The host should keep the letters and mail them the following December. Also have each person bring an item that uniquely represents the closing year to be put in a time capsule and opened at next year's party.
- Have a broom-ball party at an ice-skating rink after hours. Wearing athletic shoes and helmets, participants play hockey with brooms.
- Have a dessert bake-off, asking men to bake and women to judge. Give prizes—a Julia Child award, most attractive dessert, best-tasting dessert, most original dessert, most likely to have come from the deli, and so on.
- Have SNACS—Sunday Night After Church for Singles.
- Plan summertime fellowships with homemade ice cream, picnics, watermelon, waterskiing, or cookouts.
- Plan wintertime fellowships with snow skiing, chili cook-offs, Friday-night videos, board-games nights, or ice skating.
- Sponsor Monday-night football parties with a potluck dinner and a large-screen television.
- Have a bridal-party party. Everyone should wear an outfit previously worn as part of a bridal party. Consider a mock wedding, including a photographer.

Meaningful Missions

Some of the most meaningful relationships formed in a single-adult ministry develop as we minister to others. All of the fellowships and Bible studies in the world cannot replace ministry and missions. Every single-adult group ought to plan ministry-and-missions activities. The ideas are endless if you look at the world with a servant's eyes.

- A parents night out is a great way single adults can serve parents in the church. This is especially helpful if offered in the fall when parents can use the opportunity to shop for Christmas.
- Combine travel and missions either domestically or internationally. Work on a Native American reservation in Montana and see Yellowstone, too. Aid a ministry in New York City, Chicago, Los Angeles, or San Francisco and see the sights during free time. Go to

Wales and spend time in London on the way home. Help with missions work in Albania and spend a weekend in Rome or Athens as you return. Missions opportunities can be discovered through the International Mission Board or the North American Mission Board of the Southern Baptist Convention (see "Resources for Single Adults and Their Leaders," p. 138).
- Adopt needy children at Christmas. Nothing is as thrilling as providing wonderful Christmas memories for children. Another time to help needy children is when school starts. Several organizations in your community can put you in touch with needy children.

factoid

Some of the most meaningful relationships formed in a single-adult ministry develop as we minister to others.
Source: Chris Elkins

- Form a friendship team to support a significant leader, such as the principal of an inner-city school, the recreation director for a housing project, or the director of a social-service agency. The team should regularly meet with the leader to ask, What can we do to help you do your job even better? Be prepared to back your offer with action.
- Offer to staff a Vacation Bible School for a mission church, supplying leaders, materials, and refreshments. Include the mission church as much as possible, but don't expect it to provide much.
- Sponsor an Easter-egg hunt for a housing project or an inner-city recreation program. You'll be surprised by how many kids show up! Your single adults can have fun, and it's a great time to tell the children about Jesus and why we have Easter.
- Offer to paint or do other labor at a mission church. Perhaps you can even purchase the paint and supplies.
- Sponsor a foreign student to come to America and study or one who is already here. This is a big undertaking but one that can make a difference.
- Adopt a family or a retiree for a year. Make sure your ministry can follow through on the needs you find. A denominational annuity board can identify hundreds of retired pastors who need financial assistance.
- Volunteer to read for the blind and/or elderly.
- Help a nursing home celebrate a holiday.
- Take needy children to a fair or an amusement park.
- Provide blankets and/or food for homeless persons.
- Help a women's shelter with child care.

Creative Small-Group Studies

Some of your single adults want to go deeper into God's Word than is possible in Sunday School/Bible study. Regularly offering studies in faith, lifestyle, and Bible content develops leaders and promotes spiritual maturity. The following guidelines can help you establish creative weekday Bible studies and keep them fresh and alive.

- Maintain a focus on the Bible. Find a teacher who knows not only content but also ways to lead single adults to apply Bible truths to their lives.
- Offer age-specific studies. Some single adults may not like this approach, but it is especially effective for prospects and newcomers who are trying to build relationships with persons who are their ages. In addition, some subjects are age-specific.
- Offer studies on lifestyle issues and the daily Christian walk: dating, communication, conflict resolution, personality traits and issues, spiritual gifts, sexuality, and others.
- Don't change the location too often. If you meet in someone's home, try to complete an entire study in the same location. This minimizes confusion and offers your host an end in sight.
- Use different teachers for different subjects. Beware of building personality followings.
- Regularly use interactive materials that require individual homework and small-group discussion. Courses like *Experiencing God*, *MasterLife*, and *The Mind of Christ* guide participants to discover more about God and to apply biblical truths to life (see "Resources for Single Adults and Their Leaders," p. 138).
- Have a name-your-subject night when participants submit questions or topics that are selected at random and are discussed by the group.
- Occasionally take a break. Everyone needs time off. If you don't offer it, members will eventually take it on their own.
- Offer a variety of teaching styles. In addition to lecture-style studies, occasionally offer a discussion-group approach.
- Poll members to discover what topics and studies they would support if they were offered.
- Continually promote your Bible study. Week by week always announce the current study and where it is conducted. Never assume that people get the message. Keep telling them.

Leading Leaders

Single-adult ministry is in a constant process of change. New persons join, and members get married or are transferred. Recruiting and training leaders is vital to stable, effective single-adult ministries. Below are ideas that can help you develop your leadership team.
- Plan an overnight leadership-development retreat.
- Have a leadership-recognition banquet.
- Plan a leadership-development miniretreat and encourage persons to attend who would not normally be able to stay more than one night. Many churches hold leadership lockins, starting with dinner and closing with breakfast at midnight.
- Invite leaders to learn more about single adults by subscribing to *Christian Single* magazine or by receiving it from you via bulk-mail order. This magazine, interdenominational in style, addresses the needs and interests of single adults who are Baby Busters and Boomers (see "Resources for Single Adults and Their Leaders," p. 138).
- Provide your single-adult leaders copies of *Single Adult Ministries Journal*. This is the best publication for leadership information and motivational training (see "Resources for Single Adults and Their Leaders," p. 138).
- Provide special fellowship opportunities for leaders around holidays.
- Meet with leaders for lunch or coffee in the workplace or hold periodic dinner gatherings.
- Assign every leader a prayer-and-accountability partner.
- Communicate and pray with leaders over the telephone and in person.
- Periodically provide leaders motivational books.
- Regularly encourage leaders to share with one another their personal needs and concerns, as well as those of their groups.
- Conduct a quarterly informational survey of leadership needs.
- Affirm leadership achievements in church publications.
- Provide an accomplishments/concerns sharing time at regular leadership gatherings.
- Have a regular leadership-planning meeting weekly, monthly, or quarterly, with an agenda and the goals to be accomplished.
- Encourage leaders to set short-term, achievable goals. Celebrate with them when they accomplish their goals.
- Develop with leaders a single-adult ministry leadership mission statement.
- Take leaders on a field trip to discover what other successful ministry churches are doing and how they are doing it.
- Take leaders to a local or national leader-training conference.
- Fax or mail notes of encouragement to leaders. Remember their birthdays with cards.
- Invite the pastor to give words of appreciation for single-adult ministry leaders from the pulpit and in

factoid

Recruiting and training leaders is vital to stable, effective single-adult ministries.
Source: Chris Elkins

church publications.

- Consult an experienced and objective single-adult ministry leader for help in guiding your ministry through difficulties and transitions.
- Put leaders' pictures on bulletin boards in the single-adult area or print them in the church or single-adult newsletter. Include their phone numbers.
- Sponsor a single-adult-leader-of-the-year award.

Pumping Publicity and Promotion

Whatever your ministry is doing, if no one finds out about it, you're spinning your wheels. Anything worth doing is also worth publicizing. Although word of mouth is an effective, vital part of promotion, it cannot be relied on to be accurate, timely, or thorough. Here are some ideas for getting the word out. For information on marketing your single-adult ministry, see issue 6, solution 5 in this manual.

- Explore avenues for free advertising in your community. Some stores let you display announcements and posters. Radio and television stations make public-service announcements free. A press release in your local newspaper often gets you a few inches of newsprint. Build a relationship with the person responsible for each communication outlet.
- When buying advertising, be sure you understand your target market and have a precise, clear message to send. Compare costs of all forms of media—print advertising, television, radio, and billboards. Don't assume anything. Some of these channels are more affordable than you think. Often, competition makes good rates available.

factoid
Volleyball is the number one recruitment event in single-adult ministry.
Source: Chris Elkins

- Use fun, creative announcements in group meetings through skits, charades, or videos.
- Use walls and bulletin boards to get the word out.
- Produce newsletters, fliers, and mailers. Be sure they answer the questions who, what, where, when, how, and why. Prominently display your church's name and single-adult ministry on the piece. Keep it simple. Send mailings from 10 days to two weeks before the event.
- Dedicate a phone line at the church for a single-adult ministry answering machine with current, updated announcements about programs and events. Publish the phone number in the personals column and on the entertainment page of your newspaper.

Special Events That Build Attendance

As you plan special events and publicize them widely, they can feed your ministry's ongoing growth.

Single adults night out at the supermarket. In cosponsorship with a grocery store, set aside 10:00 p.m. until midnight on a Friday night for only single adults in the community to shop together. Sponsor in-store cooking demonstrations, provide product discounts and coupons, and play contemporary Christian music. Promote the event through the media. The cost could be absorbed by the store, subsidized by your church budget, or covered by an entry charge.

Solid-rock cafe. Sponsor a '60s and '70s oldies, alcohol-free club setting, with karaoke music and sing-alongs. Special decor can include buttons and shirts with messages such as "Save the Planet" and "John 3:16." Fund the event with a cover charge or the sale of food. This is an excellent fund-raiser, as well.

Mystery theater. Host a formal dinner followed by a murder-mystery play that involves guests in solving the mystery. Recover costs through ticket sales.

Group-date night. Invite single persons to meet at the church, where blind dates will be chosen from a pool of participants. Then the entire group goes to dinner and any other activities planned. This event allows couples to interact in a secure group setting rather than one-to-one. Participants pay for their own expenses.

At your service. Enlist men to grill steaks and chicken and prepare baked potatoes, salad, and dessert; then ask the women to serve and clean up. The next time the women return the favor, generally trying to be more creative than the men. This can become a long-term contest.

Volleyball: the number one recruitment event in single-adult ministry. Play regular volleyball or a variation such as sand or beach volleyball or water-balloon volleyball. Enlist a Christian athlete to bring an inspirational message in the middle of the evening. Provide refreshments. Cover the cost through your church budget or recover the cost from participants.

Single-adult metro Bible study. Hold an interdenominational, areawide Bible study on a weeknight, utilizing a contemporary worship team, drama, and a professional motivational Christian teacher or speaker. Promote the event in the local media and place fliers on windshields. Hold the study in a church, meet in a neutral facility, or rotate among churches. Churches' combined efforts to reach a larger number of single adults in the area can be very successful. Collect a love offering to cover the cost.

Perhaps there's not a single new idea to be found. Many ideas are simply recycled older ones. Keeping your ministry fresh and alive is as much a product of a fresh, vital vision as of new ideas. Being flexible and adventurous enough to try new approaches keeps you out of the ruts.

Tools for Discovering Fresh Ideas

The Anatomy of an Idea

Use this process to find your own ministry ideas.

1. Look for the Big Glaring Opportunity (BGO). It is often found in the familiar.

   Record a BGO for your ministry.

   _____

   _____

   _____

2. Retain some of the familiar. Implementing an idea in small steps often prepares your constituency for the full impact of change that a new idea may bring.

   Name the familiar found in your BGO.

   _____

   _____

3. Throw out unnecessary rules. Get rid of the box of rules that walls in new possibilities that try to emerge. Don't throw out all of the rules; they may take on new forms as you look at them objectively in various contexts.

   Identify one rule or tradition you may have to break to do something new.

   _____

   _____

4. Think individualistically. Put yourself in the presence of individualistic thinkers. They may be too extreme, but you can carry the seeds of their ideas into the mainstream that needs it.

List the individualistic thinkers in your group.

_____   _____

_____   _____

5. Keep notes. Carry a small notebook for recording thoughts and ideas you have in various circumstances. Periodically review these to glean the seeds of fresh ideas.

Start now! Write one ministry idea you've had recently.

_____

_____

_____

6. Have fun. Often, new ideas are fresh because they are fun. In a survey of ministries volleyball is the number one single-adult activity. It combines action, fellowship, team building, and coed involvement. When an idea works, find out why and apply these principles to other areas of your ministry.

Take time to dissect a good idea that's working. Answer these questions:

Why is the idea working?

_____

_____

_____

How can these dynamics transfer to other ministry areas?

_____

_____

_____

7. Pray. Call on God, and He will show you great and mighty ministry ideas (see Jer. 33:3). Never underestimate God's inspiration in discovering new ideas.

List prayer concerns for areas in which you need God's new ideas.

_____

_____

_____

Now pray.

Planning a Single-Adult Activity/Conference

Determine which actions will help you plan and implement the activity. Check off the steps as you accomplish them.

General Actions

❑ Determine dates and place them on the church calendar.
❑ Determine and manage a budget (church allocation and cost-recovery).
❑ Enlist resource persons.
❑ Form a planning group.
❑ Instruct the planning group.
❑ Promote and publicize the activity.
❑ Conduct the activity.
❑ Follow up.

Actions for Planning Groups

Publicity and Promotion

❑ Produce publicity flier: secure visual, write copy, estimate quantity, determine size, estimate cost, formulate use plan.
❑ Distribute flier according to use plan.
❑ Arrange for other publicity actions, such as posters, announcements, mailings, church newsletter, bulletins, local newspapers, radio, other media, other church channels, and community contacts.

Enlistment and Registration

❑ Arrange ticket sales/reservations: when, where, who, how.
❑ Organize phone calls and enlistment of members and prospects.
❑ Organize registration process and secure materials for conducting registration: registration card, name tag, packet/program materials coordinated to distribute.

Program

❑ Determine schedule.
❑ Have program printed.
❑ Reserve rooms with appropriate space.
❑ Arrange for a theme banner and staging needs.
❑ Obtain sound and lighting equipment and arrange for its operation.
❑ Enlist a master of ceremonies.

Decorations and Food

❑ Plan materials for decorating and cleanup.
❑ Determine food requirements and costs. Arrange for preparation and cleanup.
❑ Plan locations and hosts for lunch.

Book Store
❑ Arrange for a book store or a table with appropriate materials.
❑ Order resource persons' materials to sell.
❑ Establish change- and money-handling procedures with salespersons.
❑ Handle setup, selling, and cleanup.

Follow-up
❑ Organize quick follow-up plans that include mail, phone calls, and visits.
❑ Assign all visitors' cards to appropriate Sunday School/Bible-study units for prospect follow-up.
❑ Enlist persons to assist with follow-up.

Child Care
❑ Enlist staff, arrange for appropriate facilities, and plan for meals.

Sample Conference/Retreat Program Schedule
As you examine these suggestions, write on another sheet of paper a schedule and budget for your next conference or retreat.
• Friday evening: registration, fellowship activities, testimony, music, and presentation.
• Saturday morning: cost-recovery continental breakfast, registration, fellowship activities, testimony, music, presentation, break, testimony, music, and presentation.
• Saturday afternoon: Dutch-treat lunch. Participants sign up by restaurants with hosts. Free time follows, perhaps with planned recreation.
• Saturday evening: registration, fellowship activities, testimony, music, and presentation.
• Sunday morning: all-single-adult Sunday School/Bible-study groups with fellowship, testimony, music, and presentation by conference leader.

Coffee House/Cafe Format
• Have red-checked tablecloths and dish candles on tables.
• Have snack foods, soft drinks, and flavored coffee on tables. Or serve food and drinks at stations for single adults to serve themselves.
• Arrange tables in a semicircle facing center stage.

Cost-Recovery Planning
Consider a ticket/registration fee. Apply the money to activity/conference costs: food, lodging, decorations, promotion, resource persons, and so on.

A Guide for Booking Artists and Speakers
Check off these steps as you plan.
❑ Determine a budget amount for a musician or a speaker before you call an agent or an artist.
❑ Choose the right style of artist or speaker for your group's likes and needs. Request a free promotional copy of the most recent recording, video, or book.
❑ Sign and send contracts and deposits back on time.
❑ Begin your promotional campaign for the event at least six weeks in advance.

❏ Talk about the activity. If you are excited about the event, your single adults will be. Encourage them to tell their friends.

❏ Promote aggressively. Don't expect the Lord miraculously to bless something you haven't promoted.

❏ Personally make sure that hotel and meal arrangements are made prior to your guest's arrival.

❏ If you sponsor a weekend event, consider making it churchwide or citywide.

❏ Have your guest's honorarium ready to present before the event begins. Don't make the person search for the paycheck.

❏ Provide the best sound system and sound person possible. Nothing ruins a great program more quickly than poor sound. Rent a system if necessary.

❏ Plan the event at least six months in advance to allow you adequate time for preparation.

❏ Plan ad packages with your local Christian radio station and with the weekend section of your newspaper, especially if you are featuring a well-known artist or speaker.

❏ Have volunteer assistants on hand for the artist or speaker's needs, such as recording sales, running errands, and assisting with transportation.

❏ Pray for the event and for the artist or speaker while preparing for the event.

❏ Make the event special with simple stage decorations such as plants, flowers, balloons, a backdrop, and so forth.

the single-adult ministry solution
study guide
Tim Cleary

Introduction

Become familiar with the Single-Adult Ministry Great Commission Sampler and Planner on pages 10–11. This valuable tool provides you a definition of effective ministry based on biblical principles and a practical planning process. As you study the leader manual and develop ministry actions, remember to note the Great Commission principles being applied through the actions. Write down the actions and principles. After you finish the leader manual, place key actions on the Single-Adult Great Commission Planner.

Issue ① Understanding Today's Single Adults

Solution 1: Welcome to Single Land

- "Understand Single Adults' Demographics and Viewpoints"—Review the data by George Barna and decide whether it describes the demographics in your ministry situation and locale. List actions to take in response. Refer to issue 5 and the toolbox following issue 5 to discover ways to gather this data locally.
- "Understand Single Adults' Lifestyles"—Name several lifestyle challenges single adults face in the immediate future. Suggest ways churches can help individuals cope with these. On a scale of 1 (low) to 10 (high) rate your church's current capacity to help single persons with these challenges.

Solution 2: Meet Mr. and Ms. Single Adult

- Reviewing the needs of the single-adult identity groupings, determine which ones include generational categories to which your church is ministering or could minister effectively. Why? How?

Solution 3: Understand the Micro Viewpoint: Solutions for Smaller Churches

- List one idea smaller churches can use to encourage ministry with single adults. Brainstorm others.

Solution 4: Use the Single-Adult Ministry Toolbox

- Use one of the many toolbox resources to plan for ministry in your church and community.

Issue ② Empowering Single Adults for Christian Living

Solution 1: Determine the Primary Ministry Model to Meet Single Adults' Needs
Solution 2: Choose the Empowerment Model
- Review the various ministry models. Determine your ministry's primary model and the extent to which other models may be represented. Give examples.

Solution 3: Use These Principles of Empowerment
- List the six principles of empowerment and identify the one most prominent in your ministry. Name one you would like to work on.

Solution 4: Use the Single-Adult Ministry Toolbox
- In addition to this leader manual, the book *Start a Revolution* can help you empower single adults in your ministry. Use the training plan to decide how you can use the book with your single adults.

Issue ③ Developing Your Single-Adult Ministry Leadership Team

Solution 1: Cultivate a Passion for God
- Write one goal you have as a leader for growing in Christ this year. Example: Have a daily, five-minute quiet time with God.

Solution 2: Develop a Leader's Heart for Single Adults
- What are the four fabulous *E*'s that can help church leaders develop a dynamic concern for motivating your church to reach single adults?
- Choose one of the fabulous *E*'s and describe how this principle functions in your church.

Solution 3: Learn the Dynamics of Team Building
- Name five principles that develop teamwork on a leadership team. Describe the one you think is most important in your situation and why.

Solution 4: Build Your Single-Adult Ministry Leadership Team
- "Peer Listeners"–Describe how to organize a peer listening ministry and list results you may expect, based on this group's experience.
- "Single Adults Are Leaders, Too"–List several ways your church incorporates these principles in encouraging single adults to become active leaders in your single-adult ministry.
- "The Role of Married Leaders in Single-Adult Ministry"–Discuss the pros and cons of having single-adult leaders who are married or single. Give your opinion of which option is better and why.
- "Resolving Conflicts Among Leaders"–Describe ways to deal with conflict among leaders in your single-adult ministry. Which of these ideas have you utilized? What were the results?

Solution 5: Develop Your Pastoral-Leadership Team
- List ways you can help your pastor relate to single adults and ways single adults can support their pastor.

Solution 6: Understand the Micro Viewpoint: Solutions for Smaller Churches
  • Why do single adults often choose smaller churches? How can a smaller church capitalize on this reason?

Solution 7: Use the Single-Adult Ministry Toolbox
  • Choose a tool from the toolbox, complete the activity, and discuss.

Issue ④ Incorporating Single Adults into the Body of Christ

Solution 1: Understand the Biblical Foundation for Single-Adult Ministry
• List biblical ideas to inspire and encourage a church's single-adult ministry.

Solution 2: Integrate Single Adults into Your Church's Ministry and Leadership
• Name and discuss the four essentials for maintaining life and vitality in your single-adult ministry and in your church.

Solution 3: Make Your Church User-Friendly for Single Adults
• List several ways your church is user-friendly for single adults.

Solution 4: Understand the Micro Viewpoint: Solutions for Smaller Churches
• Brainstorm ways single adults can be involved in smaller churches.

Solution 5: Use the Single-Adult Ministry Toolbox
• Select a tool from the toolbox for incorporating single adults into the body of Christ. Use it and record what you learned.

Issue ⑤ Organizing for Effective Single-Adult Ministry

Solution 1: Use the Paper-Clip-and-Pipe-Cleaner Principles
  • Review the 12 essentials for starting and strengthening a single-adult ministry. Circle those you have already accomplished. Check those you want to work on.
  • Which single-adult ministry paradigm describes your church's single-adult ministry and why? If the paradigms do not apply to your situation, describe your paradigm in your own words.

Solution 2: Choose an Organizational Style to Meet Your Unique Needs
  • Name seven issues to consider when organizing for effective single-adult ministry.
  • Utilizing the suggestions, write a purpose statement for your church's single-adult ministry.
  • Look for the Jesus-style leadership concepts that empower effective single-adult ministry. Determine the ones at work in your ministry and those you would like to utilize more effectively.
  • Review the options given. Then develop your own single-adult leadership team based on your church's ministry dynamics.

Solution 3: Take Advantage of These Special Ministry Opportunities
- Review the content and describe single-adult target audiences or special ministries specific to your church and community. How can knowing your audience help you minister more effectively? List priorities to consider in ministry to your audience.

Solution 4: Use the Single-Adult Ministry Toolbox
- Choose a tool from the toolbox and use it to develop related ministry plans.

Issue 6 Expanding and Growing a Single-Adult Ministry

Solution 1: Understand the Dynamics of Single-Adult Sunday School/Bible-Study Ministry
- What do churches face without an aggressive plan to reach single adults? Do you agree or disagree?

Solution 2: Build a Growing Sunday School/Bible-Study Ministry
- Name six tasks of a single-adult Sunday School/Bible-study group. Which tasks are utilized in your church's ministry, and which tasks need to be developed?
- List six characteristics of growing single-adult groups and give examples of those that are present in your group.

Solution 3: Reach Single Adults Through Small Groups: The WillowCreek Model
- Name the four basic functions of a small group.
- Discuss with other leaders the need for small groups and what kinds of groups your church might want to begin.
- True or false? Single-adult ministry should always employ small groups without any large-group activities.

Solution 4: Apply the Great Commission Factor
- Write a paragraph describing how single adults can be led to Christ through single-adult ministry. Tell the story of a single adult who has come to Christ through your church's single-adult ministry.

Solution 5: Market Your Single-Adult Ministry
- List marketing principles that you currently use in your single-adult ministry and those that could be used to improve the marketing of your ministry.

Solution 6: Use the Single-Adult Ministry Toolbox
- Diagram your single-adult ministry's Sunday School/Bible-study organizational structure. Compare it with the suggested structures and related roles. What have you discovered from this solution that would improve your ministry's effectiveness?

Issue ⑦ Facing the Challenge of Critical Issues in Single-Adult Ministry

Solution 1: Lead Your Church to Face the Challenge
- List several ways your church can face the challenge of ministering to single adults' critical issues.

Solution 2: Utilize Counseling Techniques and Resources
- Name techniques for counseling single adults. Describe how your church provides counseling for single adults.

Solution 3: Tackle These Critical Issues
- Choose a counseling issue and apply the information to a single adult you know. What did you learn? What would you do in addition to these ideas?

Solution 4: Use the Single-Adult Ministry Toolbox
- Use the toolbox to plan a counseling strategy for your church.

Issue ⑧ Discovering Fresh Ideas for Ministry with Single Adults

Solution 1: Find Ideas That Work
- What are three points to keep in mind as you search for ideas for your single-adult ministry?

Solution 2: Use This Catalog of Ideas
- Pick an ideas category from the material. Choose what you consider the best idea. How would this idea work for your ministry? Brainstorm additional ideas.

Solution 3: Use the Single-Adult Ministry Toolbox
- Use the toolbox to develop a new idea for your ministry.

While recommending the following resources, we do not necessarily endorse all contents of each. If any are out of print, check your church or community library.

Use these resources to—
- train leaders;
- build a personal leadership resource library;
- start support groups;
- develop a year-round discipleship and support-group ministry;
- stock your church's media library;
- discover new ideas and the latest ministry trends;
- provide a mediagraphy for your single adults and leaders;
- make single adults aware of personal-growth resources;
- build a resource center in your single-adult Sunday School/Bible-study area;
- share selected resources with single adults in crisis;
- provide gifts for new group members or visitors.

Resources indicated by an asterisk (*) are available from the Customer Service Center; 127 Ninth Avenue, North; Nashville, TN 37234; 1-800-458-2772.

AIDS

Allen, Jimmy. *Burden of a Secret: A Family Journey Through the Shadow of AIDS*. New York: McCracken, 1996.

Banta, William F. *AIDS in the Workplace: Legal Questions and Practical Answers*. New York: The Free Press, 1987.

Barth, Richard B. *Families Living with Drugs and HIV: Intervention and Treatment Strategies*. New York: Guilford, 1993.

Gage, Rodney. *Let's Talk About AIDS and Sex*. Nashville: Broadman and Holman, 1992.

Blended Families

Anderson, Neil T. *Steps to Freedom in Christ*. Ventura: Regal, 1995.

Cutler, William, and Richard Peace. *Blended Families: Yours, Mine, Ours*. Littleton, Colo.: Serendipity, 1990.

*Dunn, Dick. *New Faces in the Frame: A Guide to Marriage and Parenting in the Blended Family* (interactive with leader resource). Nashville: LifeWay, 1997.

Dunn, Dick. *Willing to Try Again*. Valley Forge: Judson, 1993.

Frydenger, Tom and Adrienne. *Resolving Conflict in the Blended Family*. Grand Rapids: Chosen, 1991.

Budgeting and Financial Management

*Blue, Ron. *Master Your Money* (interactive with leader re-

source). Atlanta: Walk Thru the Bible, 1990.

Burkett, Larry. *The Complete Financial Guide for Single Parents*. Wheaton, Ill.: Scripture, 1992.

Building Friendships

McGinniss, Alan. *The Friendship Factor*. Minneapolis: Augsburg Fortress, 1979.

Purnell, Dick. *Becoming a Friend and Lover*. Nashville: Thomas Nelson, 1995.

Counseling

Collins, Gary. *The Biblical Basis of Christian Counseling for People Helpers*. Colorado Springs: NavPress, 1993.

———. *How to Be a People Helper*. Wheaton, Ill.: Tyndale House, 1995.

*Drakeford, John W., and Claude V. King. *WiseCounsel: Skills for Lay Counseling* (interactive with leader resource). Nashville: LifeWay, 1988.

Fagerstrom, Douglas L. *Counseling Single Adults*. Grand Rapids: Baker, 1995.

Dating Relationships

Purnell, Dick. *Free to Love Again: Coming to Terms with Sexual*

Regret. San Bernardino, Calif.: Here's Life, 1989.

Rollins, C. E. *Are We Compatible? Strategies for Making Your Personality and Background Differences Work for You, Not Against You*. Nashville: Thomas Nelson, 1995.

*Springle, Pat. *Untangling Relationships: A Christian Perspective on Codependency* (interactive with leader resource). Nashville: LifeWay, 1993.

Talley, Jim, and Bobbie Reed. *Too Close, Too Soon*. Nashville: Thomas Nelson, 1990.

Discipleship/Equipping

*Blackaby, Henry, and Claude V. King. *Experiencing God* (interactive with leader resource). Nashville: LifeWay, 1990.

*Blackaby, Henry, and Richard Blackaby. *When God Speaks*. Nashville: LifeWay, 1995.

Experiencing God Bible. Nashville: Broadman and Holman, 1994.

Floyd, Ronnie W. *Reconnecting: How to Renew and Preserve the Three Vital Elements of a Powerful Spiritual Life*. Nashville: Broadman and Holman, 1993.

*Hemphill, Ken. *LifeAnswers: Making Sense of Your World* (interactive with leader resource). Nashville: LifeWay, 1993.

*Hunt, T. W., and Catherine Walker. *Disciple's Prayer Life: Walking in Fellowship with God* (interactive with leader resource). Nashville: LifeWay, 1987.

*Hunt, T. W., and Claude V. King. *In God's Presence*. Nashville: LifeWay, 1994.

*———. *The Mind of Christ* (interactive with leader resource). Nashville: LifeWay, 1994.

*Neighbour, Ralph W. *Living Your Christian Values*. Nashville: Convention, 1989.

*Neighbour, Ralph W., and Bill Latham. *Survival Kit*. Nashville: LifeWay, 1996.

*Willis, Avery T. *MasterLife* (interactive with leader resource). Nashville: LifeWay, 1996.

Divorce and Remarriage

*Akamine, Hale. *Healing the Wounds: Teenagers Learning to Cope with Divorce* (interactive with leader resource). Nashville: LifeWay, 1995.

Bristow, John T. *What the Bible Really Says About Love, Marriage, and Family*. St. Louis: Chalice, 1994.

Grissom, Steve. *DivorceCare* (interactive video series). Call (919) 571-7735.

Hunt, Angela. *When Your Parents Pull Apart*. Wheaton, Ill.: Tyndale House, 1995.

Kniskern, Joseph W. *When the Vow Breaks: A Survival and Recovery Guide for Christians Facing Divorce*. Nashville: Broadman and Holman, 1993.

*Pitts, Cindy. *KidShare: What Do I Do Now?* (interactive with leader resource). Nashville: LifeWay, 1994.

*Smith, Harold Ivan. *A Time for Healing: Coming to Terms with Your Divorce* (interactive with leader resource). Nashville: LifeWay, 1995.

Tannen, Deborah. *You Just Don't Understand: Women and Men in Conversation*. New York: Ballantine, 1994.

*Weber, Ellen. *Single but Not Alone*. Nashville: Broadman and Holman, 1990.

Whiteman, Thomas. *When Your Son or Daughter Is Going Through a Divorce*. Nashville: Thomas Nelson, 1994.

General Ministry with Single Adults

Barna, George. *Unmarried America How Singles Are Changing and What It Means for the Church*. Glendale, Calif.: Barna Research Group, 1993.

Christian Single magazine.

*Cleary, Tim, comp. *The Single-Adult Ministry Solution Resource Pack*. Nashville: LifeWay, 1996.

Harbour, Brian. *Famous Singles of the Bible*. Nashville: Broadman, 1980.

DeLap, Rollin. *Helping the Local Church Through Evangelizing Single Adults*. Alpharetta, Ga.: The Home Mission Board of the Southern Baptist Convention, 1991.

Fagerstrom, Douglas L. *Single to Single: Daily Devotionals by and for Single Adults*. Grand Rapids: Victor, 1991.

*Felts, Stephen. *Start a Revolution: Nine World-Changing Strategies for Single Adults*. Nashville: LifeWay, 1996.

Gray, Gary. *Single Saints, Single Sinners*. Oklahoma City: Christian Single, 1996.

Hughes, Robert Don. *Satan's Whispers: Breaking the Lies That Bind*. Nashville: Broadman and Holman, 1992.

Koons, Carolyn A., and Michael J. Anthony. *Single-Adult Passages: Uncharted Territories*. Grand Rapids: Baker, 1991.

Peterson, Paul. *Creative Weekends: 29½ Ready-to-Use Ideas for Your Single-Adult Ministry*. Chicago: David C. Cook, 1995.

Singles and Leaders Newsletter. Contact Hazel Bell; P.O. Box 842; Norman, OK 73070-0842.

Leadership

Barna, George. *User-Friendly Churches*. Ventura, Calif.: Regal, 1991.

Fagerstrom, Douglas. *Singles Ministry Handbook*. Wheaton, Ill.: Scripture, 1988.

———. *Single-Adult Ministry: The Next Step*. Wheaton, Ill.: Scripture, 1993.

George, Carl F. *Prepare Your Church for the Future*. Grand Rapids: Revell, 1994.

George, Carl F., with Warren Bird. *The Coming Church Revolution: Empowering Leaders for the Future* (Grand Rapids: Revell, 1994).

Hershey, Terry, and Rich Hurst. *Giving the Ministry Away:*

Empowering Singles for Leadership. Elgin, Ill.: David C. Cook, 1993.

Ideas for Associational Single-Adult Ministry Christian Single Resources (booklet). Available from Christian Single Resources; 127 Ninth Avenue, North; Nashville, TN 37234-0151; (615) 251-2231.

Jones, Jerry. *Idea Catalog: For Single-Adult Ministry.* Elgin, Ill.: David C. Cook, 1991.

———, comp. *Growing Your Single-Adult Ministry.* Elgin, Ill.: David C. Cook, 1993.

Miller, Calvin. *The Empowered Communicator.* Nashville: Broadman and Holman, 1994.

———. *The Empowered Leader.* Nashville: Broadman and Holman, 1996.

Network of single-adult leaders video catalog, (616) 956-9377.

Patterson, Sheron C. *Ministry with Black Single Adults.* Nashville: Discipleship Resources, 1990.

Single Adult Ministries Journal; P.O. Box 62056; Colorado Springs, CO; 80962-2056; 1-800-487-4SAM.

Wilkinson, Jerry and Lana. *Developing Ministries with Single-Parent Families.* Convention, 1993.

Marriage Preparation and Readiness/Divorce Prevention

Bilicki, Bettie, and Masa Goetz. *Getting Back Together.* Holbrook, Mass.: Adams, 1990.

*Chapman, Gary. *The Five Love Languages* (video pack with book). Nashville: LifeWay, 1995.

———. *Hope for the Separated.* Chicago: Moody, 1982.

Gray, John. *Men Are from Mars, Women Are from Venus: A Practical Guide for Improving Communication and Getting What You Want in Your Relationships.* New York: Harper Collins, 1994.

Greeley, Andrew M. *Faithful Attraction.* New York: Tor, 1992.

*McManus, Michael J. *Insuring Marriage: 25 Proven Ways to Prevent Divorce* and *Marriage Savers Resource Collection.* Nashville: LifeWay, 1994.

PREPARE Premarital Inventory and M. C. Remarriage with Children Inventory; P.O. Box 190; Minneapolis, MN 55440-0190.

Warren, Neil. *Finding the Love of Your Life.* Colorado Springs: Focus on the Family, 1992.

*White, Ernest. *Counsel for the Nearly and Newly Married.* Nashville: Convention, 1992.

Wright, Norman, and Wes Roberts. *Before You Say I Do.* Eugene: Harvest House, 1978.

Organizations

Christian Single Resources. Contact Tim Cleary; 127 Ninth Avenue, North; Nashville, TN 37234-0151; (615) 251-2231.

The International Mission Board of the Southern Baptist Convention; 3806 Monument Avenue; Richmond, VA 23230.

The North American Mission Board of the Southern Baptist Convention; 4200 North Point Parkway; Alpharetta, GA 30202-4174.

National Single-Adult Events. Contact David Hassell; 127 Ninth Avenue, North; Nashville, TN 37234-0151; (615) 251-2865.

The Network of Single-Adult Leaders (interdenominational organization of professional and volunteer leaders). Contact Doug Fagerstrom; P.O. Box 1600; Grand Rapids, MI 49501; (616) 956-9377.

Single-Adult World-Changers (mission-service organization); 1548 Poplar Avenue; Memphis, TN 38104-2493; (901) 272-2461.

Singles Ministry Resources. Contact Jerry Jones; P.O. Box 60430; Colorado Springs, CO 80960-0430; (719) 635-6020.

The Southern Baptist Association of Ministers with Single Adults is an organization of professional ministers. Contact Tim Cleary; 127 Ninth Avenue, North; Nashville, TN 37234-0151; (615) 251-2231.

Stepfamily Association of America; 215 Centennial Mall South; Suite 212; Lincoln, NE 68508; 1-800-735-0329.

Senior Single Adults

*Endicott, Irene. *Grandparenting by Grace* (interactive with leader resource). Nashville: LifeWay, 1994.

*Jakes, David. *The Decision Is Yours: Help for Senior Adults and Their Families with Housing Options.* Nashville: LifeWay, 1995.

Mature Living magazine.

Morgan, Richard L. *I Never Found That Rocking Chair: God's Call at Retirement.* Nashville: Upper Room, 1993.

Sisk, Ginny. *This Too Shall Pass: Being a Caregiver for the Elderly.* Nashville: Broadman and Holman, 1992.

Sexuality

Consiglio, William. *Homosexual No More: Practical Strategies for Christians Overcoming.* Wheaton, Ill.: Scripture, 1991.

Smith, Harold Ivan. *Singles Ask: Answers to Questions About Relationships and Sexual Issues.* Minneapolis: Augsburg Fortress, 1988.

Stafford, Tim. *Love, Sex, and the Whole Person.* Grand Rapids: Zondervan, 1991.

Stedman, Rick. *Pure Joy! The Positive Side of Single Sexuality.* Chicago: Moody, 1993.

Single Parenting

Brandt, Patricia, with Dave Jackson. *Just Me and the Kids* (interactive with leader resource). Elgin, Ill.: David C. Cook, 1985.

Burkett, Larry. *The Complete Financial Guide for Single Parents.* Wheaton, Ill.: Scripture, 1992.

Christian Single magazine (includes single-parenting section).

*Crase, Dixie Ruth, and Arthur H. Criscoe. *Parenting by Grace: Discipline and Spiritual Growth.* Nashville: LifeWay, 1996.

Cynaumon, Greg. *Helping Single Parents with Troubled Kids.* Elgin, Ill.: David C. Cook, 1992.

Marston, Stephanie. *The Divorced Parent: Success Strategies for Raising Happy Children After Separation.* New York: Morrow, 1994.

*Morgan, Robert J. *Empowered Parenting.* Nashville: LifeWay, 1996.

Nelsen, Jane. *Positive Discipline for Single Parents: A Practical Guide to Raising Children Who Are Responsible, Respectful, and Resourceful.* Rocklin, Calif.: Prima, 1993.

Single-Parent Family magazine. Available from Focus on the Family, 1-800-232-6459.

Sunday School/Bible Study

*Dodge, Richard. *Toward 2000: Leading Adults in Sunday School.* Nashville: Convention, 1995.

*Peak, Gerry. *The Leading Edge.* Nashville: Convention, 1995.

A Single Pursuit (Bible-study curriculum).

*Taylor, Bill. *Teaching to Make a Difference.* Nashville: LifeWay, 1995.

*Wilkinson, Bruce. *The Seven Laws of the Learner.* Nashville: LifeWay, 1995.

Support Groups

*Jones, Johnny, *LIFE Support Leader's Handbook.* Nashville: LifeWay, 1993.

*Kubetin, Cynthia, and James Mallory. *Shelter from the Storm: Hope for Victims of Sexual Abuse* (interactive with leader resource). Nashville: LifeWay, 1995.

*Laaser, Mark. *Faithful and True: Sexual Integrity in a Fallen World* (interactive with leader resource). Nashville: LifeWay, 1996.

*Lewis, Carole, and Kay Smith. *First Place: A Christ-Centered Health Program* (interactive with leader resource). Nashville: LifeWay, 1992.

LIFE Support Group Series Training Video. Nashville: LifeWay, 1995.

*McClain, Frances. *Quitting for Good: A Christ-Centered Approach to the Nicotine Habit* (interactive with leader resource). Nashville: LifeWay, 1995.

*McGee, Robert S. *Search for Significance LIFE Support Edition* (interactive with leader resource). Nashville: LifeWay, 1992.

*McGee. Robert S., and William Drew Mountcastle. *Conquering Eating Disorders* (interactive with leader resource). Nashville: LifeWay, 1993.

*McGee, Robert S., et al. *Conquering Chemical Dependency* (interactive with leader resource). Nashville: LifeWay, 1994.

*——. *Conquering Chemical Dependency: First Steps to a Christ-Centered 12-Step Process* (interactive with leader resource). Nashville: LifeWay, 1994.

*McGee, Robert S., Pat Springle, and Jim Craddock. *Breaking the Cycle of Hurtful Family Experiences* (interactive with leader resource). Nashville: LifeWay, 1994.

*Pillow, Larry. *Family and Friends: Helping the Person You Care About in Recovery* (interactive with leader resource). Nashville: LifeWay, 1995.

*Sledge, Tim. *Making Peace with Your Past* (interactive with leader resource). Nashville: LifeWay, 1992.

*——. *Moving Beyond Your Past* (interactive with leader resource). Nashville: LifeWay, 1994.

*Springle, Pat. *Conquering Codependency* (interactive with leader resource). Nashville: LifeWay, 1993.

*Springle, Pat. *Untangling Relationships: A Christian Perspective on Codependency* (interactive with leader resource). Nashville: LifeWay, 1993.

Widowed Persons and Loss Recovery

Cutler, William, and Richard Peace. *Dealing with Grief and Loss.* Littleton, Colo.: Serendipity, 1990.

Gibberman, David. *What to Do When Your Spouse Dies: Decisions to Make—Legal and Financial Considerations—Planning Ahead.* Chicago: Commerce Clearing House, 1991.

Smith-Greer, Becky. *Keepsakes for the Heart.* Pomona, Colo.: Focus on the Family, 1990.

Tetured, Wesley. *Caring for Widows: You and Your Church Can Make a Difference.* Grand Rapids: Baker Book House, 1993.

Westburg, Granger. *Good Grief.* Minneapolis: Fortress, 1962.

*Wright, H. Norman. *Recovering from the Losses of Life* (interactive with leader resource). Nashville: LifeWay, 1995.

Witnessing

*Atkinson, Donald A., and Charles L. Roesel. *Meeting Needs, Sharing Christ: Ministry Evangelism in Today's New Testament Church* (interactive with leader resource). Nashville: LifeWay, 1995.

DeLap, Rollin (national single-adult evangelism consultant);

3705 Faulkner Drive; Nashville, TN 37211; (615) 833-0787.

The Four Spiritual Laws (tract). Orlando: Campus Crusade for Christ.

How to Have a Full and Meaningful Life (tract). Nashville: The Sunday School Board of the Southern Baptist Convention, 1971.

*Kelley, Chuck. *Learning to Share My Faith* (interactive with leader resource). Nashville: LifeWay, 1994.

*Smith, Jack R., and Jennifer Kennedy Dean. *Witnessing Through Your Relationships* (interactive with leader resource). Nashville: LifeWay, 1994.

Young Single Adults

Barna, George. *Baby Busters: Disillusioned Generation.* Chicago: Northfield, 1994.

Directions: Bible Studies for Young Adults (curriculum).

*Edwards, David. *Spontaneous Combustion* (video series). Nashville: LifeWay, 1997.

McIntosh, Gary L. *Three Generations: Riding the Waves of Change in Your Church.* Grand Rapids: Fleming H. Revell, 1995.

Rydberg, Denny. *20-Something: Life Beyond College.* Grand Rapids: Zondervan, 1991.

Smith, Harold Ivan. *51 Good Things to Do While You're Waiting for the Right One to Come Along.* Nashville: Broadman and Holman, 1994.

Young, Ed. *Been There, Done That. Now What?* Nashville: Broadman and Holman, 1994.

the single-adult ministry solution

the christian growth
study plan

In the Christian Growth Study Plan *The Single-Adult Ministry Solution* is a resource for course credit in three diploma plans. To receive credit, read this leader manual and complete the activities suggested in the study guide; read *Start a Revolution* and write a summary of the strategies or lead a study for your single adults; show your work to your pastor, a staff member, or a church leader; then complete the following information.

Send this completed page to the Christian Growth Study Plan Office; 127 Ninth Avenue, North; MSN 117; Nashville, TN 37234-0117; fax (615) 251-5067. This page may be duplicated.

For information about the Christian Growth Study Plan refer to the current *Christian Growth Study Plan Catalog.* Your church office may have a copy. If not, request a free copy from the Christian Growth Study Plan Office at (615) 251-2525.

Course Credit Information
Check the appropriate box indicating the position in which you serve your church. You may check more than one. You will receive course credit toward the diploma designed for your position(s).

❑ Single-Adult Ministry (LS-0034)
❑ Associational Family Ministry (LS-0067)
❑ Pastor and Church Staff (LS-0083)

PARTICIPANT INFORMATION

Social Security Number	Personal CGSP Number*	Date of Birth

Name (First, MI, Last)	Home Phone
❑ Mr. ❑ Miss	
❑ Mrs. ❑	

Address (Street, Route, or P.O. Box)	City, State	Zip Code

CHURCH INFORMATION

Church Name

Address (Street, Route, or P. O. Box)	City, State	Zip Code

CHANGE REQUEST ONLY

❑ Former Name

❑ Former Address	City, State	Zip Code

❑ Former Church		Zip Code

Signature of Pastor, Conference Leader, or Other Church Leader	Date

*New participants are requested but not required to give SS# and date of birth. Existing participants, please give CGSP# when using SS# for the first time. Thereafter, only one ID# is required. Mail to: Christian Growth Study Plan, 127 Ninth Ave., North, MSN 117, Nashville, TN 37234-0117. Fax: (615)251-5067